F

THE
ZUCCHINI
PLAGUE
AND
OTHER TALES
OF
SUBURBIA

WILLIAM GEIST

ORIGINALLY PUBLISHED AS
TOWARD A SAFE AND SANE HALLOWEEN AND OTHER TALES OF SUBURBIA

A FIRESIDE BOOK
PUBLISHED BY SIMON & SCHUSTER, INC.
NEW YORK

First Fireside Edition, 1987
Published by Simon & Schuster, Inc.
Simon & Schuster Building
Rockefeller Center
1230 Avenue of the Americas
New York, New York 10020
Published by arrangement with Times Books, A Division of Random House, Inc.
All articles originally appeared in *The New York Times* and *The Chicago Tribune*.
Originally published by Times Books under the title
Toward a Safe and Sane Halloween and Other Tales of Suburbia.
FIRESIDE and colophon are registered trademarks of Simon & Schuster, Inc.
Designed by Robert Bull
Manufactured in the United States of America
10 9 8 7 6 5 4 3 2 1 Pbk.
Library of Congress Cataloging in Publication Data

Geist, William.
    The zucchini plague and other tales of suburbia.

"A Fireside book."
    Reprint. Originally published: Toward a safe and sane
Halloween and other tales of suburbia. 1st ed. New York :
Times Books, © 1985.
    1. Suburban life—United States—Anecdotes, facetiae,
satire, etc.   I. Title.
HT351.G44   1987   977.3'1'0091733   86-31891
ISBN: 0-671-63434-8 Pbk.

FOR JODY

ACKNOWLEDGMENTS

These columns are reprinted by permission of *The New York Times* and the *Chicago Tribune,* where they originally appeared. A few appear here in somewhat altered form, either as a combination of two columns on the same subject or as written prior to changes by newspaper editors.

Contents

THE ZUCCHINI PLAGUE AND OTHER TALES OF SUBURBIA

INTRODUCTION

Fresh out of journalism school and eager to put public officials—each and every one—behind bars, I rode hard into Chicago and was immediately farmed out to the suburbs, to the suburban section of the *Chicago Tribune,* a tabloid insert they called *Suburban Trib.* Cute.

Readers, such as they were, referred to it as "the Little Trib" or "the little insert" or "that little stuffer," many of them finding it an altogether annoying little section that they had to throw away with the Kmart ads. The office was out in the western suburbs just off one of the expressways that would wear several sets of my radials bald before it was over. The expressway took wide berth of the city and offered a view of Chicago's skyline way off in the distance.

It was 1972. A guard had just discovered a door ajar at the Watergate in the dawn of a new era of investigative journalism. Bob Woodward had grown up in Chicago's western suburbs, and his application for employment at *Suburban Trib* had been rejected, according to the editors. If they had hired him, perhaps his slot at *The Washington Post* would not have been filled when I applied there.

As he and Carl were becoming the most rich and famous journalists in the world, I was attending suburban board meetings in Bob's stead, meetings where debates droned on until the wee hours concerning the unconscionable raising of school towel fees or getting those infernal pimientos out of the corn in the cafeteria.

"New Traffic Lanes in Des Plaines" our headlines screamed—a headline that, incidentally, rhymes. When a jetliner went down in the suburbs, we just kept typing up our meeting stories, leaving one of the worst air disasters in history to the real reporters from downtown. It was the kind of place that could deaden a man. John Belushi grew up in the western suburbs, too, and his high school yearbook listed him as a hall monitor, member of the student council, and recipient of the American Legion Citizenship Award.

It seemed the heart of journalistic darkness. In attempts to break out, suburban reporters stayed after the board meetings, listening to gadflys tell unsubstantiated tales of local corruption. I measured a lot of tree stumps in one suburb, where the mayor was suspected of paying his friend entirely too much to cut down the city's trees. The mayor was doing it, too, but I couldn't quite prove it in the two days allowed by suburban editors for massive investigations. I stuffed a folder full of scary-looking documents—my old tax returns, some insurance forms, a few favorite recipes, and other bulk fillers—and barged into the mayor's office to press for a full confession. I had the goods on him, as he could plainly see from the thickness of the folder. He offered me a complimentary cup of coffee and suggested I get my ass out of his office and out of town.

When once I managed to detail the activities of an illegal pyramid sales firm in the suburbs, the suburban editor thought it safest to leave names out of it. So, when three officials of the firm were indicted and convicted, no credit was forthcoming.

I failed in numerous attempts to blow the lid off organized crime, although I did get a good story in the process on a guy who had inadvertently knocked Tony "Big Tuna" Accardo's stuffed tuna off the wall of a restaurant. It was the very same tuna caught by Tony that had given him his nickname, and the air-conditioning repairman who knocked it down fled to another state, where he lives to this day.

It wasn't pretty. One of Chicago's newspapers went out of business, and some of its writers sought jobs at *Suburban Trib,* where the staff was growing exponentially in this never-never land of market demographics. The suburbs were the future; my career path had led to a cul-de-sac.

I was, however, developing a fascination for life in the suburbs. It seemed to be the kind of fascination that prisoners in solitary confinement develop in old gum wrappers. Maybe this was how origami got started.

I had grown up in a normal place—in Champaign, Illinois, which is not far from Normal, Illinois, actually. My mother and father had run a small-town newspaper, *The Fisher Reporter,* during the Depression, and the only strong piece of advice Father had given me was to "stay the hell out of journalism." He died in 1975, with the peace of mind, I suspect, that comes from knowing that rebellious offspring have come to realize the wisdom of your words. He never took me to Fisher. I visited the newspaper myself recently, and the owner's eyes were wide with the hope that maybe I had dropped down from the heavens—Thank you, Jesus!—to buy the damned thing.

There are those who say that suburbia is normal—so normal it hurts—but they have not developed an eye for the telling detail that suburban journalists come to have. The polyethylene flamingos, the leisure suits, the Tupperware parties, the Weber outdoor grills, the subdivisions, garage sales—it was all starting to add up, to something. This was a whole way of life, one not documented by Margaret Mead, a subject that journalists and sociologists had deliberately avoided as devoid of reflected glory. More than one third of the country's population lives in the suburbs.

I began to find sport in traveling to and from my assignments along suburban blight strips, with their repeating patterns of Dinette Citys, McDonald's, Foam Rubber Worlds, Midas Muffler shops, Carpet Barns, Fotomats, Velvamatic Car Washes, and Liquor Corrals. The newspaper office was a half block from a veritable Champs-Elysées of shopping strips, of blight continuity that stretched for four miles.

If you left early to cover night meetings of village boards, school boards, and library boards, you could stop in at the lawn ornament shops, with their pink flamingos, black- or white-faced jockey boys (for customers with differing views on "the civil rights issue"), reflecting balls, and rare finds, such as the Madonna-in-bathtub with Day-Glo orange and green sea-serpent legs uplifting her.

You could take note of the new housing developments being thrown up. Some of the names were deceptive in nature, such as Lake View Oaks, which was ten miles from a lake and two from a tree. Others lived up to their names, such as The Landings, a development with a seaside motif situated in the landlocked suburbs but at the end of a runway at O'Hare International Airport.

You passed suburban educational institutions, such as Hamburger University operated by McDonald's, which is based in Chicago's suburbs, and the Muffler Institute of Technology.

He who sought culture in the suburbs was rewarded. There were sofa-sized-art fairs. There was the unveiling at a community college of a locally done statue of astronaut Eugene Cernan, a local boy, which was so hideously rendered that a group of guerrillas, led by the president of the school, knocked it down late one night with a bulldozer and buried it somewhere. My own investigation had revealed the truth, and even though Bob Woodward's president resigned and mine didn't, I rather liked my story as well. Maybe it was possible to be a journalist and not even write about subjects discussed on *Face the Nation*.

There was garage-door art. Homeowners painted wonderful things on their garage doors: tall ships, Hawaiian scenes, trout, a trompe l'oeil stable so finely done that it looked from fifty feet as if the horses would move at any second, and, of course, the ever-popular first initial of the family's surname. Making sport of this, Dolores Hinko painted a big *B* on her garage door. Her neighbors thought she was crazy.

Didn't she know who she was? She and other kindred spirits knew perhaps better than anyone else who they were and where they were. Members of the Lake Bluff Power Mower Precision Drill Team, who performed every year in the little Fourth of July parade in that suburb, understood.

The man selling "Sofa-Sized Art" understood about the suburbs, too.

Calls to the office were always entertaining. In summer there were the calls from gardeners who had grown tomatoes or squash in the shape of some famous personality's head—usually Nixon, with the ski-slope nose. The reading of local suburban newspapers for style and content became a hobby. Of special interest were school lunch menus—"turkey loaf à la king or pizza burrito; tater barrels; corn with pimientos or carrot cubes; chilled cling peach sections in syrup; apple brown Betty; Seven-Up"—and crime reports: "A man reported Tuesday that someone physically broke in, took a large bite out of his tuna fish sandwich, and fled." And there were the usual reports of summonses issued for lawns that had grown too long.

A journalist who sees a woman arrested for watering her petunias during a sprinkling ban, then placed on probation for two years is never quite the same. The sprinkling ban was wholly unnecessary, but authorities panic easily in the suburbs. One sleepy suburb put together a fully trained, fully equipped S.W.A.T. team just in case things got out of control at a block party or church supper.

Yet another of Chicago's daily newspapers folded. I covered the county courts for a while, then became a suburban editor as expansion of the paper continued. We installed three clocks in the bureau with little signs under them reading, "Skokie," "Highwood," and "Wheeling," suburbs in three zoned editions of the paper. The writers won some awards, and some went on to better lives at other newspapers, wire services, and television stations. But a few too many Frisbees and firecrackers flew through the bureau, and executives of the paper seemed only too happy to grant my request to write a column about the suburbs—something I would do there and in New York for the next five years, between 1978 and 1983, a sampling of which is in this book.

It was as if someone had let me sneak into a grand buffet early. I could write up all of these things that interested me about the suburbs, things that had nothing whatever to do with sewer bond referenda and new traffic signals. No one else seemed to be doing it.

I was free to write three times a week about everything from the plastic flamingos and the phenomenon of suburban malls to cases of child abuse and local officials driving black and brown people out of town by condemning their apartments. In two suburbs, through which even Dr. Martin Luther King had deemed it unsafe to march, residents threw stones at black people. More genteel suburbs built cul-de-sacs along borders with black neighborhoods so blacks couldn't drive through, and a number of suburban police departments routinely stopped those who did for questioning. Unpleasantry was not much written about or discussed in the suburbs, a point brought home by the film *Ordinary People,* shot in the Chicago suburb of Lake Forest.

I was fortunate enough in my career as suburban columnist to interview four nude women at a glass-topped table in an establishment that was recruiting bored suburban housewives as go-go dancers; I fried bacon and eggs while driving to work, using a revolutionary new line of cookware for commuters that plugs into the cigarette lighter; and I placed third in the Illinois State Fair Bake Off for a column on baking off. I covered the grand opening of a funeral home, a Tupperware party, and the Witches and Pagans Convention. I traveled to Las Vegas with a group of suburban women who go there regularly rather than to psychiatrists.

I interviewed a suburban cult hero, a man who had not mowed his lawn in thirteen years and who successfully fought his police summonses in court by claiming he was a naturalist letting his lawn grow back to natural prairie. I staked out Salvation Army drop-off bins to watch suburbanites lower their children by the heels into the bins to pick out the goodies. It is something to see.

A call came from the editors of *Chicago Magazine,* who wanted to do a cover story on the suburbs. They worked on Michigan Avenue and needed a guide. I realized then that I had come to be an expert on suburbia—a questionable distinction. I could not let them go into the suburbs alone; they who knew nothing of the food, fashions, customs, flora, or fauna of this, the Mild Kingdom. I signed on for ten baby harp polyester skins and ten Ultra-suede pelts. We rented a gracious and spacious recreational vehicle with two dinettes, a bathtub, and a wood-paneled family room and set off on a seven-day, eight-hundred-mile suburban safari, camping overnight in mall parking lots. I laid in the provisions: Velveeta, Miracle Whip, and Wonder Bread for sandwiches—and Twinkies, Pop Tarts, and Froot Loops—because breakfast is the most important meal of the day. I also stocked Tupperware, in case we had to buy off unfriendly natives, and many bottles of vodka, to fight off the deadly tedium indigenous to many areas of suburbia. There is nothing quite like dawn in a mall parking lot, with the sun breaking over Lingerie and Notions at Lord & Taylor.

The newspaper touted my new suburban column as the first of its kind in any major newspaper, and the editor gave me free rein, on the theory that any "reader involvement" was good.

After my report of a tour through one particularly tacky suburb, residents drove bags of mail to the office because their outrage couldn't wait for the postal system. The plumbers union put up billboards in response to a column about their usurious fees. An Arab threatened to kill—me!—after a column about Americans being upset with the "towelheads" during the gasoline crisis. The Jay-Mar company threatened to sue over a reference to their Sansi-Belt slacks that they found uncomplimentary. Things were picking up.

I lived in the suburbs with my wife, Jody, and two children, Willie and Elizabeth, and as a suburban resident of impeccable credentials—right down to the Japanese station wagon—I believed that I had license to write whatever I pleased.

I was out there among them. I had chlorophyll stains on my tennis shoes from mowing the lawn. I knew the nuances of status associated with various brands of outdoor grills, and I knew not to answer the door during the season when neighbors were trying desperately to pawn off their extra zucchini. I knew the embarrassment of walking into a hardware store unable to put into words what I wanted. I had heard the debates over just which three goddamned beans were going to go into the three-bean salad at the block party. I coached Little League. I was made to spend all of the money we had saved for a trip to Paris on new gutters.

Although most of my columns were intended to remind suburbanites of the foibles of suburban life, I often felt called upon to defend the suburbs when outsiders attacked. Suburbia had become so diverse and vast—four million people spread out over Chicago's suburbs, for example, compared with three million in the city—that all that was said of suburbia in praise and damnation was true. There were industrial suburbs, bedroom suburbs, ethnic suburbs, wealthy suburbs that would not allow McDonald's restaurants to be built, and poor suburbs with dirt streets that looked like rural Alabama. It was all there, just more spread out than in the city. The view held by many critics of the suburbs as one homogeneous glob was no closer to the truth than the view held by many suburbanites that immediately upon crossing the city line they would be assaulted by drug-crazed youths.

There are more children in the suburbs than the city, and critics often used that as a basis for attack. A University of Chicago sociology professor criticized the suburbs as "the nursery of the republic." He charged that the suburbs offered a "feminine" style of life, meaning overly "passive" and "domestic," and said that the nation's "serious work" takes place in "the masculine province of the city." He seemed to think that devoting one's life to the increased profitability of a corporation was more important than raising children, a notion that seemed to me to be the essence of the middlebrow conformism that critics such as he so often attribute to the suburbs.

Specific criticism, such as spending one's life car-pooling or commuting, seemed more appropriate. When artist George Segal unveiled in New York his sculpture of three bedraggled commuters waiting for a bus to the suburbs, he offered the opinion that there is something "heroic" in commuters spending a good part of their lives in trains, buses, and traffic jams so that their families can live in more pleasant, safer surroundings. Like a lot of others, I live in the suburbs because I enjoy a place of serene retreat from the frenetic world outside—a patch of green, a garden, flowers, and trees. It is axiomatic that suburbs can be dull.

I don't want to have to take our two children down the elevator and several blocks away to a park when they want to play. It's Not Normal—too much like recreation period. Our nine-year-old son rides his bicycle to his friends' houses or to the school to play ball. We play catch in the yard. My five-year-old daughter heads out the side door on her own, to play in the yard, to see her buddies up and down the street, and to stop at one woman's house to see if she happens to be doing any baking that day. No, she will not grow up streetwise—a critical failure in upbringing—but if that means she will not know when she is in the presence of muggers and the like, I prefer that she isn't, thanks.

There are trade-offs to living in the suburbs, of course. But my guess is that my kids see the inside of city museums nearly as often as do a lot of city children. Tolerance is not a strong suit of suburban life, although I find that my son has black, brown, and yellow friends from his class at school, where they are probably represented in as great a proportion as they are at many of the private city schools our friends feel compelled to use.

There is criticism that suburbanites are neither fish nor fowl, living in a bourgeois netherworld between city and country, riding pathetic little lawn tractors. A certain small-mindedness can creep into suburban life, leading to such extremes as local policemen giving tickets for long lawns. That is born of the police not having enough to do in towns where we can still walk the streets and sit on park benches at night. Suburban residents will tell you that they prefer this to living behind triple-locked doors.

Since I live in the suburbs, sometimes my columns were based on things going on in my neighborhood, and one column was about something that I hadn't realized was going on. While interviewing prostitutes in a club near a suburban Army base about the economic impact of the base's proposed closing (see page 78), I was found out to be a reporter and was taken by a bouncer to a back room with a bare bulb, where the owner sat in his bathrobe. He spoke in the gravelly voice of the Godfather, which it turned out he was. I escaped with life and limb after we struck up a nice conversation about the injustices of the grand jury system.

A few days later I was washing my car in front of the house when the prostitute whose views on the importance of a large standing Army were featured in my column drove slowly by, yelled something at me then sped away. I was concerned. These were not nice people. The owner of the club had died in an unfortunate shotgun accident in the parking lot of the club shortly after I spoke to him.

A few days later I sat on my porch and noticed the same car pulling up to the curb two doors down. The prostitute stepped out of the car and walked into the house of a neighbor who happened to be a dean at a local university. House calls? A week after that, I was upstairs washing a cat (fleas) when one of the neighbors ran up the stairs excitedly. "You should *see* what showed up for the block party! A woman with tattoos all over her body!" I knew those tattoos, having seen them on the woman when she danced at the club. She turned out to be the long-lost adopted daughter of the neighbor two doors down and had showed up for the block party scantily clad and carrying a half-gallon of bourbon.

Between talk at the block party about how the tomatoes were growing and the latest developments in charcoal briquettes, she piped up with shocking little tidbits, such as the physical discomforts of riding naked on a motorcycle. The block party lasted a lot longer than usual that year, going well into the wee hours of the morning.

It was to be our last. I left to write about New York's five hundred suburbs, which are pretty much the same as Chicago's two hundred and those everywhere else. Now I'm writing about New York City. I like it. It's Not Normal, either.

I

FLORA
AND FAUNA

ON PINK FLAMINGOS

Although plastic was brought into industrial use in 1909 by L. H. Baekeland of Yonkers, New York, it was not until after World War II that the modern miracle substance was used in a wide variety of consumer goods, among them speedboats, dentures, and flamingos. Previously, flamingos were made of cement. Before that they were made by other flamingos.

When the flamingos return to Kmart, summer is nigh in suburbia. For years they have flocked by the hundreds to discount stores and garden centers. And by the time of the summer solstice, when the ceremonial Lighting-of-the-Grills was past, and the drone of the power mower was upon the land, one could observe flamingos posed on lawns and grazing in shrubbery in all their shocking—especially to the neighbors—pinkness.

Shirley Bernell stopped at the display of pink plastic flamingos in a Fairfield, New Jersey, garden center the other day and asked her husband, "Dick, do you think we should get some of these?" Mr. Bernell stared at her, frozen and speechless, as if all their years together had meant nothing. He walked slowly to the checkout counter with a can of mosquito repellent, shaking his head.

When the couple had gone, Jim Fernicola, manager of the Fairfield Home and Garden Center, admitted, "I'd never put flamingos on my lawn." At Gloria's Garden Center in Milford, Connecticut, customers could be heard snickering at the flamingos. "They're kind of a joke," said a manager there. A customer at Hoverman's Garden Center in Paramus, New Jersey, who had come to price a cement reindeer for his lawn, had this to say of plastic flamingos: "They're tacky."

He seemed to be stating the prevailing attitude toward pink plastic flamingos. While the flamingos still return each year, it seems to be in ever-decreasing numbers. Most of the major suburban chains of lawn and garden stores don't even carry them anymore, and the flamingo fancier can often drive mile upon mile—deep into the very cul-de-sacs of suburbia—without seeing a single one.

A spokesman for the Unnatural Wildlife Federation and Holistic Leisure Suit Clinic, if there were one, would undoubtedly express shock and dismay at the flamingo crunch and announce that *Flamingus Polyethylus* has been placed on the endangered list of blow-molded lawn products. That there is no one to speak for the pink plastic flamingo is no doubt part of the problem.

And a perplexing one it is. The gradual disappearance of these flamingos could not be caused by the encroachment of man, for it is we who shell out the $7.99 a pair to buy them. The flamingos are impervious to pesticides. And the problem can't be traced to industrial pollution, for the flamingos are of its essence.

"People just want other things," explained Mr. Fernicola, whose sales of lawn statuary have risen steadily in recent years. He said that people want mirrored glass balls in a variety of colors; red and aqua cement gnomes that are reading books and playing musical squeeze boxes; cement reindeer with antlers of bent reinforcing rods; big plastic daisies that spin in the wind; and little signs that warn: "Chipmunk Crossing."

Professors of landscape architecture, anthropology, popular culture, and other subjects were questioned about this situation and had remarkably little of interest to say on the subject. One said he had never even considered the question, busying himself most recently with a study of timber depletion. The squeaky wheel gets the grease.

Lloyd DeGrane, a photographer who has for some reason recorded hundreds of suburban lawn-statuary displays in recent years, said owners give him a variety of reasons for owning the things, ranging from buying them during weak moments on vacations to wanting to express strong religious beliefs. Many cement or plastic Madonnas are placed in grottos that are bathtubs turned on end and buried halfway into the ground—bathtub Madonnas they are called.

Mr. DeGrane said there are some socioeconomic and religious patterns among owners. He rarely finds such displays in well-to-do neighborhoods, save for a few large statues of Greek goddesses. Others have noted that lions and pineapples in natural, unpainted cement are popular in more affluent neighborhoods.

As whimsical remembrances of suburbia past, flamingos are selling rather well at such stores as Johnny Jupiter in Greenwich Village, where a clerk said the birds have adapted nicely to the urban environment and do quite nicely on fire escapes. In the suburbs, salespeople say that many flamingo purchases are made as gifts and sometimes for placement on the lawns of unsuspecting neighbors.

Midnight marauders have recently tried to take matters of taste into their own hands, stealing lawn statuary. A rash of plastic flamingo thefts last year in Quincy, Illinois, was reported in newspapers across the country. In 1981 David Ramsden, leader of a group that called itself CARAT (Committee Against Racism and Tackiness), was fined $200 and placed on two years probation for stealing flamingos and jockeys with black faces in Peterborough, Ontario. (Most jockeys seen these days have had their faces painted white.) A similar group was implicated in the theft of lawn statuary in West Hartford, Connecticut.

But to flamingo owners such as Bill Borden, a shopper at the Fairfield store, plastic flamingos are pleasing to the eye and certainly an improvement on the original, being of tough, unibody construction, having galvanized metal legs, and sporting colors more radiant than any found in nature. They are relatively carefree, with no messy cleanup or late-night searches for an open store that sells flamingo food.

The flamingos at Fairfield Home and Garden are manufactured by Lawnware Products, where plastic resin beads were observed coming into the plant from enormous silos. "This is plastic in its natural state," said Leo Niemiec, president of the company, running his hands through the beads. Hot pink dye is added as the plastic is heated to a fluid and funneled into a blow molder, which within seconds yielded one fresh, piping-hot flamingo after another.

The birds are then moved to the painting room, where beak, feathers, and eyes are blackened before shipping. Mr. Niemiec explained that the coloring had an ultraviolet inhibitor to reduce fading. "We don't want them to turn into egrets," he said with a laugh, slapping his palm on a four-pack of plastic Madonnas.

Mr. Niemiec noted what seemed an inexplicable paradox. At the same time that fewer flamingos are being observed on lawns, Lawnware is making more of them than ever—about fifty thousand pairs this year. He believes that the recession has prompted people to stay at home and spend more money on flamingos and other yard items.

Rose Palermo, a representative for Union Products, which makes a complete line of polystyrene lawn ornaments, said, "Right now flamingos are our hottest item. There has been a real flamingo boom in the last two years, and we'll make forty-thousand to fifty-thousand pair this year.''

"A pair of plastic flamingos in front of your house," said Mr. Niemiec, "was a sign of class twenty-five years ago." But he notes that front porches are long since gone and that people now live in their backyards. And that, Mr. Niemiec believes, is where all the vanishing flamingos have gone: into backyard landscape gardens, around patios, and alongside swimming pools.

You know who you are.

THE TREE

There are issues that continue to divide this nation, and the plastic Christmas tree is one of them.

As Wanda Bryant stands at the checkout counter of a Christmas-tree store in suburban Long Island, she notices a woman with a natural blue spruce and is compelled to speak: "That's a lovely tree," she says, "but how can you stand having it in your house with all the needles and the mess all over?"

"I certainly wouldn't have a fake one in my house," the woman with the blue spruce shoots back. "They're awful." Taking that, Mrs. Bryant picks up a large cardboard box containing her polypropylene "Natural Mountain King Quick-A-Tree model number AT 84-355-90" and stalks out.

Deeply held beliefs on this emotional issue are always close to the surface at this time of year. "This stuff happens all the time," says a manager of the store, Gardner's Village. "It's a very touchy issue. If you ask the wrong person walking through the artificial-tree section if you can help them, you have to jump back fast. They'll let you have it."

Salesclerks at other Christmas-tree stores in the area say that they frequently overhear such arguments between customers, between husbands and wives, or between company employees sent to buy a tree for the lobby.

"People who still buy natural trees have to be yo-yos," says Martha O'Neal, taking a long look at a plastic Presto Pine that folds up like an umbrella. "Why put up with the needles and with spilling water on the carpet?" Others on the artificial side of the issue cite such factors in their switch to synthetic trees as "standing out in the cold every year and tying the damned thing on the roof of the car," "stepping on the needles until March in your bare feet," and "I don't like to see all the trees cut down."

The manager says he can recommend the artificial tree as safe, economical, and convenient. "You can pay $40 or $50 for a seven-foot tree these days," he says, "or you can get an artificial one for $75 that lasts fifteen years." He notes that the artificial tree is also flame-retardant and easy to set up in these hectic times, particularly if one leaves the decorations on the individual panels from one year to the next. He also says, "There are some pretty lifelike units now."

He admits, however, to a personal preference for natural trees. "When I think of Christmas," he says, "I think of a nice-smelling tree and a fireplace."

That is no longer much of an argument, say the artificially inclined. Gardner's Village sells aerosol pine scent for plastic trees, as well as life-sized cardboard fireplaces with "electric simulated firelog." They are moving well, as are plastic wreaths, holly, and mistletoe.

Salesclerks say that even the natural trees must wind up looking unnatural, judging by the decorations customers are purchasing. They buy glow-in-the-dark aerosol flocking; wire the trees with (the recommended) 1,350 four-way lights that are synchronized to flash in time to the Christmas carols played by electronic microprocessor ornaments; garnish them with (the recommended) 125 feet of two-tone metallic garlands; and place them on rotating stands equipped with four-color floodlights.

The natural-tree faction wonders if Santa or even the local bomb squad would want to get close enough to place presents beneath such a thing. At that end of the spectrum, salesclerks say, is the reactionary traditionalist, who might come in wearing a sweater with holes in the sleeves, buy a cheap natural tree with three bad sides, and decorate it with a single, frayed string of large colored bulbs purchased on their return from the Big War.

Observers point out that there are fewer problems when the two factions in the Christmas-tree brouhaha stick to their own kind, shopping in segregated tree lots that offer one type of tree or the other. "We don't have any trouble," says Richard Muskin, assistant manager of Harrows, a store in Hempstead that sells only artificial trees. "We don't get the natural-tree types in here. They are a dying breed."

Harrows sells eighty-six styles, exhibited in predecorated fashion in a showroom with walls of crushed red velvet and a ceiling draped in metallic gold and silver garlands. The Christmas music is deafening. For added realism, some of the artificial trees have "planting instructions" rather than mere assembly instructions for the color-coded, numbered, and alphabetized pieces. Others have the standard pan-shaped stands for water or whatever liquid substance one might feed a plastic tree. "Tang" was the guess of one man particularly critical of plastic trees.

Another spokesman at Harrows says that the trend to artificial trees means that Christmas trees are put up much earlier in the year, because plastic doesn't dry out. Nothing rankles the traditionalist more, of course, than rushing the season.

Down the Hempstead Turnpike at Christmas Tree Wonderland, natural-tree devotees shivered in an outdoor lot illuminated by strings of bare bulbs, as they went about examining the fragrant natural blue spruce, Douglas fir, balsam, and Scotch pine trees.

Sooner they would eat rubber Christmas goose than have a plastic Christmas tree.

☛ CROP FAILURE

When George Walsh arrives for work at the suburban lawn and garden center, they are already there waiting, holding little bags that contain patches of their sick lawns and hoping that somehow he can cure them.

Yesterday at the West Hempstead, New York, center Tom and Marion Conroy brought in a tuna-fish can filled with dirt and brown grass. "We are very concerned," said Mr. Conroy. But it was too late; nothing could be done; dead on arrival.

Mr. Walsh, the assistant manager, said that he is often the one who has to tell them. "It isn't always easy," he said softly.

By way of autopsy, he showed Mr. and Mrs. Conroy color photographs of lawns afflicted with various bugs and diseases, asking which most resembled the appearance of their lawn. When they told him, he began asking pointed questions about where they walked the dog. "No," said Mrs. Conroy, "our dog would never do that." Mr. Walsh relented, listing cause of death as overwatering.

Suburban symbols come and go—patios giving way to redwood decks, plastic flamingos to home computers—but it seems that the suburban lawn has never been more important.

"People spend more time and money on their lawns every year," said Bob White, the owner of the West Hempstead lawn and garden center. "Most all of it on front lawns. That tells you something." A Cornell University study estimated that about $200 million a year is spent on Long Island lawns.

At the Nassau County Cooperative Extension Service, Maria Cinque, turf-grass specialist, said a seemingly never-ending stream of people are coming into the association's diagnostic laboratory with sick grass. "Some of these people," she said, "are as upset as if they were rushing their sick child to a doctor." The association has four telephone lines for giving advice to the public, and those lines are constantly busy during this midsummer period.

"You really find out," said Mr. Walsh, "how much lawns mean to people. Some are hysterical." This is the time of year when homeowners battle against the browning of suburbia caused by the awful combination of searing sun and watering restrictions and the onslaught of all sorts of lawn fungi and bugs.

Death and discoloration are rampant. Everywhere sprinklers are oscillating and pulsating and "walking" automatically across lawns at all hours of the day and night, putting strains on municipal water-well pumps and water supplies—not to mention drenching the clothes of all who try to move them from one sector of the lawn to another. "It takes me a half hour to fill my bathtub," complained a customer at the lawn center, explaining that all of the lawn watering lowers the water pressure.

Summer water-use restrictions are instituted in many suburbs, including Hohokus, New Jersey, where the borough administrator said that police cars with loudspeakers had patrolled the streets recently informing residents of the restrictions, sometimes awakening them at 3 A.M. to turn off their sprinklers.

Suburban police issue summonses for illicit lawn watering, and residents have been known to be put on probation for the offense. In Hohokus one woman was openly violating the restriction on a recent day and proclaimed loudly: "I will not let my lawn die."

"The importance of the lawn cannot be overestimated," said Jack Bienstock, a suburban area manager for Lawn-A-Mat, one of the many franchise lawn-care services that have become popular in recent years. The services charge between $100 and $350 a year to spread seed, fertilizer, and chemicals that control weeds, insects, and disease.

"Lawns are reflections of how people keep their houses inside," Mr. Bienstock said. "If he has a lousy lawn, it indicates he doesn't care, or maybe that he can't afford the neighborhood." Mr. Bienstock said that he has been teased unmercifully about his name since emigrating from France.

Robert Frank, a customer at Gardner's Village lawn center, said that heated arguments could be heard at social gatherings at this time of year about whether it is best to water during the day or at night and about whether to catch grass clippings during mowing. Experts disagree.

Not everyone is caught up in the lawn game, as Mr. Frank calls it. While his neighbors are dethatching and aerating and spreading pulverized lime, Weed-B-Gon, Turf Builder, Weed and Feed, and preemergent Crabgrass Killer, and otherwise treating their lawns like the golf course at Pebble Beach, he is "leaving things in God's hands," he said.

He said he would never think of subscribing to a lawn service, because "they fertilize and make the grass grow faster, and I would have to cut it more often."

Mr. Walsh noted that some people become so fed up with trying to maintain their lawns that they color the grass green with a new paint made for that purpose, and a few have even put down Astro-Turf.

As Mr. Walsh was prescribing all sorts of granular systemics and liquid preemergents, he said that some of his customers admit that their lawn care has a lot to do with keeping up with the Joneses, but others argue that it must be done to maintain property values.

Mr. Walsh said that some of his customers regularly measure blades of grass to make sure the lawn is uniform, sharpen the mower blade after every use, install automatic sprinkling systems, subscribe to *Weed, Trees and Turf* magazine, attend regular seminars on lawn care, and keep track of their lawns' pH balance with electronic equipment.

And he said that when he has to tell them that their lawn is dead, sometimes they cry.

THE CATERPILLAR WARS

An uneasiness grips New York's suburbs as the populace braces for an onslaught of voracious gypsy moth caterpillars.

The dreaded moth was brought to this country for experiments in 1869 by the French naturalist Leopold Trouvelot and escaped from his laboratory. With none of its natural predators here, it propagated into billions and billions of moths over the next century to become the caterpillar that ate suburbia. There may well be a movie in all of this—a drive-in movie, probably—and one that is entirely true.

In this spring of 1982, authorities conduct extensive aerial and ground reconnaissance, issuing regular bulletins on egg-mass counts and warning of the impending invasion. Citizens are advised on the problem at local "preparedness seminars." The government introduces new species of predatory flies and wasps into this country. Helicopters and fixed-wing aircraft can be heard at dawn in the suburban skies, raining down the latest in chemical and biological warfare.

Still, the caterpillars come. At approximately half past six one evening in Paramus, New Jersey, one of the hairy brown worms plunges from the trees over the patio onto Margaret Mueller's nose. Her scream pierces the suburban calm. Her husband, James, has had enough. Within minutes he is skidding into the gravel driveway at the garden shop of Alexander's with blood in his eyes.

He wants vengeance and finds plenty to choose from at the store's Gypsy Moth Control Center. The shelves of this store and those throughout suburbia are bulging, deadly arsenals in this war on worms. Mr. Mueller will take no prisoners.

He inspects chemical and biological insecticides that poison the caterpillars or infect them with viruses. Also, there are the sticky tapes that can be seen on nearly every tree in surrounding neighborhoods, tape that holds their squirming little legs as they try to climb the trees.

There are even more insidious traps, such as Lure 'n' Kill and Bag-a-Bug, which seem to violate all notions of fair play. They lure adult males using a synthetic form of the female moth's sexual attractant odors, or pheromones, and once inside, the males cannot get out, and die. It's just tough luck for those male moths who don't want to mate and are just looking to meet a nice female.

State entomologists and other experts report that infestations are spotty but that overall they expect about the same amount of defoliation as last year, when millions of acres in the metropolitan area were denuded.

Although body counts would indicate humans are winning, there are infinitely more caterpillars. "I put that sticky tape on my trees," said Mr. Mueller, "and the live ones just crawl over the backs of the dead ones." Like Chinese Communists at the Yalu River, they come wave after wave.

Human casualties have been light, although a number of suburbanites are being delivered to hospital emergency rooms after falling off ladders while trying to hang moth traps or to spray the upper reaches of their trees. Several mothers have reported skin rashes on their children that they believe the hairy caterpillars have caused.

The conflict has caused considerable civil unrest. Petitions are being passed and demonstrations held in front of town halls protesting government involvement in the worm war. They protest the use of taxpayers' funds for spraying as well as the widespread use of a controversial insecticide, Sevin. The spraying controversy often sets neighbor against neighbor, as many homeowners contract with private concerns to spray their trees.

Opponents of spraying argue, and the experts concede, that much of the counteroffensive is being conducted not because the worms pose much of a threat, but just because the little bugs are "so icky," as one entomologist put it.

At a Little League baseball game in Paramus, two parents sit under umbrellas listening to the caterpillars bounce off. Others at the game note that even when they go indoors they have to watch the insects on countless television pesticide commercials. "In July last year," says Ann D'Angelo, another shopper at the Gypsy Moth Control Center, "I could lie in bed and hear them eating the trees."

Many suburban residents have been taking the caterpillar matter into their own hands, or under their own feet, as the case may be. Many are smearing tree trunks with Vaseline or axle grease, or wrapping them in burlap, aluminum foil, or Saran Wrap to interdict the insects' climb.

Although spraying with insecticides can help, these more inventive measures are of little value, according to entomologists and other experts. "But they help the homeowner psychologically," says Richard Weir of the Nassau County Cooperative Extension Service, "who feels he just has to get out there and do something."

Unfortunately, Mr. Weir says, the pheromone traps just draw more moths. "If you feel you have to buy one," he says, "we suggest you hang it in your neighbor's yard."

Cooperative Extension officials report that one suburban Connecticut woman doused her tree with gasoline and set it on fire to kill the caterpillars, and that a homemaker in Nassau County has been putting the caterpillars in her kitchen blender, then spraying her trees with the gruesome goo, in hopes that some of the emulsified caterpillars were infected with a virus that will be passed along to those eating her leaves.

Mr. Mueller purchases some Sevin liquid, Tree Tanglefoot goo, and Repel 'M II tape. He says that he will take them home and add them to what the salesclerk refers to as an "integrated pest-management program."

Mr. Mueller confesses that his integrated pest-management program has so far consisted largely of his twelve-year-old son and a few fiendish friends in tennis shoes doing battle with the worms on his driveway. War isn't pretty.

MEGA-GAGGLES

A combined force of federal, state, and local agents swooped down on Loantaka Pond in a placid Morris Township, New Jersey, park shortly after dawn today, startling early-morning joggers and dog walkers, and scaring the honk and quack out of the geese and ducks.

The raid netted 135 Canada geese in the first of many such operations to be conducted this week in New York's suburbs, plagued as they are by what one official called "a goose menace."

Officials here said that mega-gaggles of geese have taken over parks, beaches, and golf courses, brazenly intruding on picnickers, sunbathers, and people trying to putt. They said that the geese were getting in the way and, moreover, turning these areas into slippery messes.

"They're aggressive," said Jon Rosenberg of the Morris County

Park Commission. "They move in and take over. We fire blanks over their heads, but they don't even move anymore for that."

Park districts, municipalities, corporate office complexes, and golf courses throughout the suburban area have called on the federal government for help.

The overpopulation, officials said, stems from tens of thousands of Canada geese that are no longer migrating from Hudson Bay and other areas of Canada to Florida, the Caribbean, and Central America, choosing instead to make the New York metropolitan area their year-round place to be.

This has nothing to do with the rising cost of wintering in Florida and the Caribbean, nor with political unrest in Central America, according to Al Godin, of the U.S. Fish and Wildlife Service. Mr. Godin is coordinating this week's collection of more than one thousand "nuisance Canada geese" in New Jersey and on Long Island, while other agents are collecting them in Westchester County and Connecticut.

Rather, no longer flying south seems to be a matter of today's modern goose believing that, while migrating for thousands of miles may be a fine tradition, why beat your fool wings off if you don't have to?

First of all, each goose comes equipped for winter with a 100-percent-natural down coat. "And people feed the geese here all year," Mr. Godin explained. "The birds have good grazing and water on the golf courses, usually a reservoir or two somewhere that doesn't freeze over, and they seem to know that there are laws against hunting them in the metropolitan area. They are very, very smart."

John Frampton, an agent from South Carolina, who is here with two trucks to transport about six hundred of the unwelcome geese back to his state, said many hunters insist that geese are reading the statutes. "They seem to know where they are safe," Mr. Frampton said. Agents from the Georgia Department of Natural Resources are also here to take back about six hundred geese.

Some geese have been stopping here to winter for generations. Thousands more just do not migrate at all, although they may go up and fly in formation for old times' sake, maybe over to another protected area close by. They are ideal, then, for creating new colonies in states that want them. Mr. Frampton said that of the 553 geese relocated to South Carolina last year, about 85 percent had stayed right where agents put them and that none had been lost in transit.

Using trucks, a boat, and agents on foot, the collection party at Loantaka Pond adroitly herded the birds, still looking drowsy at this hour of a Monday morning, into a pen. Feathers flew and puffs of down filled the air as the birds were lifted by furiously flapping wings into the truck.

They seemed shocked and were strangely quiet. Geese can be collected at this time of year because their primary feathers are molting and most cannot fly. A few mallard ducks herded into the pen eventually recalled that there was no reason they could not fly and went over the top of the pen. One Canada goose still had all its feathers but just went along silently with the crowd on the truck.

"I wouldn't squawk if the government was taking me to Georgia and giving me a home either," commented Frank DeGennaro, who was out for a stroll by the pond.

Maybe. But many of the geese will be relocated to areas where hunting is permitted, and some are wanted specifically for hunting. "Farmers ask for them so that they can charge up to $100 a day to hunt on their properties," said Vic Van Sant, a Georgia agent. A woman walking her dog said that she had mixed feelings about the geese leaving. "They're beautiful out on the water, but they make an awful mess on the shore," she said. "My husband just about wrapped a golf club around one of their necks this year. He believes they should all be pâté."

"Luckily no citizens had been attacked before they got the geese out of here," C. P. Babbit, a park district policeman, said solemnly. "We had no incidents, but the goose can be mean in nesting season."

Others on the scene told stories of geese walking around on neighbors' lawns and lounging by their swimming pools. There have been campaigns in the suburbs to stop feeding the birds in winter so they will migrate again, and there have been campaigns to have open season on them.

At the Bergen County Duck Pond, where the collection crew plans to call Tuesday, nearby shops sell bags of "duck food," but people complain that the geese are pushing the ducks out of the way and eating all of it. Paula Angelino said that when children come to the duck pond with ice cream cones they have purchased across the street, "it's like Alfred Hitchcock. Fifty geese attack them."

By the time the truck drove away from Loantaka Pond Monday, the mallards had stopped protesting the treatment of their captured companions and began briskly swimming what almost looked like figure eights in the pond that they now had all to themselves.

☛ TOUGH TIMES FOR THE DINOSAUR OWNER

The Mesozoic Era was a tough 165 million years, no doubt about it. With great upheavals of the earth's crust, dramatic changes of climate, mountains forming, volcanoes erupting, flora and fauna coming and going, the swamp draining one day then going under fifty feet of water the next, you could become extinct. But for a twenty-six-foot pink dinosaur that is standing out on Route 6, life is no picnic in this day and age either.

Serving nobly for twenty-seven years as the trademark of the Dinosaur Gift and Mineral Shoppe—day and night, whatever the weather—the fabric, wood, and chicken-wire dinosaur has been punched, kicked, lassoed, shot at with a .38-caliber pistol, and recently was attacked repeatedly by a GMC Blazer. Had it not been for a protective fence topped with barbed wire that was erected around the dinosaur by its owner, Ronald Januzzi, the Blazer would have finished it for sure.

"A lot of people around here apparently don't like it," Mr. Januzzi said. And it is not just the vandals—the teenagers or the middle-aged men who fortify themselves for the attacks at local saloons. There are the more sophisticated types, those who have moved to the edge of suburbia and ride the trains to work or drive to the new campus-style corporate headquarters in these picturesque hills. They ask Mr. Januzzi if he would mind taking the dinosaur down, because, well, yes, of course, it is fun and all of that, but doesn't it look a little out of place in this increasingly fashionable neighborhood area, a little, you know, tacky?

"I am insulted," said Mr. Januzzi. "I don't go into their living rooms and tell them that their $15,000 modern art paintings of one black brush stroke are a joke."

Mr. Januzzi opened the shop in 1955, doing a good business

with carloads of families who cruised the wooded hills on week-ends and vacations. His mineral exhibit is of surprising size and quality, a display of more than two thousand specimens from around the world, some of which are sparkling and valuable and others that look to the untrained eye like chunks of the parking lot.

He painted the dinosaur pink at the suggestion of a Madison Avenue advertising executive who lived in the area. Then he built Dinosaurland behind the shop, the kind of roadside attraction that entrepreneurs were erecting across the country, theme parks built by individuals with a tool kit and with what amounts today to a week's grocery money.

Sights such as Dinosaurland and the pink dinosaur were once relatively common on suburbia's fringe. There are still examples of this "highway architecture" around New York, such as the Big Duck, a roadside building shaped like a big duck and selling same; the Gallon Measure Service Station, shaped like an oil can; and the Orange Julep, which looks like an orange. But aficionados say that these are relics of a bygone age, when motoring was an adventure of burial caves and reptile gardens, of motel units shaped like te-pees, and of shops selling "authentic" Indian artifacts—polyethyl-ene wampum beads and belts of Hong Kong tribes.

Tours of Dinosaurland start just out the backdoor, where a guide points out several dozen "research bins" of "research materials"—lidded garbage cans full of rocks. Next on the weeded path is a replica of a "mine dump," or pile-of-rocks, the kind mineralogists like to rummage through, Mr. Januzzi explained. Next are several models of dinosaurs, then fossilized dinosaur tracks from suburban Connecticut, dinosaur stomach stones, and also coprolites, which Mr. Januzzi said many visitors drop upon discovering that coprolites are fossilized dinosaur droppings.

"It would be better," he said, "if I'd had some money to spend. But the children like it, it's for them." What Dinosaurland lacks in thrills, its owner has tried to make up for in education. "But the older ones want Disneyland and Adventureland so they can scream and yell," said Mr. Januzzi, whose knowledge of dinosaurs and minerals is considerable.

"Kids today often think that because a place is small, it is of low quality, but sometimes the opposite is true. Frankly, those big places lack the educational punch," he said firmly, holding a fist in the air.

The idea of his place is education, particularly since the big road went through. Interstate 84 has sapped all but local traffic from Route 6, speeding Mr. Januzzi's former customers—the ones who bought his 25-cent plastic dinosaurs, candy, and Dinosaurland pennants, bumper stickers, and ashtrays—past the rear of his property at fifty-five miles an hour on their way to more distant and glamorous attractions. "I finally ran out of pennants last year," he said, raising his voice above the truck traffic. "I'm not going to re-order."

He believes that he may soon close Dinosaurland, which is also plagued by vandals. The interstate that has taken traffic from his door is also playing a part in the rapid development of this exurban area, making his land more valuable and the property taxes too much to bear.

The pink dinosaur should come down for repairs from all the vandalism, but Mr. Januzzi believes that if he does that, highway officials will not let him put it back up. It is too close to the roadway but has been allowed to remain since it was already there when modern standards were adopted. He would like to replace it with a dinosaur built of steel and concrete, something more able to stand up to the attacks of man. It would be just as big. And as pink. If only he had the money. "The little places are dying," lamented Mr. Januzzi. "People around here now seem to want nothing but corporate headquarters on this road, and franchised restaurants and hotels, the kind that advertise 'no surprises.' They seem to want everything to look alike. And everyone to be alike."

Tough times for pink dinosaurs and those who own them, no doubt about it.

II

FOOD, CLOTHING, AND SHELTER

THE ZUCCHINI PLAGUE

Zucchinni. It's a difficult thing for me to write about. For one thing, it's really hard to spell. For another, someone I know almost died in a zuchinni-related incident.

Her husband came home and caught her in the act—slipping zucinni into a casserole. She said they have a garden, and that he has grown to hate the little green squash after eating them every day all summer. She said he's warned her not to serve any more of them and probably would have tried to kill her if she hadn't been brandishing a large zucini in her left hand.

A suburban man—a neighbor of mine—went out the other day to find his four-ycar-old boy and returned with seven zuccinnis. He had been accosted in front of his own home by zuccini-wielding neighbors, who forced them on him.

My wife went outside recently and was hailed by a friendly neighbor who she assumed just wanted to talk. She didn't realize until it was too late that she was about to have a piece of chocolate-zuchini bread foisted on her, now just another sad statistic in the zukini plague.

Another neighbor returned home from work on his birthday for what he hoped would be a nice party. But things got ugly when his wife presented him with a pineapple-zucchinni birthday cake.

We never used to have trouble with zuchinni around here.

Very few people even had gardens. Life was simple for most of us. Vegetables tended to be either corn or beans and came in either tin cans or plastic pouches. There was no flavor or nutritional value ("That's Our Pledge") to worry about with these Factory Fresh vegetables, so Mom could just serve yellow or green according to the principles of Plate Color Management (PCM) she'd learned in Home Ec classes. She felt a little guilty about just opening a can, so she'd slow-boil them for sixty minutes before serving.

Then, four years ago, the number of home gardeners increased astronomically to an amazing 49 percent of American households, according to a Gallup survey. Food prices had gone up. There was an emphasis on nutrition and eating fresh, natural, organic foods. There was a lot of interest in trying to mellow out and improve yourself through vegetarianism. (Gandhi, Plato, Mussolini, and

Hitler were all said to be vegetarians.) Vegetables became immensely popular. Gerald Ford was nearly elected to a second term.

All manner of previously unheard-of vegetables were being served up: okra, kale, kohlrabi. Then: "Two or three years ago came a tremendous boom in zucinni," according to Edna, Ray's wife, down at Ray's Quality Produce stand and u-pick-'em in Chicago Heights. Spokesmen at Vauhhan's Seed Co., Downers Grove, and the George J. Ball seed company in West Chicago agree.

"Zucini broke out of the Italian neighborhoods, just like broccoli did after World War II," says Jim Wilson, of the National Garden Bureau. (He makes it sound quite dramatic—don't be surprised if you see Al Pacino in the starring role.) Wilson says zuccini has now moved up to the number five spot on the vegetable-from-seed hit list, noting it wasn't even mentioned in a similar Top 25 list in 1973.

"It's much, much more popular for some very good reasons," says a spokesman for Burpee's, the world's largest mail order seed firm. "You can prepare it in a thousand different ways. It grows easily and anywhere in the world. It's relatively impervious to bugs and disease and seems to never stop producing."

That gives you an idea of what we're up against—we who choose not to grow zuckini, not to accept zuckinni bread as Christmas gifts, not to grow it, eat it, sit next to people who do in restaurants, and not to take in the unwanted zucceeni dropped off on our doorsteps by neighbors.

We support Zero Zuccini Growth. According to our calculations, about three hundred new zuchinis come into this world every second during the summer growing season. Every second. This according to Gallup estimates of 35 million gardens, U.S. Department of Agriculture figures on the percentage of gardens that grow zuchini (the federal government may have missed those Russian troops massing in Cuba, but these things they know), and a conservative estimate of the number of zucchinnis grown in every garden. And that isn't even counting the commercial production. Friends, there are easily more zuchinnis on U.S. soil thàn Americans.

The harvest starts early and doesn't end until the first frost. The people who grow zucinni wind up putting it in every recipe—conceivable and inconceivable—just to get rid of it. Not only is there zucini birthday cake, but pie, pizza, soufflés, fritters, omelets, creole, casseroles ad nauseam, lasagna, sticks, bisque, quiche, pancakes, tempura, and of course the ubiquitous zuckini breads.

And when their families turn on them, they take to the streets with their concoctions and there is the Knock-on-the-Door. You can turn the lights out and lie on the floor, but sooner or later you have to come out of the house. And when you do, they're waiting. They have zuccinnis for you. Long, green zuccinis. In bulk quantity. There are fourteen in my kitchen right now waiting to be eaten. If only they were waiting for something else. Fourteen. Today.

"It can be boiled, baked, broiled, breaded, sautéed, grated, you name it," says one of our neighborhood's largest growers. "You can stuff it or can it," she continues.

My sentiments exactly.

☛ THE LAST LEISURE SUIT IN AMERICA

This is alarming.

The American people, already facing the critical problems of inflation, rising crime, and energy shortages, are living under the assumption that they can walk into any suburban Kmart, anytime, and purchase a nice polyester leisure suit.

Well, they can't. This is not a test. This is not a fashion advisory. This is an alert.

The situation appears critical. This country's polyester leisure suit reserves are suddenly and without warning almost totally depleted. Know this: The leisure suits that you continue to see on patios, at Rotary meetings, and in Ponderosa Steak Houses on Saturday nights were not purchased this year. What is worse, none of the petroleum-based leisure wear is even in the pipeline.

Under the current administration, stores that once bloomed with double-knit leisure suits of burgundy, sienna, banana, robin's egg blue, and orange (the choice of state legislators) now have none. And there appears to be a shortfall in white belts and white shoes with the shiny patina.

Worn together, of course, the leisure suit, white belt, and white shoes have come to be known as "the full Cleveland"—the backbone of suburban fashion for at least five years. The FCI (Full

Cleveland Index) has fallen below 50 percent in Midas Muffler waiting rooms for the first time in years.

The spun, aerated plastic suits were first introduced for wear during time away from work, newly defined as "leisure time." Eighty percent of business firms allowed them to be worn to work by 1976, and John Molloy, author of the book *Dress for Success*, stated that the credibility ratings of people in white shirts was plummeting, while those ratings for people wearing leisure suits and "mod" clothes had leaped. His explanation was Watergate.

"Now," said David O'Brien, a national menswear buyer for Sears, "the dress-down era is ending. Leisure suits are going out. Double knit has been totally replaced by woven polyester."

Leisure suits: out. Double knit: gone. Think of it. The disappearance is sudden and mysterious: short supply despite continued demand; Sears now shipping a lot of their leftover leisure suits to England and Africa; silence on the leisure suit crisis at the White House; the so-called doctor appearing on the television show *Fernwood Tonight* claiming that leisure suits cause cancer.

The likes of Ralph Lauren and Bill Blass are pushing the all-American double-knit polyester leisure suit with the wide collar and white top stitching off the racks in favor of natural fabrics. (Remember: silk is worm discharge.) We sensed trouble when we were told we couldn't talk about the problem with Sears's national fashion coordinator because he was in Europe. Europe!

Those designer labels mean nothing to us. We want more petro-togs from Monsanto and Phillips 66. We in suburbia look for that "100 percent polyester" label. It is a fabric by suburbanites for suburbanites, said to have been invented right here in our own Amoco Research Center in Naperville, Illinois—as was lead-free premium!

Let's look before we leap. *Good Housekeeping* reports that natural fibers often can't stand up to the heavy air pollution of urban areas. Pollution can fade their colors, yellow whites, and weaken some fabrics to the point of destruction.

Let's say a fellow wants to sit out on his patio in Hodgkins (a suburb and a disease) to drink Blatz beer and watch the Sox. If he's wearing, say, a cotton T-shirt, he could be in serious trouble. According to *Good Housekeeping*, if there is any humidity the natural fibers swell, letting in oxides or nitrogen and ozone plus sulfur dioxide. If our suburbanite begins perspiring from all the Blatz, Mom can just set one less place for dinner—our suburbanite would be eaten alive by the acidic fluids.

No such problem with polyester, first introduced in 1942 as a material for boat hulls. And with polyester, there's no chance that moths will attack your natural-fiber clothing, not to mention boll weevils.

In the course of our investigation, we called about thirty suburban men's shops targeted as likely to have leisure suits. None did. A clerk at the Hanover Park Zayre's said that, despite continuing demand, the store does not carry them anymore. At the Bolingbrook Kmart, a clerk said, "I know, I know. My husband loves them, too, but we just don't carry them anymore."

Finally, after two days of searching, some were found. There were a few nice leisure suits ($18) and tops ($8.77) still available on the clearance rack at Wards' Budget Store in Villa Park. Down the street, the J. C. Penney Catalogue Store seemed desperate to move their last remaining leisure suits, pricing the suit units at $9.99 and the tops at $1.99! What value.

The end is near. It is time to take stock. What, for example, will you wear to 1970s nostalgia parties? At Penney's, a clerk issued this chilling and only slightly overstated sales pitch: "That's right. People don't realize you can't get them anymore. In your size that could be The Last Leisure Suit in America."

NEED DOOHICKEY; GIZMO'S BROKE

Into the suburban hardware store strode the few hundred—complaining of faucets dripping, drains clogging, toilets running, plaster falling, mowers stalling.

"I need a . . . a thing," said Nicholas St. George, a homeowner groping for words and using his hands in an attempt to explain his problem to Fanny Schaefer, proprietor of Schaefer's Hardware Store in Lyndhurst, New Jersey. "The door thing," he continued, "closes too far, past the other thing, and the thing catches, see what I mean?" Within a minute, Mrs. Schaefer handed him an item and he shrieked, "This is it!"

She explained modestly that she has had years of experience interpreting this primitive form of communication used by the weekend suburban handyman. Her customers believe that she has extrasensory powers.

Customers ask for "gizmos" and "what-cha-ma-call-its" and "doohickeys," and they make crude drawings on paper bags of what it is they think they need. But on this Saturday, none will stump the seventy-year-old Mrs. Schaefer, her grandson, Mark Bolatin, or any of the several young clerks she has trained.

There is something of a traffic jam outside the store. A majority of suburban residents own their own homes, which continually fall apart in annoying, perplexing, and incalculable ways—making the hardware store the busiest place in town on weekends. The emergencies of those double-parking in front of Schaefer's range from the man who has a leaking pipe that has brought down his dining room ceiling and who knows what next, to the one who has graciously rushed out during halftime of a football game to buy a rake so his wife can do the leaves.

"The thing falls off my garage door," said Geri Brooks, raising her voice above the key grinder and the paint shaker, "then my garage door falls off." It is determined that a push nut will solve her problem. She is given ten minutes of instruction in precisely what to do, along with a sketched diagram. The charge: 39 cents.

Few sales are for more than $3 this day. Mrs. Brooks is somewhat embarrassed at her lack of knowledge. "But that's why I love this store," she said. "They know you're dumb and they help you." She said that sometimes she wished that all the world were a hardware store.

She and others did say, however, that there is something slightly unnerving about stepping up to the counter and ordering in a hardware store, but the clerks assure her that even the guys in flannel shirts, paint-splattered pants, and work boots make mistakes. When one of these working types was told this day that his order of a "half-inch sweat globe valve" was the wrong thing for the job, he was so humiliated he nearly ran out of the store.

"We teach," said Mrs. Schaefer, and sometimes she and the others just go ahead and do the job. One helpless handyman, a certified public accountant by trade, brought in a leaky faucet. "The plumber wanted $45 just to look at this," he said. Mark fixed it with a rubber washer. The charge was about 10 cents.

Discount stores carrying hardware have greatly diminished the ranks of these local hardware stores in recent years, Schaefer's being the last of nine in Lyndhurst. Schaefer's and others like it ward off this threat by offering service, free advice, and the ability to find just about anything in their dusty catacombs. "You can't ask a plastic package in a discount store any questions," said Michael Foerster, a customer.

Joseph Carlozzi, who noted that his father was the store's first customer fifty-two years ago, said that the store had not changed much. It is what suburban hardware aficionados call a "real" hardware store, as opposed to a relatively new species that carries quiche pans and wine racks along with little packets of screws and nails. Schaefer's has creaking, unfinished wood floors with metal plates in several spots to keep customers from plummeting through holes to the basement. The aisles are two and three feet wide and the merchandise a conglobation of clutter.

That an item can be found among the tens of thousands of nuts and bolts, nails, screws, washers, roach tape, Dragon Skin, cotter pins, pick mattocks, lag screw shields, grommet kits, scratch awls, spokeshaves, ten thirty-seconds flat-head steel-plated machine screws, and Ever-Flex vinyl-coated Monkey Grip gloves seems a miracle. Mrs. Schaefer's dog, Teki, sometimes blocks access to the cash register, and nails are sold by the pound or the handful, not in packages.

Mrs. Schaefer took a break, going up a few steps by the glass cutter through an open doorway into the kitchen of her home. On occasion, a customer will be found up there having a cup of coffee at her dining room table. A most favored customer might even be offered a blintz. The house is filled with her paintings, which she did until her husband died fourteen years ago and she didn't have time for hobbies anymore. "I was bewildered by all the things in that store," she said, "but I decided to learn the business and run it."

Back downstairs at two minutes before 6 P.M. closing time, a customer called, pleading that the store stay open until she got there, an occurrence so common that they have stopped the clock so that it always reads 5:58.

A stylishly dressed woman about thirty years old ran in ten minutes later and announced angrily to Mark, "This is the worst day of my life. We just moved into our new house and when they delivered the dryer they didn't hook it up. And the washer is hooked up wrong. What a horrible day."

"Don't look so unhappy, honey," said Mrs. Schaefer, bobbing up from beneath a counter. "You should say, 'Thank God' that you have a dryer. You should say, 'Thank God' that you don't have to wash your clothes in a river as our ancestors did. You should say, 'Thank God' that you are able to have your own home."

"Thank God," the startled woman whispered.

"That's better," Mrs. Schaefer said. "Now let my grandson give you some flexible hose and some adapters and sealant, and you'll feel a lot better."

Do-IT-YOURSELF FOOD, CLOTHING, AND SHELTER

With less than seven months left in the "Me Decade," I'm still looking for mine.

Why is it that "they" seem to be having the best of the "Me Decade?" At the dawning of the 1970s, gasoline was about twenty cents a gallon. They pumped it, they checked your oil, they washed your windshield, and they gave you Green Stamps.

I drove into a gas station in Northbrook, Illinois, the other day, and there with me at the new self-service island was the driver of a new Cadillac Eldorado, pumping his own gas. He had a pained expression on his face as he removed the nozzle from his tank and gasoline dribbled on his shoes. I hope he wasn't on his way to apply for membership in an exclusive club or to lunch with a glamorous socialite. When you're trying to make it in high society there's nothing quite like the scent of unleaded to give you away as a self-service kind of guy.

Inflation is wreaking havoc on the suburban middle class in the "Me Decade," leaving us with no cash for esting, Rolfing, primal screaming, hang gliding, or any other form of seventies self-actualization.

The newspaper today says, "The president's anti-inflation program has been undermined by a surge in the prices of food, shelter, medical care and energy." Other than that, he seems to be doing pretty well.

Self-service is more to the point than self-actualization. Self-service, do-it-yourself, and no-frills: no-frills homes and no-frills flights; no-frills economy cars designed for midget wrestlers and unattractive enough for use by telephone company personnel; and no-frills-no-service discount department stores selling clothes hand-tailored in Korea—North Korea, apparently—by people who hold a grudge.

Franchise stores that sell do-it-yourself home kits—home kits!—are sprouting up along suburban shopping strips. Stop whimpering. Is it asking too much that you build your own home?

And, of course, there are the no-frills food stores selling the new generic foods. These stores go out of their way to avoid aiding or abetting customers. Some turn the heat down and the electric doors off. They use low-watt light bulbs, dump packaged foods in piles on the floor, and make you bring your own bags. They do everything they can to create an unpleasant atmosphere so you will think you're really getting a bargain. Next, they should hire some employees just to push customers around.

All suburban food stores now have generic food departments, which look like the pantry of the Fifth Army, with their plain white boxes marked with black letters: "Corn Flakes," "Cola," "Breakfast Drink," "Detergent," and the like.

Shoppers are paranoid about being seen in the generic food departments by neighbors across the store buying Perrier and Swiss Emmenthaler cheese at $4.79 a pound. People worry that they will be drummed out of the country club or the Junior League. In dreams, I see my wife diving into the dairy case to avoid being seen in the generic food department. I see myself telling lies to neighbors who notice big boxes of Gravy Train in my shopping cart and who know I don't have a dog. And what about all those cow brains and tongues in my shopping cart? "Oh, heavens no, we don't *eat* this stuff. My son and I are building a cow. Model Cow Club."

New in the stores this week is generic meat—something to help us adopt a totally integrated recessionary life-style; something to serve when your family has had it up to here with the new-and-cheaper-by-far thirty-percent soyburger. "Terrier Helper" must surely be on the way.

Generic beef is coarser and tougher and of a somewhat different hue than other grades. The butcher explained that it is from older animals in which bone ossification has occurred. I'm not sure what that means, but these are probably animals who figured they had it made, figured that they could live out their lives playing shuffleboard and Mah Jongg out in the pasture, until somebody came up with the big idea of generic beef.

Generic beef is not Prime grade, not Choice, not Good, not Standard, and not Commercial grade beef. It is USDA Utility grade. "Utility" is not a pretty word. Utility beef sounds like something you might carry in your trunk for patching a flat. It comes from animals graded by government inspectors as "Utility-grade animals," which must make the cows feel lousy about themselves.

Utility beef is sold with special cooking instructions. Disregard those instructions. Remember these: remove wrapper or don't (a personal preference); check meat for rabies tags that could chip a tooth; marinate meat a fortnight in one part Vaseline Intensive Care Lotion and one part liquid tree-stump remover; take meat outside; slam it repeatedly in car door; affix meat to vehicle's rear tire (unless you have front-wheel drive) and drive meat 55 mph for twenty minutes on each side of the expressway; using jumper cables, shock meat with standard twelve-volt battery; pistol-whip meat with handgun (warning: don't get trigger-happy; bullets will ricochet off meat); then ask meat: "Do you want some more?"; toss meat into street and call the road kill squad of your local highway department for pickup; or invite the President to dinner.

There was a full-page layout in the newspaper two days ago on a line of new, trendy cardboard furniture—"so right for today"— called Corrugates.

A spokesman for Corrugates said the best part is that it is not only trendy but affordable—a one-bedroom apartment could be furnished for $1,000. The article said that the furniture is perfect for unmarried couples living together because if they have a fight, the lightweight furniture can be knocked down in a matter of minutes and easily toted away.

Accompanying the article was a photograph showing an attractive, smiling young woman, walking along and swinging an obviously lightweight, knocked-down cardboard chair with a handle on it, as well as another photograph of the woman sitting on her unfolded chair. Judging by the big smile on her face as she sat alone in a room, cardboard chairs are more fun to sit in than ordinary chairs.

She seemed serious. She was not wearing a clown's nose, nor did she have a plastic arrow sticking through her head.

This was the decade when self-service, no-frills, do-it-yourself restaurants came into their own. Places like McDonald's and Burger King, about the only places families can afford to eat, not only have us serving ourselves but doing the busboy work as well.

When the Whopper at Burger King went up to $1.15 recently the Whopper Junior was introduced. Now that the Junior is approaching $1.00, the Evanston, Illinois, Burger King has gone to a no-frills Whopper for 65 cents.

It is the same size, comes in a colorful package, and takes two hands to handle and everything, but it has no meat. It took me a while to eat one because I kept removing the bun and staring at it.

It has no catchy name yet. The bunless burger, you will recall, was named the Salisbury steak after J. H. Salisbury, who came up with the idea. But the meatless Whopper was the idea of a man named Larry Berger, so the sandwich may just have to be called "Larry."

It was an interesting dining experience, but when I walked out I must say that I was still hungry, still looking for something to sink my teeth into.

And only six months and three weeks left in the "Me Decade."

PLUMBING THE DEPTHS OF HOMEOWNERSHIP

I think it was the week after I'd spent the $454 for $200 worth of car repairs, but right before Sears refused to honor the guarantee on a week-old tire ("Our Best Tire") that disintegrated when we hit that pothole.

It was a Saturday, because I remember the ad in the Yellow Pages said no extra charge for weekend service. It was the weekend after the announcement that Cook County's gas taxes were going up to the highest in the nation and before the report that inflation is running at a 15-percent annual rate.

Yes, Saturday the seventeenth, the day we received our gas bill for the worst winter in history. We were frantically cleaning up our house and ourselves in preparation for my mother's visit. My three-year-old got out of the tub and it wouldn't drain. When he gets out of a tub, the water looks like 10W-30 with twenty thousand miles on it.

I plunged. Nothing. There are no small problems in the wonderful world of home maintenance.

I had seen fifteen *Star Wars* figures in the tub with my son. I surmised that there was a battle for intergalactic supremacy going on in the drainpipe. Or at a minimum, Luke Skywalker had taken Princess Leia down there. They don't call them "action figures" for nothing.

I was already late to pick up my mother at the airport. We decided to call a plumber.

My wife went to the Yellow Pages. It looked good. Nice selection. Little drawings of smiling, friendly men running with their tool boxes to help someone. Even the wrenches were smiling.

She picked one that had a Chicago phone number, but with offices in the suburbs: "No Extra Charge for Sat-Sun and Holidays . . . Lo-Lo Prices . . . ½ Hr Radio Dispatched . . . U-Save Emergency Service . . . Sensible Prices."

Sounded good. They said they'd be there right away so I left for the airport.

My wife told me when I returned that the plumber came about two hours later, a young man in blue jeans with identifying filth on his clothes.

It was 2:10 P.M., she remembers because the electric hair rollers were just going in.

I had already taken off the trap top and bailed out the tub. All the plumber had to do was throw the switch on his power rodder, a device that forces a rod through the pipes to clear them out. When he did, a black substance was removed from the pipes and blown all over our walls in a simple, one-step operation.

It was 2:20 P.M. The electric rollers were coming out, when he said he was finished. (I would question that he was finished. I don't like to criticize, but the black sludge didn't quite cover all of our walls in one coat.)

The bill was . . . excuse me, I get these shooting pains in my left arm . . . eighty-five dollars.

My wife was angry and upset, but she finally paid. He told her he wasn't charging her any more than anybody else, that it was a flat fee. He showed her other checks to prove it. He said it wasn't his fault that we'd done most of the work and that one time he'd spent two hours on a power rodding job.

He left at 2:25 P.M., right after he said: "I sure hope that stuff comes off your walls."

Even with my mother present, there was great wailing and gnashing of teeth when I came home.

"Eighty-five dollars for fifteen minutes!" I screamed. "Those crooks! Those robbers! That's $340 an hour! Call Ted Kennedy. We don't need national health insurance, we need catastrophic plumbing insurance!

"Why not just send the damned bathtub down to Houston for a drain bypass? I could get Michael De Bakey or Christiaan Barnard in here to work on the pipes for $340 an hour. At least you'd have a heart specialist on hand when you got the bill. And they don't make you mop up the operating room when they're done, either."

I called De Bakey in Houston to see what he'd charge for, say, a fifteen-minute toilet-float transplant. He was in surgery, so I told his secretary to tell him if the stress ever got to him, he could clear $707,200 a year snaking out pipes forty hours a week. She said he might very well be interested.

☛**P**ASSION FASHION

What we want to talk about today is crotchless underpants.

I speak of underpants that are literally without benefit of crotch; that have no crotch whatsoever.

Incredibly, there were no crotchless underpants until the 1940s. That is when Frederick Mellinger, a young combat tailor who spent World War II in Joplin, Missouri, where, he says, he "saw plenty of action," invented, discovered, or somehow fumbled upon them.

He opened a small crotchless underpants stand, selling his invention to women. (Until the position of zippers on men's pants is moved, it is doubtful the Consumer Products Safety Commission would authorize their sale to men.)

He called his small shop Frederick's of Hollywood, owing to his name and the shop's location. Even there in "Sin City," he says, he was called a dirty old man.

But hookers, aspiring starlets on their way to job interviews, and others bought his crotchless underpants. Lots of others; enough that he started opening more stores and a big catalog sales operation. People couldn't seem to get enough of his crotchless underpants.

Today thousands, maybe millions of women all across the country own and operate his crotchless underpants. And Frederick Mellinger stands as a man who became a millionaire selling dirty underwear with holes in it.

So certain is Mellinger of the universality of the sexual revolution that our crotchless crusader is opening dozens and dozens of his shops in suburban shopping centers selling his complete line of "passion fashion" among the Sears and J. C. Penney stores. He has 114 stores in 30 states, with the vast majority now in suburban malls.

The flourishing of Frederick's of Hollywood in the suburbs stands alongside the success of *Playboy* magazine as a monument to the sexual revolution.

Consider the store in North Riverside, a Chicago suburb that one village spokesman proudly says "hasn't changed much over the years." It's a suburb of solid, hardworking, middle-class Americans, predominately of Bohemian ancestry and devoutly Catholic—an area of "people with a relatively strict moral upbringing," the spokesman says.

They buy "passion fashion" like it's going out of style—like Frederick Mellinger knew they would.

"I am not sure how Harold will react to this," says one shopper at the North Riverside store, Rebecca Craddock of Oak Park, referring to her husband and a pair of crotchless underpants. "If he doesn't like them, maybe I should trade him in."

It has come to the point where high fashion is now the stuff Mellinger has been selling since 1945. Stiletto-spiked heels, dresses with leg-long slits, and see-through blouses are now seen in store windows throughout the suburbs. Some top designers steal ideas directly from his catalog.

In an apparent backlash of the women's movement and unisex, the country has leaped from the National Women's Conference just thirteen months ago to the Lycra Spandex Age of Charlie's Angels, Honey Bears, and top designers showing "exhibitionist" body stockings with breast cutouts and clear plastic jeans.

(If this means that militant feminists won't punch me in the mouth anymore for inadvertently stepping on the Auto-Door opener mat at my food store, then I'm all for it.)

"North Riverside carries almost exactly the same line we carry in Las Vegas or Hollywood or any of our stores," Mellinger says. "I used to be worried about how we'd be accepted in a suburban location like North Riverside, but no more. I worried about Omaha, too, but I was wrong.

"In the suburbs as elsewhere, there are always those who need something to frown upon," he says. "But if I've learned anything about such areas it's that what people say and do is two different things."

TWINKIES AS FOOD

You will remember from health class—if you weren't back there flipping ahead to the reproduction chapter—that there are five basic food groups: milk and milk products; meat and meat substitutes; vegetables and fruits; breads and cereals; and those foods developed in man's attempt to conquer outer space and develop better roofing materials.

The fifth group, referred to alternately as "fun," "snack," or "junk" foods, has emerged as the favorite of the American people. These foods are typically loaded with sugar, oil, and calories. They are of little nutritional value and the best of them rot your teeth.

I tend to like the salts and oils: Chee-tos, although the Agent Orange is difficult to get off your fingers; Pringles New Fangled Potato Chips, manufactured by Procter & Gamble, one of the leading manufacturers of washday detergents; and Doritos Nacho Cheese Tortilla Chips, because where else can your body get the nacho it needs?

My wife, on the other hand, is in the sweets camp. She craves double-stuffed Oreos, Hostess cupcakes, Twinkies, and even a nice dry brownie mix spooned right out of the box. She draws the line at eating those pink Sno-Balls, but does wear them on the toes of her bedroom slippers.

With sales of a billion annually, Twinkies is king of snack foods. Our own James Dewar of River Forest invented them fifty years ago. People don't even know that, which calls into question our entire educational system.

Twinkies are famous. Archie Bunker screams when Edith forgets to put them in his lunch box; there are Twinkie festivals and Twinkie-eating contests at colleges; a novel has just been written about a raid on a Twinkie factory; a Los Angeles man reportedly lived for seven years on a diet of Twinkies and Cutty Sark; and Suzanne Somers recently complained on television that she didn't like Monte Carlo because there weren't any Twinkies—even though she was accompanied there by Paul Anka.

Dewar sat in his living room in suburban Chicago on a recent day and spoke almost without emotion about The Creation. "We were selling Twinkie-shaped sponge cakes in 1930 for use as short-cake during the strawberry season," he said. "But the pans sat idle except for those six weeks. I had the idea to put in a cream filling—make that creamlike filling—and sell them year round. I got the name from a Twinkletoes Shoe billboard in St. Louis." It was also Mr. Dewar's idea to put the filling in the chocolate cupcakes, too. Incredible.

How long can the Royal Academy of Sciences, which has been announcing its Nobel Prizes this week, look the other way? They give awards to such people as James Cronin, the University of Chicago professor, for his work in "discovering violations of fundamental symmetry principles in the decay of neutral K-mesons." Fine. But we still can't get Egg McMuffins after 11 A.M.

Of what possible value is all this research to our lives? What's going on in the scientific community? Wasn't it the science teacher in high school who tried to tell us that the earth is hurtling through space at sixty-six thousand miles per hour and spinning around one thousand miles per hour? If this were true, do you think your hair would stay combed five seconds? Why not give an award for something practical, something you could eat?

Dewar, known as "Mr. Twinkie" by those at the Continental Baking Company, is now retired. As he reflects on the historic moment in snack food history, he continually offers candy to visitors, never failing to take some himself. He suggests repairing to the kitchen for some ice cream.

At 83 years of age, Dewar looks like one of those 145-year-old Russian tribesmen who appear younger with each carton of yogurt—just as mentally and physically fit as could be. "I try to eat some Twinkies every day," he said. He had just eaten the last one in the house, as a matter of fact, and opened a refrigerator to see what else he had to offer. Inside were a dozen Cokes, apple strudel, a canister of fudge, a box of Fannie Maes, and nothing more. The freezer contained ice cream bars, some gourmet vanilla ice cream, a bag of jelly beans, and that was it. We had our way with both compartments.

He showed me photographs of his four children, fifteen grandchildren, and twelve great-grandchildren. "They all love Twinkies," he said. "Damned right. One of my boys played professional football, but I'm the hero of the family for inventing Twinkies."

He poured himself a cup of coffee, ladled in three teaspoonfuls of sugar, then set out some brownies and chocolate peanut butter bars. "Yes, Twinkies have been very, very good to me," he said, as I drifted off into insulin shock.

Not only does the inventor of Twinkies live out here, but the little yellow torpedoes are manufactured in nearby Schiller Park. Russ Wilke, assistant superintendent of the International Telephone & Telegraph, Continental Baking Company, Hostess Cake Division Plant, gave me a tour.

He has not lost his enthusiasm for snacks in all his years with the company and was the perfect guide for this Willy Wonka tour. At every turn he said, "Isn't this fascinating?" And it was: double waterfalls of chocolate cascading onto 368 Ho Hos each minute; gargantuan taps gushing forth creamed filling; 82-foot-long ovens baking Suzy-Qs; cooling towers that spun around thousands of cupcakes; and thousand-pound vats of Twinkie mix.

Peering into a huge vat of six hundred pounds of chocolate icing, I told Russ that my wife would just jump in if she were along. Without smiling, Russ replied, "You get used to it after a while."

Several years ago, a local columnist could write that Twinkies were the one thing he could think of that nobody had ever said anything bad about. Times have changed.

A so-called public interest science and nutrition researcher recently attacked Twinkies and other snack foods. He said they are bad. Clearly they aren't. They are good. Nearly one billion Twinkies will be consumed this year, and Mr. Dewar will thereby be responsible for bringing a greater sum of unalloyed happiness to mankind than all the fundamental symmetry principle violations in China.

Nutritionists have said they are hazardous to your health and some claim that they even contribute to criminal behavior. Dr. Lendon Smith, the famous pediatrician, said in a telephone interview that Hostess should be taken to court for advertising Twinkies as "wholesome."

He conceded that people will probably go right on eating them because they evoke pleasant childhood memories, or because we have been brainwashed by advertising or have been taught to think of sweets as rewards or are addicted to sugar, or just because someone said we aren't supposed to eat them.

Smith contends that such junk foods contribute significantly to colds, coughs, allergies, hyperactivity, depression, and noncompliance with parents and teachers in the children he sees in his practice.

He expressed surprise at Mr. Dewar's health. Dewar laughed at that—laughed in the face of modern medical science!—and showed me a column written by Rex Reed saying that after Ann-Margret's nearly fatal fall in Lake Tahoe, she built herself up on a diet of Twinkies.

"Even Dr. Smith would have to admit," Mr. Dewar said with a wink, "they did a nice job."

BAKING OFF

Everywhere you look, people are baking off at this time of year. There are local summer bake-off contests written up in suburban newspapers, county fair bake-offs, state fair contests, and nationwide competitions.

I have always been interested in the bake-off and, after witnessing my first at the state fair last year, signed a card stating that I was interested in further information. This spring, long after I had forgotten that I was interested in further information, they sent me an entry blank that asked me to list five of my favorite original family recipes.

My baking experience had been limited, confined pretty much to Brown 'n' Serv items and to the occasional microwavation of a dinner designed with the TV viewer in mind. Also, I had no really original recipes, save for the occasional, unfortunate culinary accident—such as a recent one involving chop suey and Worcestershire sauce. So I telephoned Katherine, a cousin of mine with a degree in home economics and an entire repertoire of original family recipes. She availed me of five.

I sent them in to Elaine Peppers (no relation to "Red"), superintendent of the Illinois State Fair Bake Off, and a few weeks later received a letter that greeted me with "Congratulations!" and advised me that my recipe for apricot sour cream coffee cake had been adjudged by "qualified home economists" as among the finest submitted. I was to send an entry fee and a parking fee, and to enter Gate 4 at the Fair Grounds in Springfield on August 14, reporting to the stage area of the Arts, Crafts and Hobbies Building at 1 P.M. for the second four-contestant session of the day in the Yeast and Quick Breads Division.

There was exhilaration, but this wore off fast when I realized, one, that I would be standing on a stage baking off against the best in the state and, two, that Sara Lee does not make apricot sour cream coffee cake.

What to do? Fooling around was suggested. One idea was that I should wear a frilly white apron, smoke a big cigar, and bad-mouth the competition, in professional wrestler fashion, as a bunch of bag-boiling boobs—perhaps also suggesting that women had no place in the kitchen. That sort of thing.

The idea of cheerleaders had appeal: nubile young women in short skirts and tight sweaters jumping and yelling, "Mix it up, roll it up, put it in the pan; if Bill can't do it, no one can!" They would shake their pompons, while I baked competitively.

Dress would be important. My brother suggested a jump suit such as those worn by Indianapolis 500 drivers, but with patches of such companies as Pillsbury, Betty Crocker, and General Mills. More reasonable voices suggested I wear something more practical and appropriate to the occasion, such as a simple wrap skirt or housedress.

Katherine, however, asked just who I thought I was to think of violating the sanctity of the bake-off, an American institution. She was right, of course. We decided I should try something even more bizarre: try to win.

There would be no fooling around. Rules specified that contestants lost points for the slightest infractions: poor posture, uncomfortable shoes, unpressed clothing, unrestrained hair, unmanicured fingernails, dangling earrings, bracelets, or necklaces—anything "that might distract from your presentation."

Katherine came to town for a weekend to coach me: "Don't use your fingers! . . . measure all ingredients before beginning . . . chop walnuts with the French knife only! . . . put the pan in the oven sideways . . . Is that how you cream margarine?!" So much to learn.

"Practice, practice, practice," she said, backing out of the driveway. It was good to see her go.

I baked apricot sour cream coffee cake every day for a month. I ate it myself. I fed it to the family, the extended family, the neighbors, paperboy, mailman, and finally to the raccoons that tip over our garbage cans. After about three weeks they stopped tipping over the garbage cans.

There were frustrations. Sometimes there would be little outcroppings of coffee cake that the goddamned brown sugar and chopped nut topping would not—steadfastly refused to—cover. Or the apricot filling that was supposed to be in the center would surface or dive to the bottom. Or maybe a speck of batter would cling to the side of the pan, giving a slight burnt aroma, probably detectable only to qualified home economists.

It was hot in that kitchen in July and August, but I kept on training. Gradually, I worked the bugs out of my coffee cake. My friends would call up, ask if "the dough boy" was home, and hum the *Rocky* theme. Feeling strong now. The coffee cake got better and better.

Good enough that when I bent over to set down my box of utensils and ingredients in the Arts, Crafts and Hobbies Building at the state fair, the old white pants (appropriate for baking) I had dug out of the bottom of the drawer split right up the middle. Too much coffee cake. I had to wear my apron just so.

The Arts, Crafts and Hobbies Building was an intimidating temple of the homemade and the home-grown: blue plum butters, hand-loomed material, bread and butter pickles, edible doll houses (completely furnished)—everything in that vast, brick airplane hangar of a building, handmade. Had these people never heard of stores?

At one end of the building was the Bake Off stage, equipped with four counter tops and four ovens for four contestants at a time. Before the stage, in folding chairs, sat an audience of about one hundred people—apparently desperate for a place to sit down.

As we waited, it became clear that another contestant, Susan Llames, a champion suburban baker, was trying to psych me out. "Heard about your pants," she laughed and opened a refrigerator door to show me something that looked to be a Taj Mahal in frozen dessert. She had won a blue ribbon with it the day before in another category, one of three blue ribbons she had won so far this week at the fair.

This was hardball. A judge told me about a fight that had erupted earlier in the competition when one contestant showed up with premeasured ingredients and another contestant took exception. And of course there was the big scandal a couple of years ago when one of the judges hitched a ride to the fair with one of the contestants.

Several of the finalists in my division, Yeasts and Quick Breads, had already baked off in the morning session: Violet Yunker of Minooka, Rose Pfeiffer of Bath, Billie Jo Mitchell of White Heath, and the formidable Grace Hewitt, sixty-four-years old, with fourteen straight annual appearances in the finals. Grace is so confident of her original recipes getting her into the finals that she just sends in her entry fee for the finals along with the recipes. Moreover, she told me that this year she had baked "Grandma's Maple Nut Loaf," the very same recipe that she had won this division with three years before.

Could that be fair? I turned away, only to come face to face with the most beautiful food product I have ever seen, in person or magazine. It was the braided dill 'n' onion bread, baked that morning by Brenda Post, who lived on a farm, which she explained was outside of Edgewood, which is outside of Effingham.

Buddy Lee's Banjo Band left the stage, and the four of us were escorted up. "Welcome to Woman's World—Designed with the Woman in Mind," the master of ceremonies announced. Pig.

We were given the command to commence baking. As we measured and stirred, using glass bowls so that the audience could see, Mrs. Peppers spoke to the audience about where the four of us were from and what we were baking: my coffee cake, the dilly bread, the very cherry bread, and the "two small loaves of goodness." An organist accompanied us. Judges watched closely for good posture, orderly preparation techniques, and the like. Many in the audience stayed put even during the baking.

When a toothpick came out of the coffee cake clean, I snatched it from the oven and sliced three small pieces for display. Appearance actually counted for more than flavor on the 200-point scale. To get just the right plate to bring out the apricot color, and to match the place mat and the artificial flowers in my display, I had to purchase a carton of four place settings—returnable.

A new set of judges was brought in, ensuring that they didn't know who made what. They judged flavor, texture, and appearance. They sat for an hour dissecting, examining, tasting, and jotting down comments on long evaluation forms with such questions as: "Are the cells thin-walled, uniform in size, and elongated vertically?"

Finally, the judges announced that they had reached their decisions: "First place, the blue ribbon for 1984 Yeasts and Quick Breads, goes to . . . to . . . Brenda Post, and her braided dill 'n' onion bread!" The audience gasped at her astonishing score: 195 points on the scale of 200. They then announced second place: Susan Llames and her dilly bread, with 190 points.

But I was third! 189 points! My wife hugged me and the cheerleaders would have jumped up and down if I'd brought them. Grace Hewitt looked angry. I had blown the white anklet socks right off her and her Grandma's Maple Nut Loaf.

Mrs. Peppers told me that, confidentially, we were all lucky indeed that Bonnie Michaels of Ottawa, a ten-year veteran of the bake-off, had suffered a flat tire and didn't show up with her French herb swirl in time.

Brenda was asked how she stays so thin despite all the baking, and she explained into the microphone: "We chase hogs daily." Her beautiful braided bread went on to dominate the competition against winners of the cake, the casserole, and the other divisions during the next several days, and on Saturday night she became Grand Champion of the Illinois State Fair Bake Off.

Of course, I felt proud—and wholesome—about my performance. And I can tell you this: we saw our score sheets; and were it not for one little thing, I might very well be the one standing today at the very pinnacle of sport baking in the State of Illinois: "Uneven Nut Distribution."

☛ FRONT PORCH SHORTFALL

The suburbs are really short on porches.

Most of what is suburban Chicago has been built in the last thirty-five years, and they stopped building front porches around fifty years ago.

Apparently, it was about the same time people started staying indoors to listen to the radio.

Then, TV. People at first were excited about it, then galvanized, transfixed, and finally glued to the cathode ray tube, unable to move. It was like turning up the juice over a period of years on the electric chair - and with the same result: cessation of brain function.

This was followed closely by the miracle of the ranch home— Mom doesn't have to carry the vacuum cleaner up and down stairs; I remember that from *My Weekly Reader*. And she sure doesn't have to sweep the front porch, because there isn't one.

Not to mention Total Electric Living. A friend of mine, whose father hit it big pouring cement foundations for all these ranch homes, lived in a house with a big gold Total Electric Home medallion on the front. Total Electric Living meant air-conditioning, maybe even Central Air.

A body'd have to be a fool to sit out on the front porch talking with his next-door neighbor when he could be in his air-

conditioned "TV room" being talked at by the big stars from Hollywood and New York. I mean, it was almost like having Jack Paar or
Topo Gigio or Bishop Fulton J. Sheen right there in your own
home.

The known physiological attraction to a cooler, more comfortable temperature, and the dilated pupils of the mesmerized viewer
of bright, flickering images, tell us that moving inside to our cool
("It's Kool Inside") TV rooms probably wasn't even a conscious
decision.

The front porch was pleasant, not exciting. It was a place to sit.
To sit and talk—something called visiting—about anything that
came up. Sometimes nothing was said for several minutes, just
sharing the silence, the sound of the crickets, the lawn sprinkler, or
whatever. It was okay to be silent then, not a failure to communicate that you had to seek professional help for.

It was pleasant just being there with your family (see Nuclear
Family), friends, or whoever dropped by. Maybe some neighbors
who spotted you on the porch from across the street, or someone
taking a walk (see Other Modes of Transportation). It was all right if
they dropped by. They didn't expect you to be entertaining, witty,
and informed like the people on Johnny Carson. The earth's crust
was cooling and there wasn't a Johnny Carson show. If you felt like
talking, you might offer them a beer or iced tea. Or not.

Good times then generally tended to run more to pleasant than
to exciting, and the rest of the time more to "okay" than to depression over not being excited. There were exciting times to be sure,
but our threshold was lower.

Today we tend more to finding people with similar demo-
graphic profiles and inviting them a week ahead of time to our patio behind the house in a fenced-in backyard. We usually have some
ulterior motive in inviting who we do: improving our professional
or social positions. It's fine to just have a nice time, of course, as
long as it's productive.

Sitting has become unfathomable to a nation of joggers, rac-
quetballers, and tennis buffs. Where's the thrill? Where are the designer sitting outfits? How do you stop the jerking and fidgeting?
How do you deal with the guilt of doing absolutely nothing—not
even repeating a mantra?

People now having themselves surgically removed from their
TV screens are trying to relearn sociability in encounter groups,

support centers, Holiday Inn bars, human interface workshops, and interpersonal communication seminars and weekend retreats. If they've got the bucks they go to sounding-board psychologists who for $100 will say, "I hear you."

I talked with a couple of suburban developers about the possibility of building front porches on houses again.

They said front porches are gone forever. "I'd never do it," one said of putting porches on his houses. "I've thought a lot about it, because I like porches. But drive through the old neighborhoods of the city or Oak Park or Evanston. Even when people have porches they don't use them.

"They don't know how."

III

THE ECONOMY, BUSINESS, AND TECHNOLOGY

☞ WHEN A COMPANY TOWN'S COMPANY MOVES ON

The Singer Company is closing its mammoth plant here in Elizabeth, New Jersey. Moving on to a marketing strategy of more cost-effective foreign production and diversification in aerospace products; it is finished with this aging city now.

So intertwined have their lives become—this company and this city—during their 109 years together, that many people here can only shake their heads and say, as Morris Finkel did, "It does not seem possible that it's over."

In their minds echoes the racket of the ten-thousand-worker assembly lines, the cheering for the tool department's softball teams, the sounds of the best of the big bands playing at dances in the company's hall on the shore of Newark Bay. It has been more than a professional relationship, and many in the community now feel scorned. "Working for Singer was a way of life," said Mr. Finkel, who was in the plant for forty-four years. "It was the natural thing for a young man coming out of high school to do. Everyone in town, it seems, worked there at some point."

A machine operator and first baseman, Mr. Finkel recalls that the company recruited top athletes during the 1930s, 1940s, and 1950s from nearby high schools and from other area companies to work for Singer and play on its ball teams.

"Everyone in town went to those games," said Sophie Kobylinsky. She also has fond recollections of company dances on Friday and Saturday nights during that period. The company supplied soft drinks and beer, as she recalls. Women were not admitted without bringing cookies or cakes.

"Singer's recreation hall was the center of social activity for the whole town," she said. "My girl friend and I didn't work at Singer, but we went to the dances. She met her future husband there."

Harry James, Jimmy Dorsey, and other bands played at gala company affairs. Wedding receptions, bar mitzvah parties, and other functions took place in the company hall. Mayor Thomas Dunn recalls thousands of people gathering at the plant each year for a demonstration by the company's fire department in which a house specially built for the occasion was burned to the ground.

Several residents remember, as children, waiting with great antici-
pation for that springtime event.

The gargantuan redbrick plant was built here in 1873, during
America's industrial revolution. The city of Elizabeth grew up
around it, with neighborhoods representative of the waves of im-
migrants who came to the plant from Ellis Island, just a few miles
away: German, Italian, Irish, Jewish, Polish, Lithuanian, and
others.

Mayor Dunn, whose father worked at the plant for forty-one
years, has childhood memories of earning nickels by "rushing the
growler," a job that he said was as common for a boy in Elizabeth as
delivering newspapers was in other towns. He said that the German
workers lowered covered beer pails, called growlers, out the windows of the factory on ropes to the boys, who would rush them
over to Grampp's tavern to be filled. "The Germans did all the precision work," he said, "despite the beer." Joseph DiBella recalls
that the growlers he carried were heavily greased with lard to hold
down the head and allow more room for beer. Donald Wylie remembers a Catholic priest who roamed the streets knocking the
pails from the children's hands.

Residents of Elizabeth have fond memories of the long relationship but are now upset that the company is leaving them, particularly when Elizabeth is having unemployment and revenue
problems. "We're being done in," Mr. Wylie said, "by outside
influences—malls taking the shopping business and cheap labor in
Japan and Taiwan taking jobs."

Not that they are completely surprised; things had not been
right between the city and the company since Singer began gradually moving its operations overseas twenty-five years ago. The
dances and the recreational activities came to a halt, and in the
early 1970s the company deeded away the recreation hall for use
by local groups. The work force dwindled, then dropped off
sharply in 1980 when the plant stopped making all but industrial
sewing machines. Now, only about 950 people work at the plant.
Still, the final closing that was announced Friday is traumatic.

Mr. DiBella, president of Local 461 of the International Union
of Electrical, Radio and Machine Workers, said that the union will
file a $15 million damage suit against Singer for not living up to a
contractual agreement, made last year, to spend $2 million to make
the plant more efficient so that it could compete with the modern

technology of the foreign producers, and also to seek defense contract work for the plant. "They did neither," Mr. DiBella said. Congressman Matthew J. Rinaldo has also charged that the company made no valid attempt to obtain defense contracts.

Singer officials contend that the company sought defense work but could find none. The company plans to spend the $2 million to modernize the plant before it is closed at the end of this year "in order to live up to the contract," said a spokesman, Thomas Elliott. He said that the plant was closing because of "reduced demand for the industrial machines produced there."

"Singer officials told me that they'd never move their industrial sewing machine operation out of Elizabeth," Mayor Dunn said. "Their word doesn't mean a thing. We reduced their taxes by $417,000 over four years when they gave us the impression that would keep them open, but they were just taking us for a ride."

During the lunch hour at Shoban's, a shot-and-a-beer bar across First Street from the plant's main gate, a Singer supervisor wondered aloud whether the United States was not turning into a nation of two kinds of people: white-collar managers for multinational companies that produced their products overseas, and unemployed workers.

Later in the day, S. L. Jones summed up the prevailing mood of the rank-and-file workers, many of whom said they believed the company capitalized on cheap immigrant labor until the union negotiated the first contract in the 1940s, then began moving its operations overseas to capitalize on other "oppressed" workers.

"Now it seems like they just used us up," Mr. Jones said, "and left us behind."

HIGH-TECH LAWNWARE

You half expect the thing to take a jerky step on its gawky tubular steel legs and fire a laser blast that vaporizes the neighbor's charcoal grill.

The unearthly-looking structure—a dish antenna twelve feet in diameter with a rotating eight-foot tripod in the center—sits on a suburban lawn, near the swing set, whirring as it moves left and right, up and down, searching the stars for Regis Philbin.

The dish antenna, properly known as a satellite earth station, locates Mr. Philbin in geosynchronous orbit 22,300 miles above the equator on the Satcom F-3 satellite and draws him into the living room of the Burt Lerner family of Tenafly, New Jersey.

Other residents of this tidy suburban neighborhood did not know what to make of it when the Lerners installed their "dish" three months ago. Most of them treated it as a UFO come to roost. "I don't know what it is," said one neighbor who telephoned the Lerners. "But whatever it is, it moved."

Officials in Tenafly are now scurrying to gather information on the antennas so they can pass an ordinance that would at least require the planting of bushes to conceal the technological beasts.

In the neighboring suburb of Englewood Cliffs, where another dish antenna has been installed, Major Joseph Parisi said, "It's huge. It looks like, like I don't know what. Like space invasions or something!" The mayor sees the invasion of the antennas as a threat to the community that has come "out of the blue" and must be stopped.

The borough has sent a letter to Richard Turner ordering him to remove immediately the more than nine-foot-square, $7,500 dish that he has installed on his rooftop. Many dish antennas are being installed on house roofs because a direct line of sight to the satellites is needed.

About fifty-five thousand homeowners in the United States have installed dish antennas, with three thousand to four thousand more being installed each month, mostly in remote areas not served by conventional television signals or cable companies. As the prices of dish antennas have dropped, they have begun cropping up throughout the New York metropolitan area on the rooftops and in the yards of homeowners who for some reason are not satisfied with the mere two or three dozen channels that cable television offers.

The borough attorney for Englewood Cliffs is drawing up an ordinance to ban dish antennas from the community on aesthetic grounds. "They are unsightly and dangerous," proclaimed Mayor Parisi, "a threat to property values." With the prices of the home models dropping—to between about $3,500 and $12,000—and with Englewood Cliffs being a relatively affluent community, the mayor said he fears that the town will soon look like a space station.

Owners of dish antennas receive more than seventy channels, everything beamed by satellite to the North American continent and then some. Judy Lerner, who explained that her husband "is always coming home with strange things," twisted her dial through a broad spectrum of programming:

Regis Philbin exercising on the floor; Tip O'Neill live on the floor of the House of Representatives; stock quotations; Spanish soap operas; a twenty-four-hour weatherman; the Canadian Parliament; private corporate conferences; the local Hamilton, Ontario, station; the Armed Forces Network; the Eternal Word Network; the Playboy Network; *Sewing with Nancy*; *The Erotic Adventures of Pinocchio*; a man planting a garden; and a woman making chicken cordon bleu, to name a few. You want Popeye speaking French, tossing down cans of epinards for strength? You've got it.

On the Lerners' coffee table sits a copy of *Orbit* magazine, a slick publication fat with articles such as one on the new Anik D satellite and with photographs such as the one showing a man in a desert watching a battery-powered dish-antenna system, thereby "demonstrating the ability to watch television in the middle of nowhere."

Then there are the month's voluminous program listings and advertisements for hydraulic antenna activators, ferrite polarization rotors, and Dish De-Icers.

"Sometimes," said Mrs. Lerner, "it takes an hour and a half to figure out what you want to watch, and by then the programs have changed." She asks her nine-year-old son, Scotty, how to use the dish-antenna system.

Tenafly officials do not seem to agree with Mrs. Lerner's assessment that because the enormous dish is beige, "it just blends in."

Perhaps not surprisingly, the first person in this suburban area to install a dish antenna is a self-described "sports nut," Mr. Turner. He explained that his eyes were red because he had watched a West Coast baseball game until 2:15 A.M. the night before.

Mr. Turner has three television sets lined up at the end of his bed, which he supplements with a portable set for Sunday afternoon football, and watches them all simultaneously.

With his rooftop dish, he receives just about every professional football and baseball game played because most of them are telecast in one city or another using the satellite. It is not unusual for him to watch seven baseball games in an evening.

Asked if he ever had a chance to talk with his wife, he replied, "No, she's usually on the telephone." When a friend of his tried to make a joke about the irony of Mr. Turner having all of this equipment amid a football strike, Mr. Turner did not crack a smile.

Walter Kleineke, who lives across the street from the Lerners, said that he doesn't mind the dishes and recalled the uproar in the neighborhood a generation ago when homeowners began installing television antennas. Another neighbor went so far as to say that the dish antenna was something of a status symbol.

But Mayor Parisi said borough officials would adopt an ordinance banning the antennas on aesthetic grounds. The dish-antenna outbreak, the mayor said, is "the worst thing that's happened since everybody bought recreational vehicles and we had to pass an ordinance that they couldn't park them in their driveways."

THE MATRIMONIAL-INDUSTRIAL COMPLEX

"Ken and I met at work," the young woman said to the young man, raising her voice a bit over the orchestra's romantic melody. "We're getting married in the fall."

He looked into her chestnut eyes and replied: "You'll need cutware."

The man, a Cutco knife salesman by trade, was one of the merchants fortunate enough to obtain space Wednesday evening at Bridal Expo in Massapequa's Esquire Manor catering hall to ply his wares to three hundred Long Island brides-to-be. The women came to look over everything they could possibly need and more for their weddings, the anticipated cost of which ranged from $3,000 to $12,000.

"Have you thought about makeup?" asked a Mary Kay Cosmetics saleswoman, promising to come to the prospective bride's home on the wedding day, if need be.

"It's not a wedding without a limo," proclaimed the Roberts Limousines agent, offering Cadillacs, white Rolls-Royces, and stretch Lincolns.

"*Hava Nagila,*" crooned Johnny Fusco, ruffled white shirt unbuttoned to the solar plexus, gold necklaces glistening in the spotlight, his manager handing out business cards for wedding bookings.

"You'll be needing a minister," said the Reverend James

Wentz, master of church and civil ceremonies. "Fill out the card for a $25 discount on my honorarium."

The merchants recalled that ten years ago marriage was being discussed as an increasingly outmoded concept. And those who married often did so for the price of a parks department permit, vowing to have and to hold until the whole trip just became too much of a hassle.

Times have changed. This is the opening of wedding season, May to September, and spokesmen for the wedding industry believe that this will be the most profitable ever. They expect 2.5 million weddings nationwide (30,000 in suburban Long Island), surpassing the highs of the last three years and even the 2.3 million of 1946, when returning soldiers and waiting women rushed together and bonded in marriage.

Despite the recession, weddings are expected to be more extravagant than ever. "I don't know where they're getting the money," said the sales director for Murray the K's mobile disco, another entrepreneur at Bridal Expo, "but they're spending it like crazy on weddings."

William F. Heaton, president of Bridal Expos, of Babylon, Long Island, explained that lavish weddings are part of "a return to traditionalism, formalism, and quality." He said he held about five of these everything-under-one-roof wedding merchandise extravaganzas each month, each attracting several hundred prospective brides. He said his Great Bridal Expo this year drew fifteen thousand people.

At this one, there are purveyors of gowns, tuxedos, honeymoons, photography, invitations, balloon decorations, and "memory candles" (with photographs and invitations embedded in the wax), in addition to the mobile discos and bands, makeup and limos, cutware and clergy. Previous Expos have included automobile dealers, real-estate salespeople, firms that videotape weddings, carpet outlets, furniture stores, banks, food store chains, and dealers in such things as tent rentals and sensuous lingerie. Even abortion clinics have asked for—but been denied—space.

"They seem to have everything," commented Cynthia Dikeman, of Massapequa, Long Island, an "encore bride," as Mr. Heaton calls them, who is planning a smaller backyard wedding this time around. "Did you see any Porta Johns?"

Women here describe themselves as "middle class" or "working class" and said they will sacrifice for their big weddings, forgoing new cars, vacations, dining out, and college. Managers of the catering halls explain that about half of the couples are paying for their own receptions. "I think the tribulations of planning and saving may strengthen their relationships," said Mr. Heaton. One couple agreed, she saying it would "cement" their marriage, he saying she might have used a better choice of words.

There is a degree of planning in this—up to two years or more—rarely seen since the Apollo moon landing. Johnny Fusco says he has bookings throughout the coming twelve months and one for two years from now. But then, brides have changed their wedding dates for Johnny Fusco, a Brooklyn butcher and singer who attributes his two hundred wedding bookings a year to "the bridal boom." If a bride is not still speaking to her intended in two years, wedding cancellation insurance for the down payments is available.

"You must plan ahead," said Jill Santa Maria, of Lindenhurst, Long Island, who is planning her wedding for fourteen months from now. "There are so many big weddings, everything is booked."

When she called Our Lady of Perpetual Help some weeks ago, there was just one hour open on her wedding date. Miss Santa Maria, a chiropractor's secretary, is also involved in planning her honeymoon, which is an extended Caribbean cruise.

She said that many of the catering halls were nearly fully booked for next year, which is somewhat surprising when one considers that forty or fifty wedding receptions are held each day in the largest of these Astrodomes-with-room-dividers. At the Esquire Manor booth, free appetizers are passed out to give the affianced a taste of what might be if they hold their receptions here.

"Coconut chicken?" the servers ask, as brides-to-be consider the gowns and tuxedos being modeled from Mr. Tux and a local bridal shop. The more ornate gowns are selling this year, thanks to the Princess of Wales.

Marilyn Santa Maria, the mother of the prospective bride-to-be, thinks it is all "a little crazy."

"Ten thousand dollars for five hours!" she exclaimed, recalling the inexpensive "football weddings" of her day, so called, she said, because sandwiches were tossed to those who could not push through to the table at receptions held in the cramped back rooms of bars.

"You get so tired of scrimping on everything these days," said her daughter, echoing the sentiment of many other brides-to-be. "For one day in your life, you want to be queen for a day."

Still, they say, their fathers mention the consummate romance of elopement.

BREAD BRAINS AND SMART IRONS

Ruth Hanson realizes that this may sound a little silly, but she has been bothered for some time by the nagging realization that her automatic drip coffee maker is not quite so nice as the automatic drip coffee makers of her friends and neighbors.

While her four-year-old Mr. Coffee still performs dutifully every morning, "it is obsolete," she explained. It does not have all the little pushbuttons of the more advanced models. It has no clock whatsoever, let alone the digital clock that is on the newest model, which tells not only the time of day but also the time that the coffee will be ready. A lot of progress, including four space shuttle missions, has taken place since Mrs. Hanson purchased her Mr. Coffee.

On a Saturday the appliance stores of suburbia are crowded with shoppers like Mrs. Hanson who are continuing what one appliance trade spokesman described as an "almost romantic" entanglement with corded appliances.

The Long Island Lighting Company recently reported the results of a study of three thousand suburban customers that found that, despite all the talk about increased energy consciousness, there has been a 30-percent rise in peak electrical demand over the last decade and that much of the increase can be attributed to the relentless rise in the use of electrical home appliances.

"Today's electric appliances are specialty gadgets that do things rapidly," the spokesman said. "But we are not precisely sure why people want all these items. But we do."

We want about $6 billion worth this year. We want electric toothbrushes, but we want more than that in this great nation. We want Oral Hygiene Centers.

We want the capacity to drink freshly squeezed orange juice

not from concentrate. We therefore want electric squeezers—$96 squeezers with "pulp ejection."

We want electric peanut butter makers and electric bread baskets and electric pizza keepers and electric salad dryers. Food can often look peculiar to us out of its familiar boil-in-bags, so we want electric Seal-A-Meal and Seal-A-Meal II.

We want electric potato peelers and we want electric woks to satisfy our need to stir-fry. We want toasters with "Bread Brains" and "Smart Irons."

We want Super Shooter electric dough guns and 1,400-watt Super Pro Pistol hair dryers. We want electric fondue sets even though the forks are regrettably manual. We want auto-pluck capability: electric tweezers.

"I know people who own every last one of these things," said Ralph Garrett, who acknowledged that his own electric appliances are pushing one another off his kitchen counter. Yet he was in Macy's in Garden City, Long Island, browsing for more.

People in Macy's and other stores at the mall last Saturday were considering and buying electric Kabob-Its, Pastamatic 700's, Creperies, and electric whisks.

"Excuse me," said Mary Angelillo to a clerk. "What is a whisk?" The clerk replied, "It is for, like, whisking egg whites." Mrs. Angelillo put the device down. She said that she owned "all the usual appliances," including in that category an electric nail polisher and an electric foot massager. Unusual to her was her single-function electric potato baker, which was a gift.

Similarly puzzled was Jennifer Robertson. "What on earth would you use this for?" she asked of a woman shopping with her at J. C. Penney as she picked up an electric food dehydrator. She was in search of a wedding gift, she explained. A companion of hers suggested that perhaps Mrs. Robertson should give the betrothed the electric breadbasket that someone had given her as a wedding present.

Mrs. Robertson priced Crock-Pots, Crock Watchers, and Crockettes; Fry Babys, Fry Daddys, and GranPappys. She considered state-of-the-art popcorn poppers: the Poppery, the Pop Corn Now, the Popaire, the Buttermatic, and others with "flip-'n'-serve" lids and caramel corn capability.

"It's funny," said Barbara Shapiro, "how you come in looking for something simple and you walk out with some incredible contraption." She recalled shopping with her husband for a can opener. "I was thinking of a plain, manual can opener," she explained. "We walked out of the store with a $30 number." It could have been worse. They might have purchased an Opening Center with Power Pierce that also sharpened knives and opened plastic food pouches.

This day, she was looking among the electric fruit peelers, woks, and Donut Factories for the blenders. Not the electric cocktail blenders—one kind for hot drinks, another for cold—those are something else.

She wanted a food blender with enough buttons to stir, beat, puree, cream, chop, whip, crumb, and mix. But a saleswoman didn't have much trouble convincing her that $20 more would give her more buttons and the capacity to mince, grate, crush, blend, shred, grind, liquefy, and, finally, to frappe.

The lighting company study also found that electric garage-door openers, microwave ovens, trash mashers, foot massagers, Weed Eaters, and other amenities were common to suburban life. The study did not ask about a device that—inexplicably—will scramble your eggs inside their shells.

After considering the Mr. Coffees, Pour-O-Matics, and Dial-A-Brews, Mrs. Hanson settled on a sophisticated coffee maker with four buttons, a digital clock, and, if it pleases her fancy, the programming capability to make coffee while she is out of town!

She said that she did not think about such things but that, yes, with this unit she would probably be the envy of her neighbors.

For how long, though, in this age of galloping technological advance?

☛ GRILLS AND BOYS

Susan B. Anthony he is not, but Long Grove sheet metal man George Stephen has perhaps done as much as anyone lately for women's liberation.

While he has done little to further the philosophy of the movement, he has shown skill in practical, applied liberation. He makes men cook dinner, millions of men, repeatedly, and of their own volition.

The backdoor opens and we see a normal (surly, uncooperative) adult American male carrying a trayful of bloody animal parts. Though the weather is warm, he wears oversized gloves like our boys stationed in Antarctica and an apron exclaiming "Come and Get It!" beneath a likeness of little dancing, smiling weenies.

This man apparently has no shame, may not even be embarrassed—except maybe for the cute little chef's hat—and doesn't appear at all ill-tempered, as the family dog would be if you dressed him up like that.

In picturing this, I'm sure you've probably already guessed how George Stephen does it: he is a brain surgeon on the side and has performed lobotomies on millions of men who then act like this one.

We assume someone has, but not Stephen. What has made millions of men take over the cooking on a somewhat regular basis—in one of the great sociological changes in the last quarter century—is his technological breakthrough: the outdoor barbecue grill.

And twenty-seven years ago, at a time when there were only a few thousand closet male chefs, George Stephen invented the acme, the Cadillac, the ultimate, the very quintessence of grills; the grill that people I barely know have come up to me at parties and talked about for thirty minutes; a grill's grill; the grill that costs a lot and has become a status symbol; the grill of the stars, zealots, fanatics; a grill that has probably played Caesar's Palace with Sammy Davis, Jr.; and certainly a grill that needs no introduction:

The Weber Grill.

Hal-le-lu-jah.

Stephen didn't like his brick barbecue pit, so in the small Weber Brothers Metal Works, in suburban Chicago, where he worked, George crafted (presumably on his own time) the first Weber Kettle in 1951.

A few months later he made twenty-five to sell to neighbors and this year expects his Weber-Stephens Product Co., in Arlington Heights, to sell more than one million. These will go forth and join the more than ten million already out there in the world. Stephen said the company has grown to 375 employees, with a new plant in Manitowoc, Wisconsin, and a European assembly plant on the drawing boards.

"We got 'em out of the kitchen all right," Stephen says, acknowledging his contribution to women's liberation. "It's now second nature around our house that Marge, my wife, just says what we're having—steak, pot roast, or whatever—and the boys and I know we're doing the cooking.'' He has a swimming pool shaped like a Weber kettle and seven grills of varying sizes, one of them big enough to barbecue Orson Welles, if he had a mind to.

Women say this is all well and good, but is there anything further Stephen can do in the field of applied liberation?

Can he get men to take the laundry out in the backyard and beat it clean with rocks? Perhaps men would do the laundry if they could dress up like astronauts and get in the washer and dryer with the laundry. Would men clean the bathroom if we went back to two holers in the backyard?

Of the early days, when the trend started that made outdoor barbecues as American as having your car towed from the Fourth of July parade route, he says: ''The women were just smarter than we were. I think we made a big mistake and were outmaneuvered.'' And thinking back to those early days, he realizes ''a hell of a lot of those early kettles were bought by women. A hell of a lot.''

SPERM BANKING

Nobel Prize winner Ben Mottleson, a hometown boy from La Grange, says: ''It's all a lot of nonsense.''

He hasn't yet been asked to contribute to the new sperm bank for Nobel Prize winners revealed this week and says he wouldn't if they asked.

The sperm bank, called the Repository for Germinal Choice, is being set up by an Escondido, California, business tycoon—in his backyard—to produce exceptionally bright children. Already, five Nobel laureates reportedly have contributed, many more have been solicited, and three women described as having ''exceptionally high IQs'' have been impregnated. They are given a choice of sperms.

''The idea of intelligence isn't that simple,'' the 1975 winner of the Nobel Prize for physics said in an interview. ''This is a primitive approach. There is considerable arrogance involved in thinking we should populate the world with images of ourselves.''

The Nobel laureate declined to comment on the concept of forgoing all other considerations on passing intelligence on to future generations; that is, he wouldn't say if he and other Nobel Prize winners he knows have really oily hair or congenitally smelly feet. These are the sticky moral questions we will encounter on the frontiers of genetic engineering.

There are said to be a number of sperm banks already operating, and judging from the number of inquiries pouring in, this new one is going to be quite successful. It appears that there is big money to be made in sperm banking.

Its success will undoubtedly foster competition. At first the sperm banking industry will be staid and dignified. But as more of the banks crop up—"Why Have Just an *Average* Child?"— they will be forced to try and woo customers from competing institutions.

The 1st National Sperm Bank of Chicago will offer a complete line of all your favorite Nobel laureate sperms, including medicine, physics, economics, literature, peace, and lemon-lime. Continental Sperm Bank will decide to offer premiums: black satin sheets, Johnny Mathis records, and subscriptions to *Playboy.*

The Northern Sperm Trust will counter with "Prolonged Hours," a walkup window, a window for nocturnal deposits, and "No Penalty for Early Withdrawal." Someone will open 1st Federal Sperm Savings & Loan, but it is doubtful sperm borrowing will catch on with a large segment of the population.

But why just banks and why just Nobel winners? Indeed the philosophy behind the new California bank calls for donations from "famous and exceptional people" as well.

Sperm department stores and boutiques will open in suburban malls, featuring sperm of the National Football League, the Chicago Symphony Orchestra, the Academy of Motion Picture Arts and Sciences, and Phi Beta Kappa.

If you can afford exceptional children, there will be exclusive shops carrying an expensive line of Bjorn Borg, Julius Erving, Luciano Pavarotti, Paul Newman, Mick Jagger, William F. Buckley, Jr., and "An Exciting New Shipment: Eric Heiden and the official sperm of the U.S. Olympic hockey team!"

But everyone cannot. So suburban Kmarts will carry the likes of Bears quarterback, Bobby Douglas, Cubs utility infielder Paul Popovich, the K-Tel Singers, Elvis impersonators, and people smart enough to pass their driver's test the first time. Then, generic sperm.

Franchise sperm outlets will sprout up like weeds along suburban thoroughfares: Alfred Nobel's Sperm City, Sperm World, Sperm Barn, House of Sperm, Birds 'N' Bees. Baskin-Robbins-style franchises will be among them, featuring the mutation of the month—for March? Kareem Abdul Kissinger. At The Sperm Hut the basic impregnation will be $5, plus $1 for each additional ingredient: cheerful, thrifty, obedient, fun-to-be-with.

Would that this were just another short-lived southern California aberration. But the first man-made geniuses, products of the Nobel sperm bank, will be rolling off the assembly line in a few months.

Nineteen years ago a doctor started life in a test tube and kept the embryo alive for twenty-nine days. He said he could have continued, but didn't. Scientists clone frogs and say they could clone humans, too—a Cheryl Tiegs in every garage—but don't.

We already have taken eggs from a woman's body, fertilized them with the sperm from the man of her choice, and implanted them in a second woman who carries the child.

Scientists have refrained from making withdrawals from sperm banks and ovum banks, adding three cans of water, and stirring up huge batches of babies.

When they do, what will they make? Super intellects and athletes? Slaves? What will we think of kids when we can buy them to match our walls? What will they think of us, and what will they think of themselves?

How will we ever make a decision of such magnitude and importance, a decision to create such a brave new world?

In America, businessmen in places like Escondido will ask themselves if there's a buck in it.

8 33-ACNE
Hotlines!

In recent months we have been reading volumes of gripping newspaper articles about people suffering from hundreds of different mental and physical ailments no one ever heard of before. These are gripping and grim stories, all very similar, with only the names of the illnesses changed. Then come the books on these illnesses.

We have seen talk shows about the horrors of being too short.

too tall, too ugly, the first of two children, empty-nesters, or afraid to go into shopping malls. Think of that! We have seen men on the *Donahue* show talking about discrimination against them when they go to work in women's clothes—right here in America. I heard a woman on my own car radio talking about the suffering of left-handed people. Let's all be victims of something.

A new industry arises providing trendy solutions for trendy modern problems. Everywhere we look crisis intervention centers are forming, drop-in centers, rap centers, outreach centers, awareness groups, encounter groups, support groups, and Hotlines! A real favorite in the suburbs, every self-respecting Rotary Club, YMCA, church group, youth group, civic organization, township, municipal government, park district, human relations commission—everyone with half a damned heart—is starting Hotlines.

You name it, they'll listen to it. VD? PG? High? Low? Ripped off? Just want to rap? Last summer, Hinsdale had a Mosquito Hotline for people experiencing more than six bites within a five-minute period.

This week in my mail comes "a public service announcement" telling of another new suburban Hotline. That seems about the average: one a week. The number to call in Oakbrook Terrace is 833-2263.

That's 833-ACNE. An acne Hotline. It's sponsored by Acne Health Care Centers in Oakbrook Terrace and Wheeling.

"People get acne and they say, 'Why me?' explains a woman with Acne's public relations firm who says the Hotline is definitely not just for those with serious, disfiguring acne. "They feel alone with their problem. They can call the Hotline and talk about their problem. We try and answer any questions they have, and we send them free information on the disease. They can also come in and see a videotape on acne if it will help. People get terribly upset about their acne. The emotional effects are tremendous even in the minor cases.

"We try to treat the whole person."

Dr. James Fulton is the driving force behind the Acne Centers. He is owner and medical consultant to the Acne Centers as well as a research scientist at the Acne Research Institute in Miami.

Dr. Fulton is a member of the National Acne Association and the Society of Investigative Dermatology. He is author of a paper on "The Effect of Chocolate on Acne Vulgaris." And he is author of the book *Farewell to Pimples*.

His is a moving story. In *Farewell to Pimples*, he tells of his adolescent years: "Night after night I prayed that my acne might disappear before daylight. Then I gave up hoping for magic and decided that if any cure were possible for acne I would have to discover it myself. This inner drive chased me, drove me, and plagued me for the last twenty years."

Today Dr. Fulton has opened a chain of Acne Centers in Illinois, and also in Florida and California, to help those who suffer as he once did. Still there is no cure for acne. In *Farewell to Pimples*—soon to be adapted to the stage?—Dr. Fulton lambastes his fellow doctors for paying too much attention to other diseases and not enough to acne.

And well he might. Dr. Fulton says the millions of people who have sought medical help for their acne represent the tip of an "acne iceberg" in this country, because only 10 percent of acne sufferers reach physicians. Perhaps if we had trained para-acne teams with helicopters.

There is an Acne Crisis facing this country. Dr. Fulton says more than 80 percent of Americans and Europeans suffer from it. You'd think NATO could do something. Caucasians are far more prone to acne than others. Stress, birth control pills, and pollutants are causing Growing Numbers of "career persons and housewives" to have recurrences of acne in middle age. Not to mention, acne can attack babies in their cribs!

I can see Dr. Fulton being interviewed by concerned-looking television reporters about this crisis. I can see him on the *Donahue* show, sitting next to a couple of teenagers with big blemishes on their noses, telling Phil what he says in his book: that there is a greater "sum of suffering from acne than any other disease."

Can we stop here or do we now move on to Hangnail Hotlines, Ring-Around-the-Collar rap groups, Static Cling Crisis Intervention, Yellowy Floor Wax Buildup Biofeedback, and Holistic Hemorrhoid Centers?

There is no end to human suffering.

There would be no money in it.

A LARGE STANDING ARMY LIES DOWN

This woman slides into the next seat and puts her arm around me.

I act startled. Since they serve no liquor at this place near North Chicago and offer you orange juice, I tell her that I'd figured it for a health food joint. The woman says no, that there is a law in Lake County against serving liquor at a place where there is nude dancing.

The waitress wants $2 for the orange juice. The woman, who says her name is Julie, orders a $4 glass of water. It's a small glass of water, but iced. I pay for the water with a $5 bill, and Julie gives the waitress my change. Dancing has apparently given her a powerful thirst because she orders another $5 glass of water.

The waitress asks if Julie and I would like to share this drink "in the comfort of a private room"—for an additional $36.

"What's your pleasure?" Julie asks.

"This may sound a little kinky," I say firmly, "but tonight I'd like to discuss this country's national defense policies."

The waitress shoots Julie a quizzical, who-is-this-guy look.

"Do you think it would be sound defense policy to close Fort Sheridan and cut back forces at the Great Lakes Naval Training Center, as is proposed?" I ask. The establishment serves both.

No response. Blank looks.

"See," I explain, "Congress wants public input on the economic impact these cutbacks would have on local businesses, and you girls don't come to the public hearings and don't have a representative on the county's special subcommittee to fight the cutbacks. So, what would you like to tell the gentlemen in Congress?"

"We ought to open more bases," says a tall, thin girl with her skirt split up just past her pierced ears. "We should have a lot more Navy bases around.

"Russia is coming out with atomic bombs and all that," she continues, "so the U.S. has to stay on its toes. Russia is a pretty heavy country." Really.

Some of the other women employed at the nightclub come over to the table. One of them, a voluptuous woman in a beige negligee speaks up: "I think we need a large military force. I like to feel well protected."

"Do you feel well protected now?"

"Definitely."

Julie, who I suspected all along was the patriotic type judging by the tattoos all over her body—all over—speaks with conviction: "We need all the —ing planes and ships we can get!

"If they close these bases down, it would be a dangerous precedent; they might start closing bases all over the place.

"The Russian Navy is so far ahead of us it isn't funny. They have more destroyers.

"I was raised in the sixties, so I'm real conservative. I worked for Reagan and Wallace."

Fund-raiser?

"No."

"I'll bet [U.S. Representative] Phil Crane is against this," she says. "I know him."

Personally?

"No."

"So," I say, about to be escorted out by a large man with complexion problems, "you all favor a large standing Army [but prefer it lying down]. Anything else you'd like to tell the gentlemen on the Armed Services Committees?"

"Yeah," says one of the others. "Tell them to come around and see us before they vote."

IV

TRANSPORTATION

DAILY COMMUTATION

For Walter Mahoney to live a normal life—a wife, children, home in the suburbs, and job in the city—he must spend an hour each morning and an hour each evening on a painful machine: the Long Island Rail Road.

"We do tend to be masochists," said Mr. Mahoney, who views his experiences riding the world's busiest commuter railroad, and perhaps one of the most infamous, for twenty-two years, to be "about average." Commuting from Syosset to his job in Manhattan and back, he has experienced breakdowns that have eaten up entire days; shorter delays that make him regularly late for business meetings and family functions; trains with doors that do not open when they stop at his station, and trains that forget to stop at Syosset at all; smothering summer rides in cars with no air-conditioning and with windows that don't open; and winter rides with no heat, no lights, no seats, frozen switches, broken switches, broken signals, and circuit failures.

Like other L.I.R.R. riders, Mr. Mahoney, a relatively mild-mannered sixty-year-old executive with the New York Telephone Company, has at times become fighting mad. He has argued with trainmen, written letters, called commuter-advocate groups for help, and tried to get through to the railroad's president. But, like the others, he has gradually become inured over the years, accepting his fate. "Finally, they wear all of us down until we just take it," he said. He is counting about eight hundred more rides until retirement.

Informed that in January the railroad posted one of its worst performance records in years—reporting that only 54.3 percent of its trains ran within five minutes of their scheduled times—Mr. Mahoney just shrugged. "It didn't seem much different to me," he said. "I think they play with those figures anyway. They say that during the summer one third of their cars don't have air-conditioning. Why is it I'm always on that one third?

"In twenty-two years on the Long Island Rail Road," he said, "service has never been much good. It may be worse now because employees don't seem to care anymore."

There have been periods of hope, he said, such as when former Governor Nelson Rockefeller announced he would make the L.I.R.R. "the greatest in the world." Mr. Mahoney commented:

"The railroad changes presidents a lot, and great promises are made. But it's like when the Mets change managers."

What was your worst experience? Riders say that they are frequently asked this question. At suburban social gatherings, stories are traded. "Well, two-hour delays are common," said Mr. Mahoney, waiting for the morning train on a recent day. "But one winter day I got on here at 7 A.M. and didn't get off until 4:50 P.M. And we weren't all the way there yet. We'd been stuck for ten hours, with no way to get off and no heat." After that, Mr. Mahoney has always carried a paperback book. One L.I.R.R. commuter said that she carries wool socks in her purse during the winter and has had to use them on several occasions. Another commuter said he always carries some food.

"Every Long Island commuter has his stories," Mr. Mahoney said nonchalantly. "The brother of a guy in the office was in an overcrowded train when the doors opened and he fell out. They found him eventually with helicopters. He's all right.

"You plan no meetings for nine A.M. when you ride the Long Island," he said. "Always ten." Mr. Mahoney's wife, Peggy, said she has frequently turned into "a raving maniac" waiting in the car for her husband's train to arrive. "You read and you read and then you fume," she said.

"He misses things at home in the evenings when his train is late," she said. "My dinners are always catch-as-catch-can, often burned."

One morning commuter said that he missed his daughter's graduation from high school because the train was two hours late. He sat on the stalled train envisioning her receiving her diploma and almost cried.

Mr. Mahoney pointed out that the devilish railroad can also work in more subtle ways. "I love fish for dinner," he said. "You can never have fish for dinner when you ride the Long Island Rail Road because it dries out so badly when it sits."

All of the riders ask themselves from time to time why they put up with it. "I've thought seriously about moving off the Island because of the trains," Mr. Mahoney said. "But I grew up here in Queens. [He points out his high school as the train passes by.] This is home. We have kids in school, and commuting is no picnic from anywhere."

Neither is trying to get a seat on the train. Mr. Mahoney queued up four minutes early on a recent morning, positioning himself directly in front of the gleaming white teeth of a television newscaster on a platform advertisement. He explained that this is where the car with the most empty seats usually stops.

"I use the center-rush technique," he said. "During rush hour, when there is a crush-loading, end arounds don't work. That would be my advice to newer commuters. That, and to think about moving to San Francisco.

"I think for $91 a month you should get a seat," he said, standing on the 7:51. Some riders on this train have driven twenty minutes away from New York, their destination, in order to board at a station where seats are still available. He said that the trains are so crowded that many people do not have to pay because ticket takers cannot squeeze through the cars. Mr. Mahoney reads, while others sleep, knit, or play cards. "The bridge players don't care if they ever get there," he said.

There are no seats on the way home this day either. Mr. Mahoney leaves his office at the same moment each day, walking briskly for ten blocks to Penn Station. He knows within thirty seconds or so what time he will arrive and steps onto the same train every day. So much for split-second timing. Then he is at the mercy of the Long Island Rail Road and anything can happen.

He retreats to the bar car. It is terribly hot. The air-conditioning is not working, and a beer can has been inserted between the outside doors to allow some circulation. "At least it's not a sleeper," said Mr. Mahoney thankfully, a term the riders use for cars without lights.

To be fair, he noted that some "happy commuters" could probably be found among those in the bar car guzzling beers and martinis and among a group of young office workers passing marijuana cigarettes.

Also in the interest of fairness, Mr. Mahoney pointed out: "It must also be said that the Long Island Rail Road is the greatest excuse for getting home late from a round of drinking with the boys known to man."

AUTO-EROTICA

"You look like you've had a tough day," I say to my wife. "Let's go out for dinner."

She thinks I'm wonderful for suggesting it and bounds out to the car. "What are all these pots and pans doing in the front seat?" she asks.

I explain that it's a new line of car cookware you plug into the cigarette lighter: "I thought I'd just drive around, and you could fry up those perch there in the glove compartment." She declines, saying that she had something else in mind.

"Fish, potatoes, hamburgers, anything you can fry in your kitchen you can fry in the front seat of your car on the Port-A-Fry," says Larry Jaffe in his Lincolnwood office. Jaffe is Illinois representative for the Metal Ware Corp., which markets Port-A-Fry and two other Travl-Mates, the Travl-Perk coffee maker and the Pot 'n' Pop saucepan.

"Like you, I was skeptical," says Jaffe. "Some of the buyers thought it was crazy, but it's selling like mad with virtually no advertising." He says a toaster and a broiler are in the works.

If the line of cookware was just being pitched to campers, it would be a little easier to understand. But they have a new coffee pot and service set coming out designed to fit over the transmission hump. They already have one that attaches to the dashboard. Publicity photographs show the saucepan (hot dogs, stew, popcorn, you name it) sitting on a fold-down armrest right there in the front seat. And the boxes say, "Ideal for the daily commuter or cross-country traveler."

"If people want to start cooking cakes and pies in their cars, we'll bring out an oven," says Jaffe, excited by the eager market already snapping up the new line.

"The next logical step would be a cookbook," he quips, "with recipes for Eggs Benedict à la Edens [expressway] and Steak Diane Eisenhower [expressway]. Julia Child on the radio is a good idea. With all the construction work, you can cook a complete meal just on the Edens."

Seriously, though, Larry . . .

"This nation is so dependent on the automobile—everything is drive-in," says Jaffe. "People are living out of their cars, so we're saying, 'Here are the appliances, start cooking in your cars.' " And they are.

I tell him it's not unusual for me to motor through the drive-in bank and the drive-in cleaners on the way to work. There are, of course, drive-in theaters, restaurants, and a drive-in funeral home where you can view the body (not recommended while cooking and eating in the car).

We won't get out of our cars.

There are magazine ads showing Mom and the kids watching television in the back seat of the station wagon. There are big smiles on their faces as there is on driver Dad's. Something like the Grand Canyon slips past outside, unnoticed.

The Warshawsky automotive catalog lists the Travl-Mates, along with other cigarette lighter items like spotlights, radar detectors, vacuum cleaners, and portable sinks. A fellow worker tells me he has four cigarette lighter outlets for appliances, including a refrigerator. Moloney Coachbuilders in Rolling Meadows will put a toilet in for you.

With reclining seats, I figure I could sell the house. Some people have, moving to vans and campers, not to mention the people who live in developments of mobile homes.

We won't get out of our vehicles, not until those last few feet from the hearse to the grave. Mobile cemeteries are bound to happen.

I leave Larry Jaffe and the next morning try cracking eggs on the expressway entrance ramp, with a pot of coffee brewing and tomato soup in the works for lunch. I arrive at the office a little deflated and hungry, having blown a fuse.

There's a press release on my desk: The Lombard Bible Church is holding drive-in church services each Sunday during July and August.

Surely the President, the Environmental Protection Agency, and the regional transit authority must realize by now: We don't care about gas shortages. We won't get out of our cars.

THE HUBCAP HARVEST

Edwin Murphy was working the road leading into the Lincoln Tunnel like a ball boy at a tennis match. He stood poised on the shoulder until traffic whizzed by, then pounced onto the roadway to snatch a hubcap and quickly darted off. Holding high a gleaming, spoked wheel cover of a late model Cadillac, he predicted that this would be a vintage year.

This is the opening of another pothole season, a time when snow and ice begin to retreat, revealing pockmarked roadways that look as though they were abandoned by highway maintenance departments and left to the Luftwaffe. Motorists throughout the metropolitan region complain that by March of each year they need lunar rover vehicles to negotiate the roadways.

Mr. Murphy, of East Rutherford, New Jersey, seemed pleased to be out again in the open air—rich and full-bodied with exhaust fumes here by the Lincoln Tunnel—pursuing hubcaps on the wing. He found on his arrival thirteen hubcaps lying just up-lane from a favorite pothole, waiting to be harvested, and was now going after the live ones.

An Oldsmobile hit the crater, appearing to send the driver's head into the car roof. The stunned driver slowed with the jolt, and his left rear hubcap shot past him, bounding up the highway, careening off the concrete lane divider, rolling slowly about, and shimmying noisily to rest.

Mr. Murphy winced at the sight of an oncoming commuter bus that flattened the sculpted wheel covering. The forty-one-year-old scavenger sells the squashed ones as scrap metal. Those that are relatively unmarred bring a higher price at auto-supply dealers.

Some beleaguered motorists who drive to work view the pothole season as providing a continuity of aggravation, filling the gap between the snow and ice that slow them down during the winter and the major construction projects that cause miles and miles of backups in spring, summer, and fall.

Mr. Murphy, however, who espouses something of a "when-the-potholes-return-to-Teterboro-can-spring-be-far-behind" philosophy, views the pothole season as a time of hope. He seemed to suggest, only half in jest, that the much-maligned pothole was good for the economy.

Indeed, Hubcap World, a store in Jersey City that buys from entrepreneurs such as Mr. Murphy, is now experiencing its annual sales boom in everything from its $5 hubcaps to the $400 Rolls-Royce models. Also reporting a seasonal surge are those who realign the front ends of automobiles, who straighten out bent wheel rims and axles, and who sell tires and mufflers to those who have encountered potholes. In addition, there's the asphalt industry, which provides patching material for the country's 100 million new potholes each year.

These are just part of what road-maintenance officials say is a growing pothole industry that has sprouted in recent years with a general deterioration of streets and highways caused by several severe winters and cuts in financing for road maintenance.

Trade organizations, such as The Road Information Program in Washington, have been formed to collect data that might encourage government to fill more potholes. TRIP, as it is known, tells us illuminating things. For example: the "average American pothole" last year was sixteen inches in diameter and five inches deep; potholes occurred that spring season at the rate of six each second and totaled 116.4 million nationwide.

A new field of law, pothole law, has opened up, and ancillary services like The Big Apple Pothole and Sidewalk Protection Corporation have been created. In response to a law stating that New York is not liable for pothole-related injuries unless the city has been informed of the offending pothole fifteen days before the accident, the company has registered between 750,000 and one million potholes. It charges $50 to tell a lawyer whether a pothole has been registered, a company official said.

The federal government has flirted with getting into the pothole-repair business several times in recent years. After complaining that he had hit the same pothole six days in a row, one congressman authored a $250 million bill, which did not pass, to fill potholes. Critics suggested that his hitting the same pothole six days in a row might say more about the caliber of people being sent to Congress than about road conditions.

Hubcap scavengers are seen in increasing numbers. A TRIP official reports having heard of one who was recently offered $100 by another scavenger for his spot at a particularly effective pothole. Radio stations and newspapers are currently trading on the pothole situation by holding contests for the worst ones and for suggested uses for potholes.

"They could stock that one with fish," said James Ward, a motorist who stopped his crippled car to survey the damage after hitting a chasm on the Franklin D. Roosevelt Drive.

Over on the West Side Highway, Martin Cohen was changing a tire after having plunged into a canyonette big enough to arouse Evel Knievel's interest. This is the highway that has had its southern reaches closed since December 1973, when a vehicle plunged through the roadway.

One of the hundreds of rush-hour motorists rolling slowly past Mr. Cohen allowed as how he had received two flat tires last year from hitting potholes on this stretch of road. And he gave a brief, profane dissertation to the effect that the Roman Empire had fallen because its roads fell apart.

New York City is viewed by many as the country's pothole capital. A taxi driver, who said he had "nearly drowned" in a massive pothole concealed by water, asked, "You know of any other cities where they declare 'pothole emergencies?' "

In addition to potholes being good for the economy, however, the taxi driver also noted that potholes slow traffic to safer speeds. And Ted Resnick, who oversees eighty pothole-patching crews in the city, had to admit: "Potholes provide jobs."

At a time of concern over the balance of payments and diminished prestige of American goods, New York is pioneering in the export of potholes. Jaguar-Rover-Triumph Inc., the automobile maker, had made plaster casts of New York's potholes and shipped them back to England for use on a test track. "The feeling," a spokesman said, "is that New York has the finest in the world."

OF PLASTIC GRAVY BOATS AND CLEAN WINDSHIELDS

Gasoline station attendants here in Englewood, New Jersey, are washing windshields, checking oil, and, in one reported instance, even saying "Thank you" as the price of gasoline falls and stations try once again to curry favor with motorists.

"One guy almost fainted when I washed his windshield," said Bob Isaacson at the Sunoco station. "He said it was the first time anyone had done that in six years." Prices are so low, Mr. Isaacson said, that some motorists demand to know what is wrong with the gasoline, and others accuse him of not filling their tanks completely.

For the moment, there is no energy crisis, no gasoline rationing, no collection of conservation tips from oil companies, no twinge of un-Americanism from driving a car big enough to fit into comfortably, and no such thing as being "fuelish."

There is now more than enough gasoline, with sharply lower prices—less than $1.10 for regular at some stations—and gasoline wars in which oil companies are giving rebates to station owners who sell at cost or below. And Bob Isaacson is washing windshields—until further notice.

Gasoline price warfare is next to Nirvana for residents of the auto-dependent suburbs, where meals are picked up at the drive-in windows of fast-food restaurants, clean clothing at the drive-in laundry, money at the drive-in bank, and commuters from the train station. Everything else is obtained at drive-to shopping malls. Children are driven to movies and music lessons; parents are driven to the brink from driving them everywhere.

In a packed cluster of eight stations along Route 4 here, not far from the George Washington Bridge, owners are busy erecting new and bigger signs—some of them with flashing lights—dusting off the colorful plastic pennants, and standing ready to climb their ladders at a moment's notice to lower the posted prices and keep up with the competition. The Mobil station has even put up a sign in Japanese to lure residents of the large Japanese community in the area.

"It's a circus out there," said Edward Pakies, Jr., owner of the Getty station, referring to his seven competitors. "We may go back to giving away teddy bears, plates, glasses, and little flashlights again before it's over."

At the Amoco station, John Majewski, an attendant, said many New York motorists are paying the $1.50 bridge or tunnel toll to buy here. "Many of them bring five-gallon cans, too," he said. Mr. Pakies said that on days when he had the lowest price on Route 4, he was servicing sixty to seventy-five New York cabs.

Few of the motorists were gleeful over the reduced prices, however, noting that they had been paying considerably less than 60 cents a gallon before the beginning of the energy crisis in 1973. Barbara Anderson, of Tenafly, who was having one of her family's three cars filled, echoed the sentiments of many others, saying: "Low? You call these prices low? I didn't buy all that stuff about raising gasoline prices to save democracy. I think the prices are still outrageous."

At the Exxon station, the manager, John Biango, said comparison shoppers now question him about his gasoline's octane level before buying. Mr. Pakies said that he could not lower his prices as much as the other stations and now watches cars cruise through, check the pump price, and speed on. "I just watch TV all day," his attendant said.

"I come to work every morning," said Frank Wilgo, owner of the Texaco station on Route 4, "and I see that guy next door up on his ladder changing the prices and I yell, 'Oh no, not again!' Something has to give. The rebates are not enough, and a lot of people are going to be out of business."

Kathy Moran, who was having her car filled at the Amoco station, was not sympathetic. "It's hard to feel sorry for them," she said. "We had to sit in long lines a few years ago for our little allotments of gas. The prices were ridiculous. The gas jockeys were pretty surly, too."

"Now," Mr. Wilgo said, "we are offering more and faster service to compete. Maybe we say, 'Good morning,' where before we said nothing." But James Birmingham, who has been selling leaded regular gasoline for $1.08.9 per gallon in his Sunoco station in Ridgewood, said: "Price is everything. We could wear little bow ties and smile and pump up little boys' bike tires, but for a penny less all of our customers go next door."

Telling tales of what the future holds is a popular pastime at service stations these days. There are frightening tales, grim prognostications of $2 per gallon and surly attendants. But there are also soothing tales of $1 by summer, of stuffed teddy bears as premiums, of complimentary tumblers, and plastic gravy boats.

TRUCKS TAKE TRANQUILITY FOR A RIDE

Marjorie Hoey has had nineteen tractor-trailer trucks overturn in her front yard during the last ten years, usually in the early morning, when she is awakened by a thunderous crash and the sound of heads of lettuce, sides of beef, or frozen turkeys thrown against the front of her house.

On various occasions she has peeked out the curtains to see hundreds of dazed chickens standing around, or three feet of baby-food jar lids covering most of the lawn, or a U.S. Air Force experimental plane that flew rather well off a truck rounding the bend in the road in front of her home.

"The plane was interesting," said the sixty-seven-year-old Mrs. Hoey, pushing up her glasses. About three thousand tractor-trailers a day pass Mrs. Hoey's home on the way through Milford—an otherwise picturesque community of eleven hundred people—rattling teacups and nerves and cracking windows, plaster, and the rural tranquility.

They rumble through on a stretch of U.S. Route 209 known to truckers across the country as the Ho Chi Minh Trail, a narrow, winding, dangerous road that provides a link between Interstates 80 and 84.

Townspeople finally won a ban from the federal government on trucks using the road. But word of the impending ban seemed to have spread through every hill and dale in the foothills of the Poconos, so neighboring towns—fearful that Milford's one million trucks a year would begin rumbling through their communities instead—obtained a postponement and reevaluation of the Route 209 ban.

Meetings were hastily called, petitions were signed, and members of Congress from the area were besieged with pleas to press for the reevaluation.

The forty-ton eighteen-wheel trailer trucks, carrying everything from medicine to corn chips, exit Route 80 and make their way up Route 209 through Marshalls Creek, past the Pocono Snake Farm and the Pocono Indian Museum and Ski Shop, past Henny Youngman, when he is on stage at the Fernwood resort, and through Egypts Mills and Dingmans Ferry.

Trucks by the thousands roar past the Environmental Education Center and through the Delaware Water Gap Recreational Area and into Milford, a remarkably well-preserved town chock full of Georgian, Federal, and Victorian homes.

They cannot stop at the Milford Diner anymore, a practice that filled the whole town with trucks prior to some new parking restrictions. Some say that the heat and exhaust of idling trucks killed the trees, and most say that exhaust from the trucks is ruining the paint on the exteriors of the houses. They say the trucks are cracking the walls of the First Presbyterian Church, shaking the stucco off a historic building and the ornamental wood trim off the Pike County Courthouse.

Warner Depuy, the Pike County commissioner who has led a relentless and often frustrating battle for more than ten years to ban the tractor-trailers from Milford, said he had his home remodeled so that the bedroom is in the back, farther away from the road and the trucks.

Mr. Depuy said that the Hotel Fauchere, which opened in 1842, closed two years ago because of noise from the trucks that pass just a few feet from its front door.

Martin Greenwald, the owner of the Milford Drug Store, said many residents have just moved out of town.

Cynthia Van Lierde keeps a scrapbook of news clippings about the trucks, filled with stories and photographs of them knocking down signs and telephone lines, of Mrs. Hoey and her neighbors standing in their bathrobes looking at piles of carpeting and at stunned chickens.

Although the scrapbook has its comical moments, for the most part it is a macabre album of death, chronicling dozens of fatal automobile accidents on Route 209, most of which local residents believe are attributable to the heavy truck traffic. Many residents said they were afraid to leave town in their cars.

Mr. Depuy says that 112 deaths have occurred on this short stretch of Route 209 in the last seven years. But the state Department of Transportation argues that the figure is only about half that—just as others have argued that perhaps only a mere twenty-five hundred trucks, not five thousand, go through Milford every day.

Mr. Depuy has proven a strong opponent to the trucking lobby and to various state and federal agencies. At times during the frustrating battle, he has had to convince Milford residents not to block the road with baby carriages, piles of shale, or a barrage of gunfire—all of which have been suggested at one time or another at meetings of vigilantes.

Some of his methods have been canny, such as the most recent move deeding the road to the National Park Service so that it could ban the trucks from passing through a national recreation area near

Milford. So close was he to final victory—and a planned victory celebration—that road signs announcing the ban were erected by the State Transportation Department, only to be covered over with the postponement announcement.

Mr. Depuy contends that banning trucks from Route 209 would require most of them to drive just eleven extra miles. "Tonight, tomorrow, or a week from now," he said, "someone is going to die on that road. I hate to write a letter to someone saying there is blood on their hands, but I will."

Roadway Express Inc. operates the largest of its 500 terminals on Route 80 near the Route 209 shortcut, and company officials have threatened to move the terminal and its 823 full-time jobs if the ban is put into effect.

At the Pocono Queen Diner on Route 209, truck drivers were generally peeved about the proposed ban. Herbert Hillegas, an independent trucker from Pittsburgh who makes runs to New England, said, "A ban is going to cost truckers a lot of money because of the mountains and extra mileage, at a time when companies are going out of business right and left."

"These people," he said, "think they are entitled to their private little paradise up here."

YOUR HOSTS AT THE MIDWEST'S DIRTIEST MOTEL

Meet Woody and Peggy Roe, two wonderful people, and your hosts at the Midwest's dirtiest motel.

They work their fingers to the bone getting rid of the dirt-dirt, but we're talking here about sexy dirt—you know, *Hustler* magazine, unattended medical encyclopedias, or dirty words, the kind you used to get your mouth washed out with soap for spouting.

The Ogden Motel in Downers Grove, also known as the Sybaris Inn, has hourly rates on rooms with king-size waterbeds, mirrors on the walls and ceilings, plush carpeting where the mirrors aren't, and a control panel on the headboard that only an impassioned airline pilot could comprehend.

The controls allow for dozens of lighting effects with a variety of switches, AM-FM and tape stereo, an electrical outlet for appliances (in case you might want some toast), and controls for the tele

vision, which has an extra educational channel showing films with
no dialogue—who could talk?—but moaning.

Above the bed, in the middle of the mirror, is this hook. It's
really not for petunia pots, as Woody told his mother and a minister on their tour of the motel, but for the Taiwan Basket, the specialty of the house.

This is not something used in the harvesting of Orientals but
rather a rattan, half-egg-shaped chair, which hangs from the ceiling
by a chain and is actually sold over the counter at furniture stores.
Woody has modified these, however, by drilling holes in the bottoms.

This seems like a heck of a place to start the suburban sexual
revolution: Downers Grove, in a small old vintage Ma-and-Pa motel
with twelve-foot-wide stucco units and a handwritten sign on the
door: "If no answer to doorbell, try garage by Coke machine."

It's deceptive. Underneath the Ogden Motel sign hangs a
smaller sign reading "Sybaris Inn" and showing an apple with a
bite missing. And behind those eleven stucco units sit three "Syba-
ritic Rooms," which are like three aluminum, cedar-shingled,
golden eggs.

Coming out of one, Woody stops and says, "I'd like for you to
meet my dad." His father is retired and lives in one of the older
units.

As we walk along, Woody points out the small vegetable gardens and flower beds that his father tends. We walk past the horse-
shoe pits, picnic table, and swing set. Inside the garage is a pool
table. He tells me that the place has a real homey atmosphere and
that one time a couple paying $30 for three hours in one of the syb-
aritic rooms spent the first two hours playing pool and charades
with some of the other guests before they realized what they'd
done.

He says about 80 percent of the couples who use the rooms are
married couples—except in the afternoons. "We don't ask the afternoon guests if we can send them Christmas cards," he says. He
says last weekend he'd taken a picture for some newlyweds crossing the threshold—entering the doorway—of one of the rooms.

We walk past the small apple orchard, where the swinger magazines take their outdoor photos when they're doing articles on the
Sybaris, and into the house. They live on the premises with their
four-year-old daughter, Michelle.

Peggy invites me to stay for dinner. Over pork chops and homemade pickles, they tell me it's a grueling life running the Midwest's dirtiest motel. They take tremendous pride in the place, constantly cleaning and polishing and doing the linens themselves. Running a dirty motel with hourly rates means you have to make up the rooms much more often—sometimes at three in the morning.

People are on the phone or at the door at all hours demanding to get in one of "those rooms." They come from all over the Midwest, and there are bookings as far ahead as New Year's Eve. The orange neon "No Vacancy" sign has burned out twice in the last year, and their Sybaris Inn T-shirts are going like hotcakes.

They have to be at the motel all the time, usually in the small house, which doubles as the office (the videotape for the educational channel has to be changed every hour). To relax, Woody toys with his sophisticated sound and video equipment, sometimes, as he does this evening, singing or playing his trumpet along with tapes of professional gospel groups that he used to sing with. When he can get away, he likes to go to garage sales.

As Woody sings along, Michelle coaxes Charlie—one of their two cats—out the backdoor. Peggy tells me about her reading and about the sweater she crocheted for Woody's mother. "I crocheted an entire communion dress last winter," she says, excusing herself to get up to change the dirty videotape on a typical evening at the Midwest's dirtiest motel.

V

SPORT

SPORT SHOPPING IN SUBURBIA

"I have one thing to say to that gray fox," says Fran. "I want you, I need you, I love you." She takes a bite of her tuna-pecan water chestnut on croissant.

"Think of the money you'd be saving Steve," Jackie says with a note of sarcasm, taking a bite of her avocado-chicken salad sandwich.

Steve is Fran's husband. Fran and Jackie are friends. The gray fox is a $7,500 coat that is marked down on Neiman-Marcus's fur sale to $6,000—a potentially handsome $1,500 saving for Steve. The fabulous fox is poised for sale not far from where they are having lunch, the Zodiac restaurant in the Neiman-Marcus store in the Northbrook Court mall in Chicago's northern suburbs.

They sit in a mecca of conspicuous consumption. It is rumored that anyone entering Northbrook Court with less then two designer labels showing on his or her person will be wrestled to the ground by Security. Shopping here is a sport; Fran and Jackie would seem to be world class competitors.

It is said that shopping was once done of necessity. An example might be shopping to buy a pair of shoes without big holes in the bottoms. Now we go shopping for entertainment, to get out of the house, to see those new things that are making those people in the television commercials so remarkably happy, and to mingle with people. Where else in the suburbs can we see people stripped of their cars?

The better sport shoppers at Northbrook Court would seem to be women in their thirties or forties, traveling most often in twos, and either thin or divorced. They have chic hair styles; and their faces represent the state of the art in cosmetology. Many wear "fun furs" and designer tops with designer jeans. The jeans may be tucked into new low-cut cowboy (if you will) boots. If Designer Jeans Are Not Tucked In, They Shall Be Stylishly Rolled Up—The Management.

Fran is tucked; Jackie, rolled. One wonders if this places a strain on their relationship. They are not wearing coats. Really good sport shoppers know that there are places in malls to drop off coats. The two seem as comfortable as if they were at home, which to some extent they are.

101

They are here at Northbrook Court nearly the entire day. They were here yesterday. The day before that they went into the city, to Watertower Place, one of the vertical shopping malls that cities are building to emulate the suburban malls that have been stealing away all of their business. Once Fran and Jackie even spent the night at Watertower Place, in the Ritz Hotel. They may spend more time shopping than they do at home. They aren't sure.

They are carrying shopping bags but say they haven't bought anything. "This is just something for my daughter [nine years old] to knock around in," Fran says, holding open a bag containing a Givenchy terry cloth top ($20) and Gloria Vanderbilt jeans ($32) purchased at I. Magnin, an up-scale store that just opened at the mall. "It changed my life," Fran says with a smirk about the store opening. Jackie has a one-pound box of Godiva chocolates that have crossed chocolate tennis racquets on their tops ($12).

After lunch they glide through this clean, climate-controlled shopping womb, through Ann Taylor and Lord & Taylor before stopping in Stanley Korshak to buy Fran a bikini ($58) for an upcoming Palm Springs vacation. Jackie buys a pound of freshly ground coffee—make that Ethiopian Harrar coffee—at The Coffee Factory ($5.25). Fran returns to I. Magnin to inspect a plain black piece of luggage about the size of a gym bag—but with Ralph Lauren's name on it—priced at $550. The two shoppers stop at the cosmetics department to talk with the clerks about Erno Laszlo skin care programs and to buy some cosmetics. It is a minor purchase ($9), yet still a purchase, complete with attendant conversation and salesclerks fawning a bit over these preferred customers.

Jackie takes a serious look at a Bottega Veneta Italian lambskin shoulder bag ($185) that looks to have about enough room in it for half a tuna-pecan water chestnut on croissant. It is almost time for the children to come home on the school bus. Jackie feels rushed.

She tells the clerk that she will "sleep on it." Tomorrow is another day.

At Roosevelt Field shopping mall on Long Island, Lisa D'Amico drifts through the corridors like a fish in a comfortably familiar aquarium, needing nothing in particular other than to shop. "I didn't really come today to buy anything," says the thirty-two-year-old Garden City housewife.

Roosevelt Field, a 180-store, 2.2 million-square-foot enclosed shopping center (that argues with the Woodfield Mall in suburban Chicago about which is the world's largest), was considered a risky undertaking when it was built in 1956. But now, during the celebration of its twenty-fifth anniversary, it is viewed as a visionary prototype of the mega-malls that have transformed the country's landscape and spawned a generation of shoppers such as Mrs. D'Amico.

"Shopping has become a mode of entertainment," says Frieda Stangler, a spokesperson for the mall. Shoppers describe Roosevelt Field as "pleasant," "fun," and "exciting." There are frequent special events, such as antique shows, fashion shows, car shows, boat shows, and appearances by film, sports, and soap opera stars.

"We believe that if we can get them to the mall," Mrs. Stangler says, "there will be purchases."

The purchases of 275,000 visitors a week total about $230 million a year. An assortment of restaurants and such things as lockers for coats and other belongings encourage them to stay, as do the benches and tables outside the stores, where shoppers can relax with no pressure to buy. There are no clocks or windows.

The country's more than two thousand enclosed malls are overwhelmingly successful, finely tuned selling machines, in which everything from climate to clientele has always been closely controlled to produce an impeccably pleasant shopping environment. Retailers not fitting the total marketing concept are not allowed into most malls, and the ones that are let in usually have their hours set and their store designs approved by mall management.

In malls it never rains or snows. There are no puddles to jump, no unpleasant aromas to smell, no crummy bars or people who frequent them. There are no Hare Krishnas or protestors or anyone to introduce unpleasantness of any kind. Such people have no rights here; this is private property.

Of late, however, many shopping mall managers say they have had the uncomfortable feeling that the outside world is seeping in. In suburban Hartford, for example, there is grave concern over a group of women that wants to put up a little folding card table in Westfarms Mall.

Attorneys for the 127-store mall have been battling in court for more than two years to keep out the card table where two representatives of the National Organization for Women would collect signatures on petitions supporting the Equal Rights Amendment. The women's organization argues that even though such malls are private property, they have become the nation's "new downtowns," public places where individuals and groups have as much right to collect signatures on petitions and hand out literature as on any street corner. Moreover, argues Martin Margulies, the group's attorney, "malls are the place, the only place, to see people in the suburbs anymore." The women's organization won the first round in its court battle with Westfarms Mall early last year.

Court battles on this point are being waged across the country. In Paramus, New Jersey, sometimes referred to as the shopping center capital of the country, because of its five major centers, a political candidate has sued for the right to distribute campaign literature in Bergen Mall.

The attorney for the candidate argues, "There is no real downtown Paramus. Areas of the mall outside the stores are the town's public sidewalks." He noted that community events were held at the mall and that it contained a meeting hall, a post office, and a Roman Catholic chapel.

"We in the industry are quite concerned about a loss of control," says Peter Hollis, senior vice president for the Taubman Company, one of the nation's largest mall developers and the management concern for Westfarms Mall. "The hassle-free environment is the whole basis of shopping mall development."

Mrs. D'Amico says she comes to the Roosevelt Field mall about three times a week, twice on weekday trips with friends and once on the weekend with her husband and two children. When she comes with her friends, they browse, make a few small purchases, and have lunch at a new restaurant in the mall called Houlihan's Old Place, which is decorated with old-fashioned tin ceilings and reproductions of memorabilia and has a menu awash with frothy frozen strawberry daiquiris, piña coladas, nacho platters, and Huevos California. "It's a fun place," she says.

Donna Shapiro, who is seventeen years old and says she has been coming here all her life, is at the mall after school with two friends, looking for just the right pair of jeans at such stores as Jeans West, Just Jeans, Jeans Only, and Pants Place Plus. They also meander into such places as Just Shirts and Just Cards and make purchases of opportunity as they go: one pound of very cherry jelly beans at Fanny Farmer Candies, one Bob Seger double album at Record World, and a bag of Bruce's Chunky Chocolate Chip Cookies.

They have some laughs trying on hairpieces at Wig Allure but become serious when the clerk turns the discussion to the shop's acrylic fingernails. They have also come here to troll for friends in general, boys to be more specific, and Jim in particular. As one of Donna's friends says, "This is where you see everybody."

"A lot of young people come here on shopping dates," Mrs. Stangler says. "There are not the cultural activities for young people in the suburbs that there are in the city. It is a very expensive proposition to keep teenagers amused these days, and they can come here free, where it is safe and warm. I don't think that it's bad for them."

There are many elderly people at the mall, one of whom explains that they come regularly to get out of the house without having to worry about crime or inclement weather.

They all say they can get anything they want at the 180 stores and other businesses at Roosevelt Field. Visitors to the mall can see a movie, take out a life insurance policy, have their television sets and cars repaired, have their hair styled, have their income taxes prepared, attend "jazz-ercise" classes at the health spa or weight loss classes at Weight Watchers, mail a package at the mall's post office, visit the optometrist, or have a cavity filled at Dental World. They can buy a dog or buy a Florida retirement home in a six-thousand-house development populated primarily by former Roosevelt Field shoppers.

There is a waiting list of seven to ten years for businesses to get into Roosevelt Field, and those not on the inside line every roadway to the mall, attempting to lure motorists headed for the mall's 12,300-space parking lot. Office buildings, banks, and corporate headquarters have built on the periphery. The mass, the gravitational pull of Roosevelt Field, seems to have drawn everything from miles around into its orbit, and officials of surrounding suburbs bemoan the loss of stores, jobs (with six thousand employees, the mall is Long Island's fourth-largest employer), sales, and taxes.

The downtowns of older suburbs often go out of business when malls are built. Newer suburbs often have no downtowns, just roadways to the mall.

Asked why he comes to Roosevelt Field, one shopper replies, "Everything is here now." Others say that they have not been to Manhattan for months or even years. Their most recent shopping trips there, they report, were "a hassle," "a little scary at times," or "too expensive."

Donna Shapiro and her friends are passing by Just Cards, heading toward Just Shirts. She has found the pants she was looking for, and they have seen a number of "cute boys." They have not seen Jim, but they fear not. "School's out," one of Donna's friends says. "He's got to be here someplace."

THE BASEBALL STRIKE

Stanley Reich of New Milford, New Jersey, was spotted last weekend trimming a plum tree in his backyard, something he had steadfastly refused to do for three years. A concerned neighbor went out to see if anything was wrong with Mr. Reich, who explained despondently that there was no baseball on television.

The potential is staggering. With the baseball strike and the absence of baseball from television, millions of man-hours are unleashed each week: to create, to discover, to build, perchance to take out the trash.

Many hardware stores and home-improvement centers report that traffic in their stores increased when the strike by players began, and the proprietors believe a lot of the fans are using the freedom from their television sets, radios, and trips to the ball park to devote extra time to home projects.

"We've been much busier than usual," said Evelyn Folz, cashier at Larchmont Hardware, in Larchmont, New York, "apparently because of the strike." She is a baseball fan, who said that she now spends the time she would have been watching televised baseball to talk with friends and to read books. "It's terrible," she said.

Many bars that cater to those who come in to lounge while they watch baseball on television are suffering. Tom Caplette, bartender at Dew's Tavern, in Elizabeth, New Jersey, said business was down considerably since the strike. "We aren't going to sit there and drink with a soap opera on," said one customer. The television stays on, but the volume on the jukebox has been turned up to drown it out.

Asked what the regular customers might be doing with their time, one patron answered: "Don't be surprised if the birthrate is up in nine months. These guys go home sober now, and they don't have those West Coast games to watch late at night either."

"I helped my father-in-law mow his lawn last weekend," said Richard Cunningham, of Elizabeth, New Jersey, "and I think he's still in shock. At home I take out the garbage and go food shopping with my wife. I fixed the brakes on my car and saved myself $80 or $90. I do a lot of the things I guess I normally should do." Mr. Cunningham hates it. He is coming off a twenty-hour-a-week habit.

Televised baseball is an easy substance to obtain in today's society, what with the networks and Channels 9 and 11, SportsChannel and ESPN. Dedicated watchers say you cannot fully appreciate the loss unless you have experienced watching a game from a recliner chair in a paneled recreation room with a cold beer in one hand and the remote control switch to a twenty-three-incher with zoom capability in the other.

"I considered myself fortunate," said Mr. Cunningham. "I have the cable and could watch the Yankees, Mets, Red Sox, Phillies, Braves, and some others. I also have a twenty-five-inch color Quasar I'm pretty proud of.

"Now I just walk around the house straightening things," he said. "My wife tells me to go outside to do something. So I go out on the porch and read the sports page five times."

Watching sports on television has become an acceptable, if unpopular, defense in many jurisdictions against pleas to clean the gutters, fix the garbage disposal, perform other tasks, or, perhaps, converse with family members.

Interwoven seasons of baseball, football, hockey, and basketball form an almost impenetrable shield of sportscasting, shutting out most attempts to move the viewer to action. Those who try to penetrate that shield say that the viewers, sometimes known as "couch potatoes," have long since changed from human beings to receiving components of the broadcasting system.

With the coming of the strike, fans say they are vulnerable to all manner of indignity. "Last weekend," said Lloyd Thompson, a Westchester commuter waiting for a train in Grand Central, "a question arose as to who was going to drive my daughter and her friends to a movie thirty minutes away. If I had been watching the Yanks or the Mets I would have been O.K.," he said, but when his wife saw him feigning interest in a bowler trying to pick up a spare, he did not have a base to stand on.

OUR GOLDEN GLOVES REPRESENTATIVE

Da-Da, Daaa; Da-Da, Daaa. Yes. It's another real life "Rocky" story.

Jim Halford of north suburban Mundelein is a mild-mannered sociology major at Illinois State University.

He distinguished himself as an excellent cross-country runner at the College of Lake County but decided to stop running when he went to school downstate.

He maintained an interest in competitive athletics, however, and the 5-foot-6-inch, 132-pound student decided he'd switch to boxing.

A lot of people thought he was nuts, but his girl friend bought him a punching bag. He says that he has no reason to believe that she encouraged his interest in boxing because she might want to start dating around.

Halford didn't do anything to dispel thoughts he might be crazy when he decided to enter the Golden Gloves boxing tournament for Chicago area fighters. He had never been in the ring before, but at least there is a Novice Division for relatively inexperienced fighters.

He reported to the gym in St. Andrew's School in Chicago, where he signed up, weighed in, was examined by a doctor, and was reported fit to kill.

The scene at the gym was an eye-opener. A lot of mean-looking mothers. You don't see people like this much in the suburbs, not to mention his college town—Normal. These guys were not like Normal.

He may have been a little scared, but at least our suburban representative stayed. A significant percentage of would-be pugilists do not stay. They see a couple guys get carted out and they're gone.

That night, Halford got the first big break of his boxing career. Not a cranial fracture, as you might have guessed; rather, he didn't have to fight. Maybe they hoped he'd go away.

He came back the next day, and spent another entire evening sitting on the bleachers, waiting and watching for his name to come up on the pairings board. Late on this last night of the sectionals, his name still wasn't up, and it seemed they'd just forgotten him.

He asked one of the Golden Gloves officials what was going on. The official checked his papers and told Halford that through mixups, disqualifications, guys getting scared and leaving, or whatever, he was sectional champion.

"This can't be," Halford said. "You must be kidding." He was starting to worry about this second big break in his boxing career. "I just wanted to get in the ring there in St. Andrew's gym in front of a few people and see how I could do," he explained.

So, he thought, it was on to the supersectionals the next night in the Aragon Ballroom.

But Halford was about to get the third big break of his boxing career. The official checked further and told him that through the same set of circumstances he was also an uncontested supersectional champion. And that his first fight in the Golden Gloves—his first fight ever—would be in the finals at the International Amphitheater before ten thousand boxing fans and a prime-time television audience.

Jim Halford was getting a shot at the title. Da-Da, Daaa; Da-Da, Daaa. And because he'd turned twenty-one, he wouldn't be in the Novice Division, he'd be in the big time, in the Open Division, with the killers.

What an opportunity! A chance to join the ranks of Muhammad Ali, Ernie Terrell, Sonny Liston, Sugar Ray Robinson, and so many greats who had won Golden Gloves titles here in Chicago. He'd be fighting in the finals with several fighters given a good chance of making the Olympic team. Some guys given a good chance at the Olympics didn't even make it to the finals.

What an opportunity!

"He was sick," said the official who broke the news to Halford.

"I was knocked out right there," Halford said.

He didn't own any boxing gloves, so he bought some. He got a guy down the hall in the dorm, Tony Iuro of Downers Grove, to spar with him. He trained. He was a cross-country runner, so running wasn't a problem for him like it was for Rocky. But he had no one to teach him how to hide.

And so it was that ten thousand boxing fans filed into the International Amphitheater Friday night, opened their programs, and saw James Halford.

All the other fighters had their pictures taken in the gym with their shirts off, hair tousled, and looking slightly demented. At a minimum, they looked ruggedly handsome, some holding big clenched fists up beside their menacing mugs. Next to their pictures were things like "five times Golden Gloves champion . . . ranked third in the nation . . . three knockouts to reach the finals," things like that. And of course the name of their boxing club.

Halford didn't have a boxing picture. His mother sent in his high school yearbook photograph. A thin white guy in a coat and tie, pleasant smile, you know. "James Halford, unattached . . . twenty-one-year-old sociology major . . . cross-country runner at college," the program said.

Paired with Halford's picture was that of his opponent, Wayne Ingram, definitely one of the baddest-looking dudes in the program: a black guy with a white headband on, two fists held up, and maybe a day's growth. The program described his job as "hall monitor at Waukegan East," which tells me that you're better off murdering somebody in the city of Chicago than abusing your rest room privileges in Waukegan.

A kid who grew up in the suburbs, Halford says he has never really even liked the idea of going into Chicago, much less going in to fight Wayne Ingram. I mean if you're going to get mugged in the city, at least wait for them to come to you.

But he went. He trained hard and he showed up, because this was a big chance; and in the words of Senator George McGovern, "What if . . ."

He didn't have a coach or any cornermen, so he took two friends, who wore blue jeans and long hair and generally contrasted with the sage-looking coaches and trainers who wore things like their jackets from the last Olympics.

His friends didn't look like they belonged there. But then again, neither did the guy with them. The other fighters wore silk robes, Halford had on his white terry cloth bathrobe from home.

He was in a daze. A man in a tuxedo announced his name, the bell rang, and out they came.

Ingram swung. It looked like Halford ducked the punch. Only he really ducked it. All the way to the canvas he ducked it.

He got up. Ingram swung again. This, too, appeared to miss Halford, but he went down again.

The crowd booed, something I couldn't understand. I was beginning to gain some respect for the guy.

Ingram swung and appeared to lightly strike Halford in the head with a glancing blow. Halford went down for a third time. The referee stopped the fight at forty seconds of the first round.

"My goal in training," Halford told me after the fight, "was to keep this guy from killing me." He did.

"I wanted to get into boxing to see how I could do."

He stands as the second toughest fighter in the second largest city in the nation and has a trophy to prove it.

"And," he added, "I didn't want to hurt or kill anybody."

Da-Da, Daaa.

THINKING TROUT

A bumper sticker on Harold Williamson's car reads "Think trout," and that he does. His friend, Cecil Barnett, suggests that it goes farther than this, that Mr. Williamson is unable to live a normal life and needs to be deprogrammed.

After a long winter of fly-tying in the basement, practice-casting in the backyard, and general mooning about the house, Mr. Williamson arose from a fitful sleep at 4 A.M. to join tens of thousands of other enthusiasts jamming the streams and rivers of New York State on the opening day of trout season.

Here on the East Branch of the Croton River in southeastern Putnam County, they stood almost shoulder to shoulder, occasionally tangling lines, dodging hooks, and voicing a traditional call of opening day on trout waters that seem to be just too close for comfort to the populous New York metropolitan area: "Watch it, will ya?"

On a rare occasion, a fish was actually caught, but all seemed to be either illegally or embarrassingly small and were returned to the river.

Observing all of this from a narrow bridge across the river, Tony Valeri of Stamford, Connecticut, said that he was not about to "commit suicide" by wading into the cold, numbing waters. He suggested that not for nothing does the opening of trout season coincide with April Fool's Day.

But who was he to talk? He was up early observing people not
catching fish. Now retired, Mr. Valeri admitted to having always
gone out on opening day when he was younger. "I couldn't sleep
the night before, I was so excited."

"Understand," said Mr. Williamson, "we don't care if we catch
fish or not. It's just great to be outside again." To some. Others
complained a mite of the 39-degree temperature reading shortly after dawn and of the water too cold, too swift, and too murky for
optimum fishing.

"Admittedly," said Clem Fullerton, a nearby resident who be-
longs to a chapter of Trout Unlimited, "most trout fishermen don't
have both oars in the water. But trout do not occur in slum areas.
We stalk them in some of the most beautiful landscape in the
world. When you are out there fishing along a brook with the rho-
dodendron in bloom, if your soul is not uplifted, you do not have a
soul."

Mark Johnson of Brewster, New York, arrived at 4:30 A.M., before the sun rose, to insure a good location in the river. Chuck
Carboni of Ridgefield, Connecticut, came early this year, too, explaining that last year he had had to line up on the bank to await a
spot. State officials said it is not unusual to find fishermen out at
12:01 A.M. on opening day.

Up the road at John Knapp's Sporting Center, Mr. Knapp had
what he described as a "madhouse" on his hands with dozens of
people lined up to purchase their fishing licenses, which start at
$6.50.

"This is your ritual penance," said Steve Fay of Ossining, New
York, referring to the crowds. "I hate it when opening day is on a
Friday. Too convenient for the other people. I like it better on, say,
a Wednesday or a payday. Last year it rained. It was great out
here."

Mr. Fay is an insurance salesman, a job that allows him to fish
many days, while working in the evenings. A number of the fishermen here purposely hold such jobs. And what do their wives think
of their schedules? "I took my fly rod on the honeymoon to make
things perfectly clear," said Mark Johnson.

"How did you guys all get the day off?" came an envious shout
from a car rolling across the bridge. Most of those here were absent
without leave from the commuter army that was then, at 7:30 A.M.,
zipping inbound on Route 684, one hundred yards upstream,

on a towering bridge over the river. The chirping of birds could be heard, but sounds of the traffic were drowned out by the rushing, roiling river. The fishermen were silent, throwing their lines upstream, watching them carry quickly downstream, then throwing them again seconds later—over and over and over again.

When the rod held by Angelo Carlucci of Greenwich, Connecticut, bent into an arc, the other fishermen stopped to watch. "That's just where I was standing for two hours," said a disappointed Ken Svec of Stamford, who had retreated to shore. But when the fish appeared, Mr. Svec said, "A sucker! How embarrassing." And Mr. Carlucci jerked the scavenger fish off the line in disgust.

But down the road a bit, in another pool, away from these fly fishermen with their $125 vests and $145 chest waders, a group of fishermen dangled over a bridge, on the verge of falling in. They had been fishing for trout with worms but had given up and were now snagging suckers with large treble hooks—and seemed glad to have them. This the fly fishermen regard as no more sport than withdrawing a box of breaded fish sticks from the freezer.

The fishermen who were snagging suckers said they regarded the fly fishermen as somewhat peculiar, spending long hours becoming experts in aquatic entomology, in order to replicate the insects that fish eat. "And they don't even keep the fish," said Louie Bonavenia of Paterson, New Jersey, referring to the "no kill" concept adopted by many fly fishermen of throwing all catches back.

Mr. Bonavenia was among a throng of fishermen in Fran's Diner nearby. "All of these fishermen," said Betty Reisinger, Fran's mother, "those poor, poor trout." She was told that she need not weep for trout.

Back down the road on the East Branch of the Croton River, nary a one had been caught big enough to keep, and better than half the opening day was gone. Dan Davis of Westchester dropped his $100 rod into the water and couldn't find it. Mr. Carlucci caught his second sucker. George Maravelas of Putnam Lake turned to an old man and—eyeing his foot-long gray beard—asked him just how long he'd been standing there trying to catch a fish anyway.

PUSHING DEER

Grace McGrath opens her restaurant at 4 A.M., and within minutes it is filled to overflowing with flannel-shirted, down-vested, bullet-belted, rifle-toting, pistol-packing, blade-wielding, bewhiskered hunters who begin trading all manner of stories, jibes, tales, yarns, and bald-faced lies. "This is the best part of huntin'," says one named Lem from over by Copake Falls.

"I hope none of you showered, shaved, or had sex last night," says Lloyd Hartnett to the twelve men gathered at his table at Grace's Place in Berlin, New York, and who were making short work of mounds of homemade blueberry muffins, hot sausages, eggs, potatoes, and toast. "The deer will sense you."

Lloyd is a local resident and wears a red hat because it is the first day of hunting season and he wants to be seen in the woods by the half-million lawyers, plumbers, certified public accountants, and what have you who will be storming the woods of upstate New York armed with semiautomatic weapons, ultra-high-powered scopes, and other weaponry.

Still, such fear is not enough to make the members of Lloyd's ragtag group of local hunters—who are missing, variously, a finger, a tooth, an eye, an arm—lower themselves to wearing the fluorescent-orange hats, coats, and pants worn by safety-conscious hunters from the city. One of Lloyd's group, Slippery Johnson, snidely asks one of the city slickers dressed in orange hat and coat, "Didn't Macy's have the matching orange boots?"

The opening day of deer season may as well be a declared holiday here, for all the work and the local school teaching that get done. Several hunters stop by the table to ask Lloyd, a mechanic at a local wood-products plant, where he will be hunting. He has lived here in Rensselaer County all of his forty-five years and knows every ridge, knoll, hedgerow, and, some say, deer in the area. Only about one in fifteen or twenty of the state's eight hundred thousand licensed deer hunters is expected to shoot a deer this season, and a word from Lloyd can cut the odds. He gives nothing away.

At first light, Lloyd takes a screwdriver from his pocket, winds his watch, and announces, "Time to push deer." He splits his squad of twelve into "drivers," those who will herd deer up and down ridges, and "watchers," those who will wait in ambush.

The countryside is magnificent. The hillsides shimmer with white birch trees, and there are vast meadows, rushing streams, and stone-lined brooks below. "Just being afield," says Lloyd, "with the beauty and no one telling you there's something you have to do, is the real pleasure."

Lloyd, who is also a trout fisherman, has given up hunting everything but deer. "They're smart," he explains, "and I like to see if I can't be a little bit smarter." He spots hoof prints even in the leaves and can read them for freshness; he checks tree branches for signs of recent nibbling and tree trunks for marks where the deer have rubbed their antlers.

He positions himself on the upper edge of a basin, sitting silently behind a large maple tree for about an hour as the drivers sweep up the basin with as much stealth as man can muster in the quiet woods. The hunters tiptoeing through leaves sound as if they have big bags of potato chips strapped to the bottoms of their boots.

Suddenly, Lloyd cocks his head and picks up his rifle as the heads of two deer appear, bobbing up and down from behind a berm as they run up the hillside. The deer stop about thirty yards away, staring down the barrel of Lloyd's Remington. A split second passes. Then they vanish, crashing through the woods above.

"Flatheads," Lloyds says, meaning that they had no horns, either bucks too young to have horns or does. It would have been illegal to shoot either.

There would have been time for only one shot, the deer too fleet and the woods too thick for a second try. Moreover, Lloyd uses a single-shot, bolt-action rifle.

On the next drive, Lloyd stands leaning on a tree by the side of the road as the others try to drive deer down the hillside. Several motorists stop to ask Lloyd what on earth he is doing standing there on the road. "No one ever got a deer standing by the road," says one. Lloyd just smiles, hoping they will leave if he does not speak, and eventually they do.

In a few minutes, deer come running out of the woods and across the road: five, ten, twenty deer and more. "All flatheads," Lloyd says in his low monotone. The deer run into an adjoining meadow to prance about, their white tails bobbing and wagging.

One hunter remarks that he had seen them up in the woods reading the state's big-game rules and regulations.

Lloyd hunts on private property, virtually all of which is posted "No Hunting" by owners who have given him permission to ignore the signs. Most of them have, anyway. There is one commando-style drive, however, in which the hunters ride in the back of a pickup truck, jumping out as they go down the road and disappearing into the woods. "The owner," Lloyd explains with disgust, "is a guy who people up here helped move from New York, put him up in their houses, drilled him a well and a basement, and then he went and 'posted' his property."

The hunters tell of calling owners with posted property to make sure they are in the house before sneaking onto their land. They also tell of the Volunteer Fire Department idly watching a brush fire on one property until the owner agreed to allow locals to hunt there this season. "Outsiders have been buying up farms and posting 'em," Lloyd laments.

They hunt for an hour, then stand together talking for an hour and taking infrequent nips from bottles of bourbon and vodka before moving on to the next drive. With darkness setting in and a light rain beginning to fall, Lloyd decides that it is time to do some "car hunting"—trolling the back roads to look for deer in the meadows in his hubcapless 1973 Cadillac Coupe de Ville with packages of fish hooks spilling out from under the front seat. Many others are car hunting, and some fall in behind Lloyd, using him as a guide.

He says that someone he does not care to name has been known to bag a few deer from the driver's seat. "A deer was dropped from a car right in the yard of that house there last year," he says. "Ol' Louie and Polly were gettin' ready to eat dinner, and they damned near turned the table over. You should have seen it."

Lloyd has "put out" about forty deer this day, but incredibly, none had antlers. He says he did not mind so much—"you can only take one deer a season, theoretically"—but he does take some chiding at the Colonial Inn, where two of the cars parked outside have freshly killed deer across trunks and where the plaid-flannel shirt brigades have gathered to drink thirty-cent draft beers and trade fresh stories, jibes, tales, yarns, and lies.

THE OLD SWIMMING HOLE MEETS THE EPA

Far beyond suburbia, where even the antique shops start to thin out, children still spend slow, sunny summer days in old-fashioned swimming holes, plunging in from old tires attached to swinging ropes or diving from rocks and trees. The children seem happy to share the water with sunfish, crawfish, turtles, and an occasional beaver, if not the dragonflies and horseflies—and don't seem to mind at all a little mud oozing between their toes.

There are many such swimming holes in northeastern Connecticut, but none as nice by half as Diana's Pool. It has been the local swimming hole in Chaplin longer than anyone can remember, but this year the Connecticut Department of Environmental Protection closed the state-owned property to all but those carrying fishing gear and a valid fishing permit. It has issued more than two hundred tickets—at $28 each—to people for swimming, sunbathing, walking, standing, and sitting in the vicinity of Diana's Pool.

David Rappaport was sitting on a rock out there in the wooded wilderness the other day when two policemen jumped out of the bushes and gave him a ticket. "Weird," said Mr. Rappaport.

Department officials said that the beautiful twelve-acre area was being so overrun by visitors that it had to be closed to save it. "The swimming hole does not meet state safety-code standards for a swimming facility," said one official.

"They think," one local resident responded, "that you have to have a perfectly rectangular blue cement hole with chlorine and lifeguards in order to swim." There has been considerable grumbling about outsiders from Hartford telling them what to do.

Sergeant Fred Ruhlemann, who is in charge of the department's officers issuing tickets for "Illegal Use of State Access Areas," was out this week tacking up yet more signs reading: "This Area Closed Except for Fishing." The irony of the situation, he said, is that Diana's Pool is so lovely that it had to be closed.

People from even the most unlikely spots will describe wherever they happen to live as "God's Country." But standing—unlawfully—at Diana's Pool, one has difficulty arguing that point with the people who live here.

The Natchaug River almost seems to be flaunting its beauty, as it sashays this way and that, washing over boulders and dancing between bold rock formations. Its banks are thick with maples, oaks, black gum trees, and deep-green hemlocks, its trout-filled sparkling waters so pure that botanists at a nearby university can't begin to grow algae in it.

At a point where the bedrock flattens out and the river widens is Diana's Pool—perhaps, as local folklore has it, named for a woman who died here more than a century ago. It is where local residents have always come in summer to swing on a rope attached to a tree and drop into the water or to dive from overhanging rock formations twenty feet high—the dive being a rite of passage for local teenagers. It has probably been here since glacial activity twenty thousand years ago, and it seems to many local residents that only God could rightfully be empowered to close such a place.

Two fishermen were the only ones at Diana's Pool when a state cleanup crew came through recently, sprucing up the place so that a television commercial could be filmed for the "Better Yet Connecticut" campaign, designed to lure more tourists to the state.

"Great," said one of the fishermen, Peter Galipeau, an outspoken critic of the closing. "Invite people to a place they can't come." Sergeant Ruhlemann said the problems were that word of the beauty of Diana's Pool had leaked out beyond the immediate area, that its photographs had started showing up in travel guides, and that people had begun coming here by the hundreds, trespassing on adjacent private property, making noise, drinking alcoholic beverages, throwing beer bottles into the stream, and littering the banks.

There were reports, he said, of skinny-dipping and parking problems. Officials of the tiny town of Chaplin said they were powerless to control the situation, unable to even issue parking tickets because they don't happen to have any. "No Parking" signs erected by the state now hang every thirty feet along the roadway near Diana's Pool, appearing incongruous out in the middle of nowhere.

Sergeant Ruhlemann said that state officials consider the area unsafe for swimming, particularly since so many people were coming, and were worried about liability for accidents.

"Unfortunately," he said, "these swimming holes are disappearing. If they are on state-owned land, we can't sanction them for swimming, and private land owners are finding that where local kids used to come, the general public is following. The problem is overpopulation.''

"We miss it, too," said Gregory Anderson, a local resident who complained of problems at the swimming hole and who agrees with its closing. "It was inspirational just to walk there, just to watch the cedar waxwings catch insects."

Charlotte Shead, the town's First Selectman, agreed. "We grew up in these swimming holes," she said. "You learn so much about nature while you're swimming and don't even realize it. At swimming pools, lifeguards are blowing their whistles all the time and always making you feel like you might be doing something wrong."

Upstream from Diana's Pool, before the river passes under a bridge and tumbles down a small waterfall, is another swimming hole that has now become the most popular in the area.

Lesley Ridgeway and her brother, Ben, were on their way to swim there. "Swimming pools are boring," proclaimed Miss Ridgeway, fifteen years old. She left her shoes on the bank, shinned up a thirty-foot tree that protruded over the water at a 45-degree angle, stood up momentarily, and did a full somersault dive into the emerald water.

NEW HOPE IN THE STRUGGLE FOR WATER SAFETY

John Rao stepped out of his Tillson Lake vacation home on a recent morning, shook his head to see if there was some mistake, and hurried back to tell his wife some alarming news: "The lake is gone."

Then they both went out to look and after a period of time reached the conclusion that, no, this was not some sort of mirage in reverse. The lake was gone. "The lake is gone, John," he remembers her saying.

The lake they had been coming to in Gardiner, New York, for thirty-three summers had indeed vanished. Before them instead was a defoliated crater, thirty feet deep with a small stream running through its center. The boat docks were hanging out into midair and people were roaming the lake bed with metal detectors.

July is a time of year when the Governor Thomas E. Dewey Thruway is clogged northbound with recreational vehicles and trailers and cars laden with canoes, rowboats, bicycles, dogs, children, mosquito repellent, fishing rods, calamine lotion, inner tubes, and other gear necessary for the assault on hundreds of freshwater lakes that are only two hours from the city, one hour from the suburbs.

Those turning off during the past week for Tillson Lake, where people have been coming for half a century to swim, boat, fish, dangle their feet in the water, and listen to the quiet, were in for the sad surprise that this summer was going to be something quite different.

Joseph Unanue, Sr., owns the lake and decided to drain it—or "dewater" it, to use his phrase. Most of the eighty to one hundred homeowners near the thirteen-acre lake said that the draining of the artificial lake was an act of spite carried out by Mr. Unanue, with whom they have had a long-running feud. Mr. Unanue insisted that he drained the lake for "safety" reasons. At any rate, he said, it is his lake. He pulled the plug and went home.

Mr. Rao speculated that the draining has something to do with residents successfully blocking Mr. Unanue's request for a liquor license at a pavilion on the lake. "Now," he said, "he's getting us back." Most local residents, however, believe that the draining was prompted by their opposition to the owner's proposal for developing the shoreline on the lake with a five-hundred unit trailer park—a proposal rejected by the town council.

Mr. Unanue denies any connection between draining the lake and the denials of his trailer park proposal and his request for a liquor license. He said the New York Department of Environmental Conservation has ordered him to repair structural weaknesses in the lake's concrete and earthen dam and has issued a permit allowing him to lower the level "five feet or more"—which, of course, he did.

He said that the cost of those repairs, which he said were estimated at up to $100,000, would simply be too great. He said that he had also become concerned about the risk of swimming and boating accidents on the lake. Indeed, he has substantially reduced those risks.

Scavengers wielding metal detectors have found a few dozen gold and silver rings beneath a diving board on the lake. "This is a unique opportunity," said one of them, Herman Slovitsky of Monroe. For the most part, however, the lake bottom was whisked clean of loot and debris when the entire lake was drained in two days over the Fourth of July weekend.

Below the dam, where one resident describes awakening that weekend to the sound of hundreds of fishtails flapping, is an awful sight that smells worse. "Silt pudding dotted with dead fish" is the description of Susan Boyd, who lives with her family below the dam, for what used to be a clear brook.

Mr. Rao, who was taking the opportunity to search the lake bed for a fishing tackle box that he had dropped in the lake thirty years ago, called the lake's draining "a catastrophe."

"I taught my kids to swim here," said Mr. Rao, of Jackson Heights, Queens. He looked wistfully out upon the mud with others who recalled the good old days of roller skating and dancing to live music at the pavilion, rowboat rentals, and a nine-hole golf course. "It was gorgeous," he said. "I liked to fish for bass and bluegill and brown speckled trout. But I also like to just come sit and look at the lake." Michael Cusimano, who was looking for dozens of fishing lures that he had dropped into the lake for more than eighteen years, remembered ice skating on the lake.

While homeowners are upset about having lost their lake, fed by a clear mountain stream and set against the backdrop of a towering ridge of the Shawangunk Mountains, they are also concerned about their property values. "We think they should lower our property taxes," said Antonio Martucci, referring to his former lakefront property.

The state conservation department has ordered Mr. Unanue to clean up the dead fish and to plant grass seed in the lake bed, returning the land to the pasture that it was in the early 1930s, when Hassie Tillson dammed it up and sold vacation homesites.

Mr. Unanue said he purchased the property in 1976 and incurred the wrath of residents by trying to get a liquor license, busing in city residents for a day at the lake, and boarding up the pavilion two years ago and closing the beach area.

Said Morey Gottesman, president of a local homeowners' group, "It's like when he didn't get his way with the trailer park, he took his bat and ball and went home."

"We tell the people arriving for their vacation," said Mr. Rao, "that there's good news and bad news. The good news is that they don't have to blow up the rubber raft."

VI

CULTURE

SOFA-SIZED ART

Carol Zimmerman's husband becomes one with the couch on this Sunday afternoon of televised professional football, and she leaves home seeking art.

She goes where thousands of other suburban residents go each weekend to find it, to motels throughout the suburban area where "affordable art" sales featuring "sofa-sized" original oil paintings are held during the fall and winter.

"I'm looking for something for over the couch," says Mrs. Zimmerman, of Rockland County, New York, holding a swatch of fabric beside a two- by three-foot landscape, said to be the optimal size over a standard seventy-two-inch couch, "something with blue, brown, and peach." She riffles through some of the thirteen hundred paintings stacked on the floor and banquet tables at the Hilton Inn in Montvale, New Jersey. Others have brought fabric and wallpaper swatches and paint samples to the sale, and some also insist on matching the wooden frames to their wooden furniture.

The paintings, which sell for $30 to $350, are produced by thousands of artists working at a gallop to feed weekend art sales at local motels across the country. Several hundred of the artists work for Richard Gitelman, a thirty-nine-year-old suburban resident who supplies paintings to sales in the metropolitan area and across the country. He is variously described by those in the business as "a czar of affordable art" and "the father of the motel art sale"—as well as "the Henry Ford of art" by virtue of his being responsible for original oil paintings in countless middle-class living rooms.

Paintings arrive by mail from around the world at his Long Island warehouse, where eighty thousand original oil paintings, or "units," are stockpiled. Ten workers sort them by size and category: landscape, seascape, still life, street scene, or portrait. The "product" is then stapled onto stretching frames and packed for shipping to retailers.

"Art is a tough, physically demanding business," says an employee, who has bruises on his arms, cuts on his hands, and a bump on the head to show for a weekend of moving truckloads of art in and out of motels for the viewing of customers lured by newspaper advertisements headlined "Emergency Liquidation."

125

Leonard Morton, president of a similar firm, Affordable Art Sales Inc., talks proudly of the efficient conveyor belt system he uses to move his paintings around the warehouse before they are finally shipped out in semi-trailer trucks—convoys of art, he calls them.

Mr. Gitelman was in the retail end of the business until he tired of "lugging art." He and two partners held what is believed to have been the first affordable art sale ever in the late 1960s in a New Jersey motel. It was a success and Mr. Gitelman set out across the country holding the sales. "I'd have one hand on the steering wheel, going 110 miles per hour, and another on the phone to the Chamber of Commerce in the next town, finding the best motel to hold the next sale," he says. He has a framed Texas speeding ticket as a memento of those days.

Imitators followed and the sales are now held each weekend during the fall and winter in suburban areas across the country. They have been held in such vast arenas as the Nassau Coliseum and the Houston Astrodome.

Carol Fairclough, who now works in Mr. Gitelman's office, was one of his painters. "She could kick out forty florals a week," he boasts. "She could paint with one hand and cook with the other. The paintings are quality originals, but like anything else, after a while they can do them with their eyes shut."

Most of the paintings on display at this sale are landscapes and seascapes with little detail. While each is an original, many are markedly similar, some virtually identical. Of this, one patron of the arts says, "You can find each painting in a variety of sizes. I like that." Mr. Gitelman says that most of his artists "prefer doing landscapes, probably because if you make a mistake on a landscape, who can tell?"

Of her painting days, Mrs. Fairclough says: "I could never go back to it. It's not artistic, and it's very repetitive. There's very little satisfaction in it. Sometimes I painted all night and all day to keep up." Mr. Gitelman did say that he often told the artists what to paint and what colors to use.

At the Montvale sale, Carole Laga bought a large landscape painting to put over her fireplace. "I like beige," she said, explaining why she chose it. "We have a print there now and we like the idea of owning an original oil painting. We're trying to elevate ourselves.''

Anne Silverman says that she goes to the sales regularly just as others go to flea markets and garage sales. "Browsing is a big part of their popularity," she says. "I take my kids along, too. I firmly believe that if you surround your children with culture some of it will rub off."

Critics charge that affordable art is "schlock" and that people are buying it instead of "legitimate art." Mr. Gitelman counters by saying that he is giving people what they want at prices they can afford. "We don't make claims about our stuff appreciating in value and we don't hype it. You take a painting to a gallery on the Upper East Side—where they have to get back their fantastic rents—you hang it on a wall and put a spotlight on it and what do you have? Hype.''

Mr. Morton, of Affordable Art Sales, defends his paintings: "They are good oil paintings. They really take a beating. And it's the same paint and the same canvas you get with a $10,000 painting.''

THE GOLDEN ANNIVERSARY OF ALFRESCO FILM

Dusk settled at the Ledgewood Drive-In on a mild summer evening when the air could not be felt. A chorus of horns began honking impatiently. Ken, the son of the owner, Frances Smith, rolled *Psycho II.*

Janet Leigh was stabbed repeatedly in the shower, to bring everyone up to date. Andrew Miller ordered a sloppy joe sandwich at the snack bar. Cars with just their parking lights on continued to drift in ever so slowly and silently, except for the sound of the crushed gravel beneath their tires. Jim Malcolm settled the children down with their teddy bears in the back of the station wagon. There were sounds of crickets and pop tops.

A stone-faced, overly polite teenager drove up, having decided to take in a movie on a Saturday night alone. "Good evening," he said to Mrs. Smith. "Nice evening." Mrs. Smith allowed as how "kids haven't gotten any smarter about sneaking in." She sensed that there was more than a spare tire in his trunk.

A big, slow-rising moon began to light up the New Jersey sky. Bill Bay, twenty-one, and his friend Dorothy Van Ness, nineteen, both of Boonton, come to the drive-in frequently because they can smoke cigarettes and they find drive-ins romantic. "Drive-ins show scary movies," she explained, encouraging romance.

Romance wasn't *exactly* what Leo Mohr, eighteen, had in mind. The graduating senior had a date with destiny tonight that all of his friends knew about. She was blond, just as sixteen as she could be, shrugged into tight white shorts that showed off her tan, and did not give her name. Leo took her to the snack bar, the least he could do. He explained in an interview there that he prefers drive-in theaters because "at regular theaters you can only get candy and popcorn, but here you can get cheeseburgers, pizza rolls, and egg rolls." Sure, Leo. Fine.

One night in 1933, Richard Hollingshead, Jr., took his movie projector outside, flashed a movie on the side of a building, and sat in his car to watch it. Friends and family worried about Mr. Hollingshead.

He next built up a little dirt ramp allowing the occupants of a car to see the movie over a car in front of them. On June 6 of that year he opened the world's first drive-in movie theater, the R. H. Hollingshead Jr. Theater on Admiral Wilson Boulevard in Camden, New Jersey, showing *Wife Beware*.

History did not record the first young couple unable to tell their parents what movie they attended at the drive-in or the first family that brought children in pajamas or the first teenager to enter a drive-in theater in a car trunk and leave with a purloined speaker. But old-timers in the business said all of those things happened early on and continue today.

The fiftieth anniversary of the drive-in movie theater came on and not a moment too soon, according to experts who note the rapidly declining number of drive-in theaters, one of whom called them the buggy whip of the eighties. Rising land values and taxes have prompted many owners to sell to developers of housing and office complexes and shopping centers.

"Nonsense," said Mrs. Smith, who attracted hundreds of motorists to her Ledgewood Drive-In on Saturday night. Movies were showing on 3,178 drive-in theater screens that night, most of them on the outer fringes of suburbia or in rural areas where rising land values have driven them.

Many hold flea markets and other events during daylight hours to bring in money. Following the trend in indoor theaters, many drive-ins are putting up two and three screens (one in Florida has eight), such as the Westbury Drive-In in Long Island, which shows first-run films, and the manager says business has improved in each of the last five years.

Mrs. Smith opened her drive-in in 1952, when the auto-(mobile)-erotic suburbs were booming and Americans wanted to watch movies in their commodious cars, eat in their cars, worship in their cars, and drop off their dry cleaning and their paychecks at drive-up windows. Eventually, a drive-in funeral parlor opened.

Between 1948 and 1958 the number of drive-in theaters in the country rose from 820 to an all-time high of more than 4,000. Industry officials touted drive-ins as film's only hope against the onslaught of television.

"Going to a drive-in was like going to a carnival," said Sumner Redstone, whose father built the first really big suburban drive-in theater in the country, the Sunrise Drive-In, in Valley Stream, Long Island, with a capacity of two thousand cars. Mr. Redstone believes drive-ins will be extinct by the end of the decade.

He tore down the Sunrise Drive-In and is rapidly converting fifty remaining drive-ins that his company owns to other uses. "We had all sorts of rides in the old days at the Sunrise," he said, "including a ferris wheel." Other drive-in theaters sported miniature golf courses and special nights when bingo games and live music preceded the movie or when families could bring outdoor grills for cookouts. "A lot of people came to keep cool on a summer night," said one drive-in theater owner, noting that air-conditioning was not yet prevalent then.

Nearly all provided playgrounds, which have been removed from virtually all drive-ins because of rising insurance costs. Electric heaters, which were provided by many drive-ins to prolong their seasons, have also been removed with rising electricity costs.

Early on, the drive-ins were condemned from pulpits and editorial pages as "passion pits," and some drive-ins would check cars in which no heads were visible.

"If you went to the drive-in with a boy," said Elaine Burkow, a middle-aged woman at the Ledgewood Drive-In, "your reputation was ruined with your friends." If you went in a Nash Rambler, with those reclining seats, of course, they went right ahead and planned a baby shower. She fondly recalled going to the drive-in years ago to see double features such as *Beach Blanket Bingo* and *I Was a Teen-Age Werewolf*—with that film of the dancing hotdogs in between. *Common Law Wife* was another favorite.

Mrs. Smith's daughter, Ann Carol Perry, runs the family's other drive-in theater and sees a resurgence for drive-ins: "Those of us remaining are getting all the business."

The audience at the Ledgewood Drive-In summed up nicely the pros and cons of drive-in theaters. Mr. Malcolm noted that he brought his wife and two children to a double feature for $7 (Adults, $3.50; children under twelve, free)—and no baby-sitter to pay. He brought his own snacks and drank a beer while watching the movie. He said that in good weather he brings a lawn chair and sits by the car. "I just like to be outdoors more," he said. His wife does not, complaining of bugs.

Bob Mayo, twenty years old, of Flanders, comes as often as twice a week and uses a lotion on his windshield that causes raindrops to slide off. "Sometimes several carloads of friends come on the same night and we have a little party," he said. "I like the big screen, the ones in those new four-plexes are really small. No one coughs or talks to interrupt you here." He has a stereo system in his car, and the sound at this drive-in—and most others now—is broadcast on AM radio.

"Drive-ins are nice," said Jim Golding. "You don't have to get dressed up, and you can bring your dog." One man at the snack bar quipped, "I've brought my share."

Leo Mohr left before the end of the film, because his youthful date had to be home before midnight. He said that he had not had a chance this time to take advantage of the cheeseburgers, pizza rolls, and egg rolls. He turned on the defogger and squealed out onto the highway.

☞COURTING LITERARY DISASTER

For a suburban Chicago couple, a peaceful evening at home was shattered recently when an avalanche of *National Geographic*s crashed through the attic floor into their upstairs bedroom. An hour later and the couple would have been in bed, buried alive in mounds of glossy pages of weird fish and scantily clad natives with salad plates under their lips.

Dr. George Scheer of Park Forest South, Illinois, who owns a white lab coat, brought to light the *National Geographic* problem in his *Journal of Irreproducible Results*—along with articles on "Intersex," a method for having electronic sex with partners thousands of miles away; "How to Eat and Lose Weight"; "The Relationship of Lab Efficiency to Time Spent in the Snack Shop"; and "A Study of the Amount of Seafood in Seafood Cocktails." Still nothing is being done.

By my count, more than 2,635,000,000 copies of *National Geographic* have been published, and casual empiricism suggests that none have been thrown away. A neighbor of mine set out a bundle and disbelieving garbage men wouldn't take them. Hoarded relentlessly for nearly a century, the *National Geographic* has become an instrument of cosmic doom.

Its accumulated aggregate weight has reached the disaster point. If we assume that a copy of the magazine weighs 448 grams (the weight of this month's issue), the upper mantle of the earth's crust—with a density of 3.3 g-cm3—can be expected to give way about next November under the terrible mounting pressure of monthly deliveries.

Thus will begin the most dynamic geologic process of the Cenozoic Era, although the precise chain of cataclysmic events is unclear, because—curiously—the government does not monitor dangerous accumulations of the *National Geographic*. If this is more misguided cost-cutting by the Reagan Administration, it will be rewarded soon enough by fish swimming through the submerged White House like some 99-cent aquarium novelty.

Studies would show that the contiguous forty-eight states will completely subside between Canada and Mexico (two countries where a sensible circulation of the *National Geographic* is maintained). This will, among other things, thrust the Catastrophism Doctrine to the forefront of geologic thought and render the Panama Canal strategically unimportant.

A few scientists may argue that none of this will occur within the next century or two—a patently preposterous scenario that presupposes an even distribution of the *National Geographic* (circulation: 10.2 million) over the 7,954 x 103 km2 surface of the continental United States.

Distribution is anything but even! The danger seems greatest in upscale neighborhoods, where substantial market penetration has been achieved. One needn't be religious to realize now that the downscale may inherit the earth.

The West Coast will be the first to go. The government stands by as 1.1 million copies are dropped off every month in California, already a most precarious state. This is twice the number of copies delivered to New York—a result of California's expansive "open" living areas that result in inordinately long couches and an estimated 10,471,336 meters of coffee tables for display of the magazine—the reason, of course, that it is purchased.

What to do about this cataclysmic problem? First of all, we need to know more about Gardiner Greene Hubbard, who began publishing the magazine in 1888, and about his followers, members of the enigmatic National Geographic Society, now more than ten million strong.

We must also begin to combat the notion inculcated over generations that all we have to fear from periodicals is ideology, pornography, and the occasional paper cut.

Stopping publication of the magazine is currently out of the question because of strong lobbying efforts by patient's rights groups, which complain bitterly that they would be forced to sit in waiting rooms and read about CAT-scan machines and unusual gum diseases in trade publications if the *National Geographic* were not published.

Circulation of the magazine can probably be reduced, however, simply by changing its name to something that will make it less suitable for coffee-table display—perhaps *The National TV Wrestling Geographic*.

Or the National Guard could immediately be deployed to cut two legs off all coffee tables in the contiguous forty-eight states, thereby interdicting display of slick publications.

Clearly, as a measure of first resort, we should send in the crack team from *Reader's Digest* that recently dealt so effectively with the weighty Bible Buildup.

☞ DANCE OF THE BEEFCAKE

The guys at Fotomat must be wondering just what in the hell is going on in this country.

All of these nice enough looking suburban women are driving up in their station wagons and dropping off rolls of film with these . . . these nude, these nude and lewd exposures of the same three men. Sometimes the photographs are just from the waist down, but they've developed so many of them lately, they'd know these three guys anywhere.

That one's Turk, and that's Gary. And that! That is Larry, no doubt about it. The three are male strippers at the Sugar Shack in Lake Geneva, Wisconsin, and seven nights a week, women from Chicago and the suburbs drive up to see them. They take their cameras.

Strip joints for women! Beefcake at last! For many of these Sugar Shack customers, to whom women's lib has meant freedom to scrub their floors in pantsuits, the movement is finally starting to pay off.

But what manner of wench would set foot in such a place? Oh, people like your mom, your wife, your sister, maybe your grandma—there was a table there Friday night with four patrons aged 79, 75, 70, and 64; all ages, and carved right out of the heart of Middle America.

And why do they go? Three reasons. "Curiosity," says Rita from Skokie, "I've always wondered what a strip joint was like." That's one reason. "If my husband can play poker, I can do this," says Arlene of Chicago. That's the second reason. And last but not least: "That's a really dumb question," says Nancy, of Wheaton.

"It's a new generation," owner Dana Montana tells a packed house Friday night. "Women now too have the right to enjoy watching members of the opposite sex take off their clothes." (Applause and whistles.)

"How many here tonight are from the Chicago area?" she asks. About 12 of the 251 are not.

"How many here are celebrating something?" Dana asks. Most. At the three Friday night shows, there are lots of women celebrating birthdays and impending weddings ("bachelorette parties") plus "my husband's birthday, but he's not here [cheers] . . . my twenty-fifth wedding anniversary, but he's not here [cheers] . . . my first alimony check [cheers]."

There is a real air of excitement as Guy comes onstage in a white satin gaucho outfit with fringe. "This is the first man other than [her husband] I've seen naked," Katy from Oak Lawn tells me, adding, on second thought, "in the last five years." Guy dances to some loud rock and disco tunes, splashed by a sophisticated lighting system with red, blue, strobe, and black lights.

By consensus of women at the table next to me, Guy is "really, really cute," with a black mustache, boyish smile, and a touch of modesty. Heavy eye contact with the customers. He has one of the women help him take his shirt off, another with the waist-to-floor zippers on either side of his pants. The latter cops a feel. Women are such animals.

By the third tune he is down to a G-string, into which patrons stuff dollar bills when he frolicks in the crowd, rubbing up against them, massaging their necks, and kissing them. He goes back on stage and beckons a couple of them to come up and dance with him. One is a blond bride-to-be in her twenties, of the Lake Forest private school ilk, who feigns shyness as they all do but tweaks his cheeks when she has the chance. As does the next dance partner, a woman about sixty in a polyester pantsuit.

There are shrieks and howls of laughter from the audience. Trays of colorful, frothy drinks are rushed to the tables. Drinking is important on a night out like this, particularly for the usually inhibited, and the Sugar Shack makes it easy for even teetotalers. Cards on the tables suggest Irish coffee, piña coladas, and a drink called Strawberry Shortcake. But the biggest sellers by far are the $5.50 green Shack-Ups and red Hustlers. One of these satisfies the two-drink minimum (the cover charge is $5), and you get to keep the glass that not only says Sugar Shack but has a picture of a man who sheds his shorts when liquid is poured into the glass. Perfect for getting the Avon lady out of the house.

Hat in hand, Guy covers up during the next number and drops his G-string. Still, the hat's in the way as he dances with a coy smile on his face. "Take it off!" suggests a woman in the back. So he does. The crowd goes wild as he dances through them and back on stage. Instamatics flash. A woman about fifty-five in the front row looks down at her drink, shields her eyes with her hand, and laughs uncontrollably.

That same woman will later leap onstage when Larry is dancing and cram a bill down his pants. They do have their favorites. Others will go for Turk's *Star Wars* routine, done in and out of a Darth Vader costume.

Larry, however, seems to be the star of the show. He is a good dancer and has a show business background. Whereas Guy is a former construction worker and Turk was discovered while laying carpeting in the club. Larry says he is the former bodyguard of Liberace and Debbie Reynolds. Also, his parents were professional roller skaters: his father would spin around while his mother, with her legs around the father's neck, would extricate herself from a straitjacket. "I love Larry," says Donna of Buffalo Grove, who claims she's been up to see him three times "with some girl friends from the *synagogue.*" Her mother probably wouldn't approve, she said, pointing out that Larry is not Jewish.

Guy's hat is gone now. He is dancing furiously on stage when some latecomers—a busload of women from Hillside that were caught in traffic—arrive at the door. One is dressed in a nun's habit. The crowd goes berserk. She jumps on stage. Guy leaps from the stage and cowers in the corner by the equipment. "I was brought up Catholic," Guy tells me later, "went to Catholic school. She freaked me out." The "nun" turns out to be Sue from Hillside and not of the cloth.

The shows conclude with a (decidedly) female stripper (a few men do show up for the shows), and the place clears out for the next show. The women take the glasses, the picture of the strippers on the tables, souvenir $8 T-shirts, wall posters of Larry, and free eight-by-tens. They ask for autographs—Donna of Lombard has Larry sign one arm and Guy the other, then proclaims she'll cut them both off and frame them. Some of the women come around to the back of the building for complimentary kissing and occasionally to proposition the strippers.

They laugh a lot in the parking lot, then climb back into their cars and buses, heading back to the Chicago area to further confound the poor guys at the Fotomat.

☛ Cultural Deprivation (Visual)

When "No TV Week" was announced at the Glen School in Ridgewood, New Jersey, five-year-old John Donovan charged angrily out of his kindergarten class protesting to his mother, "They can't do this. They're not the law!"

The school's 196 pupils struggled to come to grips with the staggering concept of no television—cold turkey—for seven days and seven nights. Chris Hughes, a second-grader, shook his head as the program was explained, rolling his eyes skyward as if seeking divine intervention. Lynn Dim, a third-grader, believed she just might die. Brian Clark, a sixth-grade pupil, asked how it was humanly possible to keep from watching television if your brother turned it on?

From the next desk, his classmate Drew Bloom answered, "You have to walk away, Brian. You just have to walk away." To understand the staggering proportions of this calamity, one must realize that there are televisions suspended from the ceilings of supermarkets in this suburb so that shoppers can watch while standing in the checkout lines; that small televisions are being installed in the booths of a local restaurant; that these students have as many as nine TVs in their homes; and that some watch TV an average of six hours a day.

"Nobody said this would be easy," the pupils were warned on the first day of the experiment. But by and large, and to the surprise of nearly everyone, it was.

The students turned into little zealots. They prepared halls and classrooms with antitelevision propaganda posters: "Use Your TV for Something Useful, Like a Punching Bag" and "If the TV Is Off, the Brain Is On." They wore buttons. They booed a second-grader who admitted to having watched his sister on TV.

Like so many Red Guards, they informed on their parents, about half of whom had agreed to participate in "No TV Week" with their children. "I keep one eye open when I go to bed to make sure they aren't sneaking," said Gary Horowitz, a first-grader.

"I listen for the clicking of the dial," said a classmate, Jonathan White.

Parents seemed to have more trouble kicking the TV habit than their children. Several mothers were caught watching *General Hospital.* Fathers buckled during hockey and basketball games. One of the fathers, Rick McGrath, furtively watched the sports reports using an earplug. Another, Peter Bouton, who said he could not cheat because "I have two little detectives in my house," taped the Rangers' hockey games.

Some of the pupils pulled knobs off their sets or unplugged them. Others covered the screens with bed sheets or pieces of paper reading "Sorry, No TV." And "No TV" was strictly interpreted. One mother reported her doctrinaire daughter was putting her hands over her eyes and groping about when she entered a room where a television set was on.

On Friday an earnest-looking Peter Halpern approached the desk of his third-grade teacher for confession: "Mrs. Giro, sometimes I walk into my sister's room and the TV is on and I glance at it." Margaret Giro responded, "You are forgiven, son."

At an assembly at the end of the week, Anne Cruz, a pupil, read an original poem, "The TV Disease," which declared television "decays morality" and "builds wickedness." The vast majority of pupils told Joan Wilkins, the author of *TV Guide-Away,* who was conducting the weeklong experiment, that they had gone all week without watching television. Many, such as John Donovan, had not even taken advantage of the one hour of viewing allowed on Saturday morning.

"It was easy," shrugged Michelle Rupert, a sixth-grader who claimed a fifty-five-hour-a-week habit.

"I just keep moving," explained Sara Ruffman, a third-grade pupil with a school record of nine television sets in her home and four family members who continued to watch them all week.

Kathy Shevlin and Karen Glisch spent much of the week on the telephone, supporting each other. Others made it through the week by having classmates over after school more frequently.

Many pupils built forts in their homes out of blankets, card tables, and ironing boards, where they holed up for the week doing puzzles, playing cards, and the like until the crisis passed. Chris Kipiniak, a second-grader, said he had spent the week mud wrestling.

There were critical moments, such as when one sixth-grader had to wrestle his brother to keep the set off. Another one came at 8 P.M. Friday when a popular show, *The Dukes of Hazzard,* was on the airwaves and all the pupils had to do was push a button. One first-grader, fed up with deprivation and educational enrichment, finally writhed on the floor, cried, and dropped the big one, "You don't love me anymore," before being dissuaded by his parents from turning on the TV set.

Students in every class reported spending more time reading books and talking to their friends and families. "My daughter and I rediscovered each other," said one mother, Barbara Winther.

"My three children actually played together," said another, Carolyn Bouton.

"No TV Week" ended. One pupil said that he was going home to watch TV until he was sick to his stomach. But several pupils testified that "playing is more fun" and said they would never watch as much television as they had before.

"TV is not my life!" proclaimed Joclyn Selim at the assembly, where a representative of another school that had conducted a similar experiment three months ago testified that the amount of viewing there remained diminished.

Anne Cruz and a sixth-grade classmate typed a "Secret Pact" to continue the experiment. They agreed to watch only thirty minutes of television each week for the next four weeks, and they sealed the pact with inked fingerprints.

"It's binding," Anne said, "but we do have a release form."

☛ CULTURAL DEPRIVATION (AUDITORY)

Something is missing in George Larkin's life. For two weeks, commuting had bordered on the exhilarating, as he breezed to work from New Jersey across the upper deck of the George Washington Bridge in his snappy new European car, with the spiffy stereo system blaring Puccini or Michael Jackson. All that is lost now. There is a hole where his Blaupunkt used to be.

When Mr. Larkin told at social gatherings of having the expensive Blaupunkt radio-tape player ripped from his car, people reacted as if he were talking about crab grass or something. "Welcome to the club," he recalls them saying. Police in New York and many suburbs now characterize the problem as an "epidemic," born of a trend to increasingly expensive car-stereo systems.

Every few seconds, another car stereo is stolen in the United States, and Morton Goldfein said that usually it is his. The Secaucus,

New Jersey, resident said that after three car stereos had been stolen in Manhattan from his BMW, he installed "the cheapest radio I could find." It, too, was stolen.

His next tactic was the purchase of what he called his "towne car," a beat-up fifteen-year-old Volvo, for excursions into the city. He did this because the most frequent targets of radio thieves are late-model BMWs, Audis, Saabs, and other relatively costly European cars that often come with expensive stereo systems, such as Blaupunkt or Alpine, costing from about $300 to $1,400. In most European cars and some Japanese models, these radio-tape players can be pulled out with one jerk of the knobs. "I don't think European auto builders quite understand America," Mr. Larkin said.

When Mr. Goldfein's old "towne car" broke down, he again drove his BMW. It still had no radio, but a Walkman he had locked in the glove compartment was stolen. Although the "towne car" ploy had worked for a while for Mr. Goldfein, it did not work for Dr. Stephen Lasser. He embarked on a systematic plan to always drive his AMC station wagon into the city, while leaving his BMW with Blaupunkt at home. But early on in the plan, he returned from jogging in Central Park to find the AMC station wagon's radio "eviscerated, in medical terms," not to mention the thief's exchange of some new tassled loafers that Dr. Lasser had left in the car for "some really disgusting ones" of the same size.

Jon Bittmann almost sold his Audi after losing two car radios. One was stolen at La Guardia Airport, involving $1,000 damage to the car. Many thieves do not realize the radios can be easily removed. "I met a guy who said he had lost seven stereos from his Audi and I thought, This guy isn't too smart. When I buy a car, it probably will be a different kind."

Another car-stereo theft victim claims that leaving a BMW with a Blaupunkt on a city street in New York is "like dropping a hot dog into a tank of piranhas." The problem seems nearly as severe in some suburban areas. Thieves cruise the parking lots of shopping malls in Paramus, New Jersey, with lists of foreign cars likely to have expensive radios and with master keys to open them, according to Police Chief Joseph Delaney. "In the last two months," he said, "we have arrested several of these people and recovered $115,000 worth of stolen car radios." Scott Rosen, manager of Car Tunes, a car-stereo store with nineteen bays in Farmingdale, Long

Island, said that the stereo systems are even being stolen from cars in suburban driveways.

Helpful signs, some in both English and Spanish, are sprouting in car windows now, informing would-be thieves not to break the windows, that the radio has already been stolen. Business is booming at car-stereo installation firms, largely because of replacement of stolen radios, and at many of them it takes weeks to get an appointment.

Short Stop Car Radio in Hackensack, New Jersey, sells a new item, a $49.95 alarm that sounds the car horn when the stereo is removed. Also popular is a new $5.95 item called The Decoy, which is a false front that is placed over an expensive radio-cassette stereo to make it appear to be an inexpensive AM radio. Another decoy, with broken wires dangling out the front, makes it appear as though the radio has already been stolen. Also available is a new device that allows the motorist to slip the radio out and take it along when leaving the car. Many insurance companies now require separate "sound system coverage."

Police say that fencing operations are reselling stolen radios to victimized motorists at one third of the wholesale price. The theory has been propounded that there may be only one Blaupunkt radio in existence, which moves from one car to the other.

Although having a radio stolen is now common, Allen Kopelson, who resides in New York and Morristown, New Jersey, can still draw a crowd relating his experiences with car-radio thefts. One week after he purchased a BMW, his Alpine radio was stolen. Less than a week after it was replaced, his radio was again stolen. A few days after the second radio was replaced, he stopped for ten minutes at a friend's apartment and returned to find the car missing. The car was found, with the radio missing.

Upon replacing that radio, Mr. Kopelson enjoyed "two weeks of bliss" with no thefts. Then he came out of his apartment to find the fourth stereo missing. He remembers weeping. On the next day, the car itself was stolen. And he laughed.

VII

SOCIAL STRATIFICATION

INVASION OF THE QUICHE EATERS

In Hoboken, a town of steel-toed work shoes, shot-and-a-beer taverns, and an occasional beehive hairdo, the invasion of the quiche eaters continues.

Lured by rows of relatively inexpensive brownstones convenient to Manhattan, young professionals and artists have been moving in droves to the left bank of the Hudson River. And Hoboken, which some local residents look upon with pride as perhaps the least fashionable city in the country—if not in all of New Jersey—is becoming positively trendy.

The new residents can be seen on the streets wearing designer jeans and driving foreign cars. Plants hang from macrame in condominium windows. Haagen-Dazs ice cream and *Tax Shelter Digest* are sold at the Hoboken Daily News store. Those who liked "the old Hoboken" say it may already be too late. The first croissants have been served.

Now an art gallery has opened in Hoboken, a venture one local butcher considers tantamount to opening a live-bait shop in the Mojave Desert. "Hoboken people don't buy art," Al Pierro, of the Pierro Brothers butcher shop, stated flatly.

Debra Hull, co-owner of the Hoboken Art gallery, which opened in December, admitted that "the local people think we're crazy," But her partner, Barbara Smith, said people in New York don't laugh in her face as much as before—as if not knowing that Hoboken is in is to be out of it.

Hoboken's only bookstore, Unicorn, opened last month where the Salvation Army clothing store used to be. Having never seen a bookstore before, children come in and ask how they can join. "We had a bookstore once," said Bill Phelps, a lifelong resident. "It went out of business and the new one will, too. Hoboken doesn't need a bookstore." The bookstore, with such magazines as *GQ, Gourmet, Interface Age,* and *Artforum* in the front window, would be perplexing enough. But this bookstore is also a cafe that serves wine, cheese, toasted herb-cheese loaf, and other foods of fashion. Last week, the bookstore-cafe opened an art gallery, Hoboken's second in four months.

Viola Gundersen, sixty-nine years old, stood for several minutes at the front door of the Unicorn, peering inside and trying to come to grips with something that seemed as confusing to her as if it had just dropped from the moon. "I've never seen anything like that before," said Mrs. Gundersen with a shake of her head.

"People laugh," said Lynn Spencer, one of the owners of the bookstore-cafe-gallery, "when you say you're opening a place like this in Hoboken. Ho-Ho-Hoboken and all of that." But an employee, Kevin McCloskey, said, "This bookstore has a chance. It serves beer." That could prove a stroke of genius. The Federal Writers Project stated in 1939: "To almost everybody Hoboken means two things: beer and ships." Here, in the mid-1600s, Aert T. VanPutten built the first brewery in the New World. And the town may still hold the distinction of having the most bars per capita in the United States, although the number is down from the 1940s, when there were as many as twenty-seven on a single block.

Hoboken is frequently the butt of jokes for being hopelessly déclassé and old-fashioned, to which one longtime resident retorts, "Who wants to keep up with these times?" Though Hoboken is just ten minutes from Manhattan by train, bus, or car, everything in the city, from the architecture to the price of a beer, has been remarkably preserved—protected from popularity by its own image.

Now, however, it is becoming a city of contrasts, where a woman in purple tights and a miniskirt stands waiting for a bus with three scarfed old women. Outside a new gourmet food shop, a street vendor sells potatoes for $4.25 for fifty pounds. A lean jogger spurts past a man sweeping already clean streets by hand. And the same wide, bright neckties of the 1930s and 1940s are sold to newcomers in shops catering to those interested in the latest fads, as well as to older residents in local stores that seemingly haven't rotated their stock since World War II.

Opinions are mixed about the invasion and occupation of Hoboken. "The New Yorkers have done a lot by fixing up old houses and opening businesses that hadn't been occupied in a long time. But they're messing up Hoboken in a lot of ways. Rents and taxes are way up so high, a lot of people can't afford to live here anymore," said Mr. Pierro, the butcher.

Piet Halberstadt, a co-owner of the Unicorn, said that some of the artists who had been among the first to move here from Manhattan were moving to Jersey City now, already unable to afford Hoboken.

At the Cafe Elysian, where workers from the Maxwell House

plant can bring in their bag lunches and wash them down with 35 cent beers, some of the clientele wonder how long it will be before someone buys this architectural gem and raises the prices.

"I don't understand what all the raving about Hoboken is about," said Rocky Musella, a lifelong resident of this community that has never cared much for fads that people rave about.

But newcomers opening businesses believe that Hoboken is destined to be the next SoHo or Greenwich Village. Those who want to preserve some of the old Hoboken say that an important battle was lost when the Court Street Bar, which features 50 cent beers and Gene, a local plumber, singing such originals as "Jersey City, Jersey City, Here I Come," put quiche on the menu.

The owner, Jack Talbot, acknowledged that he had given in on the quiche issue but said that was where he had drawn the line. "You don't see any hanging plants in my windows," he said defiantly. "Someone gave me one, but I hung it in the back away from the windows until it died."

SOCIETY WEDDING: A SWINGING SOCIAL SOIREE

For too long, Berwyn-Cicero society has complained of receiving all too little attention vis-à-vis the North Shore, Barrington Hills, Oak Brook, Flossmoor, and other local habitats of high society. We want to do something about this.

The Berwyn-Cicero (B-C, as it is known in fashionable circles) social season opened last weekend with the celebrated nuptials of Kyri Stella Dakis to Michael John DiMaggio at two o'clock in the afternoon on Saturday, June 21, 1980, in the First Presbyterian Church, River Forest.

Miss Dakis, the daughter of Mr. and Mrs. Peter Dakis of Berwyn, was lovely in a traditional white wedding gown. Her maid of honor, Elizabeth Conway of Cicero, wore a yellow lace gown, with her other attendants in blue lace. The groom, best man, and ushers were resplendent in powder-blue tuxedos from Henry's Formal Wear, Cicero.

Miss Dakis, eighteen, attended Wheeling High School, Wheeling, Illinois, departing prior to completion of degree requirements, and is now, hopefully, between jobs. Mr. DiMaggio, twenty-five, said that he is legitimately unemployed, receiving compensation from the state of Illinois.

Miss Dakis was given away in holy matrimony by her father in a traditional ceremony, highlighted by usher Frank Butler of Cicero yelling, "Yahoo!" as the couple exchanged rings. The remaining ten minutes of the ceremony were omitted.

The couple departed the church in a shower of rice in a late-model Chevrolet and were driven to a reception at the respected Berwyn Elk's Club.

About one hundred of B-C's smart set attended the reception, dancing to the toneful tunes of an unnamed guitar-accordion-drum band playing pleasurable polkas. Club manager and master of B-C soirees, George Lundgren, chose tablecloths, but no centerpieces, for simple elegance. Lundgren said whiskey, gin, and setups were available. He said the band broke for dinner at 4:30 P.M. as guests dined buffet style on roast beef, broasted chicken, mostaccioli, macaroni salad, and various Jell-O molds.

After dinner, ethnic dancing continued, and at about eight o'clock the traditional fighting commenced. While dancing with the groom's sister, Michelle, Mr. Butler observed his wife touch dancing with the groom's fifteen-year-old brother, Billy.

Mr. Butler subjected Billy DiMaggio to physical abuse and threatened severe physical violence. A check of the social register maintained by the Berwyn Department of Public Safety indicates our Mr. Butler is a man of his word.

The DiMaggios are a close, old-line Cicero family, and brother Jerome DiMaggio laid Mr. Butler upside the head with a full champagne bottle, according to other prominent guests. At this point several others joined in the fisticuffs, including the groom.

So many, in fact, that the uniformed Berwyn policeman on duty at the wedding reception instructed Mr. Lundgren to call for assistance. Local authorities say it is "customary" to have a policeman at Berwyn wedding receptions, where "fights are quite common."

Two local gendarmes, resplendent in dark-blue uniforms, arrived to join the festivities. "The entire place was up for grabs," said one.

Social-scene observers note that this was a truly superlative affair, attended, finally, by the entire Saturday night shift of the Berwyn Police Department—the measure of any social occasion.

Brandishing dark, solid-wood nightsticks (absolutely smashing accessories with the blue uniforms), police waded into the boisterous gathering of B-C society.

"I couldn't believe what I saw," said one veteran policeman. "Glasses, champagne bottles, and beer bottles were flying. Everyone in the place was fighting—like a Western movie barroom brawl. They didn't even pay any attention to us." (For the record—the bride and groom and their parents said it was a nice reception ruined by police intervention.)

"When we stepped between people fighting, they turned on us," another policeman said. "It was frightening: a dozen of us against one hundred of them. They'd throw us to the floor, stomp us, and go back to fighting. We couldn't arrest anybody, it was all we could do to hold on to our guns and nightsticks. They threw most of us back down the stairs.

"The bride was getting in her licks, too. Her wedding gown was torn to pieces. The band members had extended their microphone stands as far as they would go and were swinging them like baseball bats to protect themselves from the guests," he said.

Police from a local park district, Cicero, and other surrounding communities were called in, about forty to forty-five officers in all. "We restored order, announced that the reception was over, and told the guests to disperse," a police spokesman said.

The crowd went outside, where fighting continued. Guns were drawn when one guest flattened two policemen with a table leg.

Passersby reportedly joined in the fighting.

The pugilism continued inside the two paddy wagons and in front of the Berwyn Police Department, where guests not yet under arrest met the police vehicles' arrival.

More than one dozen were hospitalized. Only twelve were arrested, according to authorities, "because we wanted to get out of there while we were still alive."

A local judge, resplendent in floor-length black robes, set bonds at $5,000 to $15,000 each.

Neck braces and arm slings are the height of fashion this week at the Berwyn Police Department.

A good time was had by all, at what is being called the most exciting B-C social event since last year's Southwest Cook County Chapter 205 of the National Association of Women in Construction's candlelight bowl.

The couple is at home in Cicero following the groom's release from Cook County Jail Tuesday evening. Honeymoon plans have been postponed pending trial.

We wish the young couple all the best—in court, at future B-C welterweight wedding receptions, and in returning those armless, blood-spattered tuxedos to Henry's Formal Wear. We anxiously await the wedding photos.

ALL TOO COMMONS

Millions of suburban Americans are being deprived of the full status, satisfaction, and reward of suburban living because their neighborhoods and subdivisions do not have names.

I know. I live in such a neighborhood. I find this particularly cruel because millions of my suburban neighbors enjoy the exciting, prestigious, romantic images of their chosen subdivisions: Pepper Tree Farms, Malibu, Les Chateaux de Charlemagne, Persimmon Fields, and the like.

I think it's time to do something about it. I think the federal government should get involved in a massive program to retrofit older suburban neighborhoods and subdivisions—or newer ones that were somehow overlooked—with snappy new names and images.

In my neighborhood we are not about to wait for the federal government for something this important. I set out fo find a name for my neighborhood. I asked one of my neighbors to drape plastic used-car-lot pennants from his house, train floodlights on it, and keep it open to the public as our neighborhood's model home. I asked one of the people at the end of the block if he'd mind putting up a six-by-eight-foot billboard in his front yard with the name of the neighborhood, "Immediate Occupancy," "A Very Special Place to Live," "Financing Available," a logo, that sort of thing.

I asked someone else to give up his home as an Information Center. I want to live in a neighborhood with an Information Center. In return for a vice chairmanship on the neighborhood image improvement committee, I asked someone to demolish his home and fill the basement up with a garden hose so that our neighborhood would have a lake and a recreation area.

But first, the name. I went out driving around the Chicago suburban area, looking for a good name, something we could build a theme around. I want to live in a theme community.

I was pleasantly surprised, discovering that my neighbors and I weren't going to have to spend a lot of money changing things around to fit the name. There is no sand and there are no pebbles at Sandpebble Walk. No brownstone in Brownstone Manor. No grand vista in La Grande Vista. No olive trees in The Olive Trees. No trees at all in Wine Tree. No water at Waterbury. No sandpipers at Sandpiper South. And nothing charming about Charmingfare.

At Edgewater Walk—"Lake View Available in a Rustic Setting"—the water is not immediately obvious. I drove around the complex looking for it. I got out of the car to inspect the grounds. I couldn't find any water. Must be quite a walk.

Now, one of my neighbors made the suggestion that the name and image be somewhat appropriate to the community. What a concept! A couple of the developments I saw had hinted at this. There are several where the developer has brought in an earth-moving shovel to take a dip or two out of the ground, has filled it with water, and called the place Runaway Bay or some such. At Runaway Bay, the single-dip of bodies of water have signs posted: "Swimming and Boating Not Permitted by Police Order." Other subdividers went with the already existing drainage ditch, calling it a brook and putting it in the name.

The Landings is nowhere near a seaport of course, but it is right under a flight path and near the end of a runway at O'Hare. Eagle Chase and Pheasant Run have certainly lived up to their names, as we hope Hunter's Run has as well. Fair View has just about that. The Commons looks the part, and The Cloverleaf is next to a four-way interchange on the Calumet Expressway.

Most of my neighbors, however, leaned toward the names that sound and look good but have no substance. That is not to say they are inappropriate for their development. Some of my personal favorites were also in this category: Feather Sound, Burgundy Lakes, Shire Ru, The Clusters, Shorely Wood, Whispering Glen, Shadow Bend, Fair Oaks, Autumn Chase, The Squires, The Windings, Emberwood, and Pebblewood.

Pebblewood. Sure. So right for today.

In calling on the federal government to intervene so that each and every suburban American can live in a theme community, I don't want the Federal Trade Commission getting involved, enforcing truth in advertising and all of that. That would ruin everything. Nobody wants to live in a place called Buckling Sidewalks, Cracking Foundations, Septic Shores, Babbling Basements, Falling Plasters, DC-10 Landings, Ridiculous Heights, Barren View, Des Foliant, Bad Manors, All Too Commons, Leaning Towers, Cardboard Colonies, Bulldozed Oaks, Prefab Place, or Tedium Terrace.

The best idea would be for each and every one of you to get involved in making your own neighborhood or subdivision a theme community—just as I did.

And if you need any tips in getting your program off the ground, feel free to stop by my house—I'm calling it the Ethan Allen Goes to Puerto Vallarta model—in my newly retrofitted neighborhood: "Pollo Del Mar" ("Chicken of the Sea").

THE NEW PEOPLE

Twenty-three-year-old David Miller was raised in the lone house on a country road just outside of Tranquility, a speck on the map in Sussex County, New Jersey. There are forty-seven houses next to his now, all put up for "the new people," "a different kind of people," who moved in after "the big road," Interstate 80, was built.

"People from Newark moved in next door," he said. "The first time they heard my dad's target-shooting in the backyard, they figured somebody must be getting killed and they called the police. Sometimes they call the police on our dog. They think dogs belong in the house."

Seeking less congestion, cheaper homes, lower taxes, less crime, and a slower pace, tens of thousands of "new people" from New York and its inner suburbs have moved to the outer suburbs of Sussex County in the last decade—part of a national trend that for the first time since 1820 has seen America's rural areas and small towns grow faster than its cities. The suburbanites continue their move—out.

They have swelled this dairy farming county's population by 49.8 percent and, for better or worse, are beginning to change its rural character. There are now three McDonald'ses in Sussex County where ten years ago there were none. Guernsey cattle graze by "For Sale—Zoned for Development" signs. Stables sit beside new branch banks that are "Helping Sussex County Grow." Motorists on county roads are alternately alerted by signs to cattle crossings and the coming of shopping plazas. Bulldozer operators push ever outward here on the cutting edge of suburbia.

"It's great out here," said Louis Caruso, who moved from Clifton, New Jersey, "as long as you understand a few things, the first being that there's a long, long commute"—the price of living amid the forests, lakes, mountains, and rolling fields.

Since most working residents drive to jobs in the city or closer to it, the conversation at social gatherings now commonly turns to subjects such as the price of gasoline, when to replace worn-out cars, and to subjects such as the invariably awful music to which other riders in their car pools insist on listening. Peter Tougas, who came to Sussex three and a half years ago, car pools into midtown Manhattan, an hour-and-a-half trip if all goes well. "It's worth it," he said.

Commuters can also ride the bus. Some of those who do say that they feel a bit better, anyway, when they climb on board and see passengers from Pennsylvania who commute even farther than they do.

Many of the commuters here do not travel all the way into New York City but rather to a cluster of corporate offices sprouting along Interstate 287 near Morristown, New Jersey. The growth of outlying areas such as Sussex County coincides with the trend to businesses moving out of cities and clustering along such "circumferential freeways."

"Suburbia is out here now," said real estate agent Katherine Evertsen, who is nearing the $2 million sales mark in what is a difficult year almost everywhere else for home sales.

Houses and property taxes are much cheaper here than they are in the older, inner suburbs where a great many of the new residents come from, according to Fred Suljic, the county planner. Mr. Suljic, who walks four blocks home for lunch, moved from those inner suburbs two years ago, purchasing a nine-room Victorian house on a half-acre lot in Newton, New Jersey, for $45,000, with annual taxes of $1,060. In Newton, residents are filling the drive-in theater for the current film: *Escape From New York.*

There are other things different here that new arrivals must become accustomed to, such as the smell of cow manure, swarms of flies, the sound of farmers plowing at night and their slow-moving equipment on the roads by day, pesticide spraying, roosters crowing at dawn, and cows straying into their front yards.

"A lot of these people coming in have a pretty idyllic view of what country life is like," said Andrew Borisuk, a local dairy farmer. He, like other farmers in the area, has his own complaints, chief among them that some of the new residents are trying to rezone farmland to stop industry from moving to Sussex, greatly diminishing the value of his property.

There are signs that some of the problems of old suburbia are following the new people out to new suburbia, just as urban problems eventually found them in the older suburbs. Fearing congestion, the newcomers have joined longtime residents in opposing large housing developments, stopping a huge one that would have raised the population of a single township from 1,500 to 9,100. A few Sussex residents admit that the nation's economic problems, insofar as they have halted new construction here during the last two years, aren't all bad.

While wanting to pull up the drawbridge once they have arrived, the newcomers, accustomed to certain amenities, are demanding more services. With few water and sewer systems, 85 percent of the county relies on septic tanks and private wells. And when the wells run dry, residents often call municipal officials for help, only to be told they themselves must pay up to $3,500 to deepen or replace the wells.

And residents moving to the many Sussex towns without local police departments frequently demand them, along with a full-time county prosecutor. "There has been a dramatic crime increase," said Brian Laddey, who fills the prosecutor's post part-time. "Some is due to the population increase, but there are other factors. The new roadways make this more accessible to robbery. In the last two years we've had more murder cases than the last ten to fifteen years."

Perhaps nowhere in Sussex has the clash of the new and the old been more apparent than in Montague Township, where new residents deny wanting major changes but believe a few curbs, paved roads, and streetlights are in order. They are to recall Mayor Emma Masset, who said, "I don't know why some of these people came here if they're so hell-bent to change it."

Most newcomers, however, seem more than satisfied with Sussex County, which remains one of the least densely populated in the state, the scenic landscape as yet unmarred by enormous housing developments, the streets relatively safe, and the chicken dinners at the Plaza Restaurant still $3.25. The highway that brought many of them here, though, may ultimately drive some away. During rush hours on I-80, stop-and-go traffic jams—a full fifty miles from New York—are common. Indeed, the traffic led Peter and Deborah Constancia, who had moved to Sussex County, to move back to Denville four years later.

And lately, David Miller, a lifelong resident who has been working three jobs in an effort to come up with a down payment for a house here, has also been thinking about leaving. "The county's getting too crowded," he said. "They're building schools and libraries and starting police departments for the city people, and taxes are getting too high. Crime is getting worse. Prices are going up.

"They say you can still buy a house for $45,000 in Pennsylvania that would cost you $65,000 or more here," he added. "My sister already moved there. I'm thinking maybe it's time I moved farther out. But I guess sooner or later the city people would find me there, too."

☞ DRIVEWAY DRESS CODES

Gary Gross says that at a time when image is everything—when people wear their designer clothing tags on the outside and insist on French water that bubbles with sophistication—he should not be surprised that officials in suburban River Edge, New Jersey, have passed an ordinance forbidding him and other tradesmen to park vehicles with commercial license plates in their driveways overnight.

But he is. "The mayor wants it to look like only accountants and stockbrokers live here," Mr. Gross, a heating and air-conditioning repairman, said. "We feel like second-class citizens."

Standing in his driveway beneath a basketball hoop attached to the garage, he said that he had always viewed himself as a typical, law-abiding citizen, a suburban homeowner with patio and grill, a dog, four children, and a wife about to depart for her aerobic-dance class.

Now, however, his white van with a company name emblazoned across the side sits in his driveway, in flagrant violation of

Section 15-20.3 of this suburb's new law. The police have been to the house once, and another knock on the door could come at any time. "Aesthetically," Mrs. Gross said, "the van even matches the house."

Ordinances and covenants outlawing everything from leaving the garage door open to unduly bright house colors have become a hallmark of life in the suburbs, where residents appear before municipal magistrates, aesthetics committees, and other tribunals of taste on such charges as "long lawn" and "visible clothesline." There are those who welcome these strictures, saying that they protect property values, and there are those who denounce them as pretentious nonsense, designed to maintain a veneer of sophistication.

Mayor William M. Doyle is remarkably straightforward about his reasons for backing the ordinance: "Having all of these commercial vehicles looks bad. We want to spruce up the town." He said having them parked in driveways gives visitors "a bad idea" about River Edge. "The ordinance may be snobbery to a certain extent," he said, "but I think the trucks do depreciate property values." Plumbers, landscapers, carpenters, electricians, and other tradesmen in this suburb are banding together to protest the ordinance, which requires them to keep their commercial vehicles overnight in garages, backyards, or under tarpaulins—anywhere, as long as they are out of sight.

"The next thing you know," said Harold Lawrence, another heating and air-conditioning repairman, "they'll make us put our lunches in attaché cases and wear three-piece suits on the streets. By saying our trucks aren't good enough for this town, they're saying we're not good enough.

"The mayor and council are violating our constitutional rights," Mr. Lawrence said. "They can already tell us how high our bushes can be. Where does this all stop?"

"Here we are making an honest living," said Peter Hammer, a plumber, "and they are harassing us because they don't like the way we look." Mr. Hammer suggested the ordinance was "simple discrimination against blue-collar workers by white-collar officials." Several other truck owners said that times had changed, that many blue-collar workers now make more money than many white-collar workers and should no longer be looked down on.

At times during the controversy, Mayor Doyle's candor has put him in hot water with both the truck drivers and the residents of two nearby communities, Lodi and Garfield, which he named as examples of areas he did not want River Edge to look like.

The truck owners believe that Mr. Doyle has been less than sympathetic, admonishing one of them without a garage to "build one" and telling another man to sell his truck and buy a station wagon. To others, Mr. Doyle has suggested removing their commercial license plates and covering the names of the companies on the trucks' doors, both of which are required by law, every night and even placing dropcloths over the vehicles.

The mayor said there had been numerous complaints from residents about the trucks, although he has declined to be more specific, and the truck owners are skeptical. He also said that the presence of the trucks depreciated property values and that other suburbs had such ordinances. In neighboring Oradell, commercial vehicles must be parked in garages overnight or in a municipal lot, where their drivers rent space. "The trucks don't look good," an Oradell official said.

The truck owners and drivers in River Edge met in a park recently to draw up compromises that the mayor and council are considering. One proposal would allow smaller vans and trucks to park in driveways overnight if the lettering on the doors was covered. That way, the mayor said, passersby might mistake them for recreational vehicles, which would be fine with him.

"Still," said Mr. Gross, "it hurts a little. At the center of this is the idea that we aren't as good as they are."

Said Mayor Doyle: "I was amazed at how angry these people really are. I tried to inject a little levity by telling them that my daughter is dating a boy whose father has a seat on the stock exchange and that they are ruining my image. They didn't think that was funny."

VIII

SERIOUS CRIME

HOME BURGLARIES CAUSE ALARM

With double-cylinder dead-bolt locks secured (check); magnetic window alarms on (check); passive infrared intrusion detector system activated (check); guard dog in position, basement windows nailed shut, and the remote "panic botton" in her purse (check), a Wilton, Connecticut, resident is off to pick up a quart of milk and two green peppers.

She drives to the store on narrow, winding lanes past old stone fences and well-preserved houses of centuries gone by. The ultrasophisticated electronic security systems being installed in so many of them are unseen, the pastoral portrait unspoiled. "The main thing they want is to not see the alarm devices," said an installer in this suburban area. "I guess they don't want to be reminded."

Residents here say they are not gripped with fear over a wave of home burglaries that has engulfed suburban areas nationwide for the past two years. But a concern for personal safety has crept into life in this bucolic town, they say, a feeling that probably has not visited here since the retreat of the British Army.

"It's kind of sad," said Lee Reading, whose home has been broken into three times, twice last month. "We never used to even lock our doors out here. Now people call you when they return from a weekend away and say, 'Guess what? We weren't burglarized.'"

"It makes you angry," she said. "I came home during the last burglary, and it was foolish, but I chased one of the men down the street." She bought a German shepherd and a complete alarm system, inside and out.

Systems being installed, even in moderately priced homes, are sophisticated, many of them utilizing electronic technology that until recently was available only to military and other government intelligence agencies. "These systems are necessary," said Peter W. Orvis, a local security consultant and president of the Connecticut Security Dealers Association, "because people are no longer satisfied to protect their belongings. In the past two years they have become worried about their personal safety as well."

Infrared systems, developed for use in Vietnam, detect body heat, setting off sirens and lights and alerting central monitoring stations or the local police. Ultrasonic systems fill a room with high-frequency signals and sense changes in reflection patterns when someone or something enters. Audio sensor systems are tuned to discriminate among the sounds of breaking glass and metal and splintering wood.

There are microwave motion detection systems and networks of photoelectric beams. Some new devices, such as stress sensors that detect flex in the floor and stair supports, have been developed because burglars, too, are becoming more sophisticated, knowing too much about the older security systems, such as pressure detectors under the carpeting.

There are magnetic window-opening sensors; annunciators that alert a resident when a car turns into the driveway; seismic sensors that detect footsteps; multiple pulse sensors to detect an unusually high number of vibrations in a fence; and sensors to detect when someone jumps into a swimming pool. There are "panic buttons" that can be carried about by an individual to trigger the residential alarm system. Also becoming popular is a battery backup system or a system that alerts police when telephone or power lines are cut, something that burglars are doing with increasing regularity to bypass alarm systems.

Prices of these custom home systems range from about $1,000 to $10,000 or more. Many residents said they viewed this as an unfortunate but necessary new cost of living in a quiet suburban area that was once a retreat from the world they saw on the 11 P.M. news.

Sprouting up with the burglary wave are "lock boutiques," such as Locks R Us; discount outlets, such as the U-Do-It Alarm Super Market; companies specializing in "decorator" steel doors for homes; and a proliferation of franchised alarm companies taking their places on the strips of franchised restaurants and muffler installers throughout suburbia.

Mr. Orvis said there are new businesses that are videotaping a homeowner's possessions for insurance purposes. At least two suburban companies are advertising large roller shutters—long used by shopkeepers in high-crime urban areas—to cover suburban picture windows.

Ferdy Angelis, a Pennsylvania restaurant owner, is trying to market taped audio cassettes of his two barking German shepherds in New York's suburbs, which people can play while they are away or turn on when they hear a suspicious noise.

Local suburban newspapers carry classified advertisements for house-sitters who have their own guard dogs. There are also ads for less expensive mass-marketed alarms that depict women bound and gagged. Vertronix, a company based in New Rochelle, has sold forty-five thousand of its home alarm systems, called The Bug and base-priced at $500, in just two years. Its television ads show a menacing burglar trying to break into a home.

"We believe that our tremendous sales are directly proportional to rising burglaries due to the bad economy," said a spokesman for Vertronix. Mr. Orvis agreed that burglaries have increased because of economic conditions. Some in this Connecticut town say that it is all just because of the high cost of silver. Others say that, although crime figures are up, news reports overstate the crime problem to appeal to the prurient interests of their viewers and readers, thereby making people more anxious than need be.

"It bothers me," said Dr. Stanley Freeman of Westport, who has installed an alarm system. "It sure as hell does, to have to live like this. I don't care about my belongings, they're insured. But what about my family?"

Another suburban resident, whose home has been broken into twice, said he would never buy an alarm system. "I just won't live like that," he said, "with sirens and bars on the windows of my home."

Clark Mulford, who has been in the home alarm business in Fairfield County, Connecticut, for thirteen years, said many people once shared that view. "People hate to buy these systems," he said. "It's admitting defeat. It's admitting that this is the way things are."

His business is booming. "Never better," he said. "Too good, really. It scares you."

THE DINER CRIMES

"Things like this just don't happen out here," said Gloria McDonald, holding the hand of her three-year-old daughter at the Morton Village Plaza shopping center in suburban Plainview, New York. "They do now," Lisa Caputo responded.

On the Friday evening inaugurating this long Memorial Day weekend, as millions of festive New Yorkers began an exodus to beach and resort areas, a group of young men robbed about ten people in the elevator of an underground parking garage in Flatbush, Brooklyn, stole a Cadillac from the garage, and drove out of the ghetto to the suburbs.

They drove out along Old Country Road, mile after mile of bright, colorfully lit signs, a smorgasbord of plenty where suburbanites indulge. They eventually turned off into the residential neighborhoods. Spotting a well-lighted house with a number of cars outside, they barged in with guns drawn.

The invaders forced sixteen guests and family members to strip, hand over valuables, and lie on the floor. They struck one man in the face with a blackjack. They raped one of the women. The young men stole a television set and a small electric clock and an Atari game, then fled. The night was young.

The sanctity of suburban neighborhoods has long since been violated by crime. Burglary is common. A walk along the tree-lined block of postwar, split-level, and ranch-style homes in the town where the incident occurred does not readily reveal the burglar alarm systems, locked doors, and seeds of suspicion that have come to this neighborhood in recent years. One neighbor suggested this incident would not have occurred had the family owned a "panic button," a device being marketed successfully in the suburbs that sounds an alarm in the police station.

"You move out here, and you think you've seen the last of this kind of thing," said Michelle Zinker, who lives across the street from the house where the crime took place, a white, split-level frame home with hanging baskets of geraniums on the porch.

Neighbors said they were relieved that police had quickly apprehended five suspects in the crime, all of whom pleaded not guilty to a twenty-six-count indictment on charges of robbery, rape, sodomy, assault, and sexual abuse. "But that doesn't change the fact that it happened," said James White, one of many who have been driving by the house just to see where the incident occurred.

Residents have an unsettling sense that violent crime is increasing in Nassau County, something borne out by statistics. Murders there increased to 31 in 1981 from 22 in 1980; rapes to 37 from 26; and robberies to 1,223 from 930. Nassau County Police Commis-

5# SERIOUS CRIME   **163**

sioner Samuel J. Rozzi cites increasing "expressway crimes," those in which city residents drive out to prey upon suburbanites, as a major factor. The expressways, which were built to carry city residents away from problems of the city to their new homes in the suburbs, are now traveled by the people they ran from.

"Plainview is not a particularly affluent suburb," commented Detective Nancy Myers, "but it must have looked pretty good to these guys from Bedford-Stuyvesant."

The men next drove to the Sea Crest Diner in Old Westbury, a stone and brick restaurant with no windows, where they rounded up about eighty patrons and employees, forcing them to strip and turn over cash and jewelry. They pistol-whipped and bloodied a young man, commanded couples to engage in sexual acts, wounded two men with gunshots, and raped a woman.

"This has shaken everybody," said Shelly Domash of Westbury. "We knew there was crime out here, but we live in neighborhoods like that one, and going to diners is a way of life. It made us realize that it could have been us." She recalls the days when she laughed at her husband, who is from Queens, for locking the car doors in their suburban driveway.

"Locking your car and house doors," said Commissioner Rozzi, "not only when you leave them, but when you're in them, is basic here now."

Residents view the events of that night as isolated and bizarre, but most also recall a similar freakish mass robbery at a Jericho diner the week before; a gunman recently robbing four women playing Mah-Jongg in a Roslyn living room; a man killed when he surprised burglars in his Roslyn home; and a rash of "driveway robberies" on Long Island, in which gunmen intercept homeowners as they step from their cars.

"People were shocked by this latest spree," said Sergeant John Nolan, a detective investigating the crimes, "and I think it may act as a catalyst for people to tell legislators and judges: 'Hey, we're in trouble out here.' "

At the Sea Crest Diner a few days after the robbery, a couple discussing the incident expressed anger that some of those charged in this crime had long arrest records but had neither served prison terms nor been acquitted of the previous charges.

"Instituting the death penalty might make them think twice," said Rachel Wolfe. Her companion, Robert Richman, argued that had the criminals been raised in the suburbs and the victims in the slums, their roles would probably have been reversed. A young man came in, took a seat at the counter, and began to ask, "Is this the diner where . . . ?"

"Yes," the waitress answered and turned quickly away.

Police said that photographs were found with the young men, photographs the men had taken of each other after arriving back home in Brooklyn, smiling with arms around each other like a basketball team at a victory party, except they were brandishing pistols and great wads of jewelry and cash.

The gunmen left the diner Friday night and returned to Brooklyn on the Northern State Parkway, which flows into the Grand Central Parkway and then the Interborough Parkway. It is a pleasant drive on a warm evening. The road is winding and verdant all the way back, with the thick trees and parks that line the roadways concealing any change from suburb to city in the landscape beyond.

Then, abruptly, the Interborough Parkway ends, and the young men would find themselves descending on a jolting street of potholes that would lead them into a neighborhood of idle groups of men and burned-out buildings in Bedford-Stuyvesant, returned from the promised land.

IT CAN HAPPEN HERE

When Judge Harry Comerford signed Sarah's adoption papers recently in Cook County Circuit Court, Chicago, he hadn't an inkling he was writing the final lines in one of the most grim child abuse stories in county history—a story that has never been told.

I tell the story because to this day there are many people who see child abuse as a city problem, not a suburban problem. I'll call the woman Julie and change the other names, too, because in the eyes of the law she hasn't done anything wrong.

Julie is a thirty-five-year-old Bolingbrook housewife. She keeps her house spotlessly clean.

She and her husband, Joe, lived in Glen Ellyn when they had their first child, Mary. There were some unspecified "problems" after Mary came home from the hospital, and Julie left the infant with her mother in Chicago much of the time.

Their second child, Maureen, came two years later.

The baby died one month after she was born. Cause of death was listed as pneumonia. Julie said she died in her sleep. No autopsy was performed. These things happen.

Joe signed the death certificate, and Maureen was buried in Mount Carmel Cemetery in Hillside.

One year to the day after she was buried, Julie and Joe gave birth to their third child, naming him after his father. Two weeks after he was born, the boy was admitted to a hospital with seizures of some type. The baby was in the hospital for three weeks before they could take him home. A week later Julie and Joe again took the boy to Memorial Hospital of Du Page County in Elmhurst.

The baby was dead on arrival. An autopsy was called for, but no results were recorded and no cause of death is listed.

No outside agencies, either social or law enforcement, were called. Doctors were busy. This was several years ago, and child abuse wasn't thought about much as a cause of death, particularly in the suburbs.

Joe signed the death certificate, and his six-week-old son was buried alongside Maureen in Mount Carmel.

He went home and said he wanted a divorce and custody of their first child, Mary. He didn't get custody; husbands rarely do.

They were divorced and Julie remarried immediately, to a city of Chicago employee named Carl. Mary continued to spend a lot of time with Julie's mother.

Julie and Carl gave birth to Rachel at Lutheran General Hospital in Park Ridge.

Six months later, Rachel returned to Lutheran General, dead on arrival.

For some reason, the coroner's report was filed in Will County. Immediate cause of death was subdural hematoma, a swelling in the brain caused by blows to the head.

Accidents can happen. No agencies were called. There were no complaints, no charges, no witnesses. Two different last names in the story now, two counties, and three different hospitals miles apart. Nothing to put together.

Julie and Carl fight a lot. She files a complaint with police that he has threatened to kill her.

Eighteen months after Rachel's death, the couple has another child, Nancy.

Nancy is admitted to Silver Cross Hospital in Joliet (Carl and Julie apparently moved to a southwest suburb near there) at two weeks of age with a fractured leg and broken collar bone.

Accidents can happen.

Carl's mother becomes extremely upset and files a complaint with the Illinois Department of Children and Family Services challenging Julie's ability to care for the child.

A child welfare worker starts investigating, and at the same time Nancy is taken to St. Joseph's Hospital in Joliet suffering from malnutrition.

This time Julie has taken a child to the same place twice. Since the time that Nancy was taken to Silver Cross Hospital with broken bones, she has been brought here on another occasion with a burn on her face. The doctor checks her closely and finds some bruises on her body and a burn around her neck that raises a question in his mind about a possible strangulation attempt. He finds what looks like cigarette burns on the bottom of the left foot of the six-month-old infant.

Child welfare workers have Nancy and Mary moved immediately to a foster home in the southwest suburbs.

Mary, now seven, tells social workers that her mother chokes Nancy, holds her head under hot water, bangs her head into the counter, and "hurts her when there are too many dirty diapers."

"I used to see Mommy hurt Rachel," she tells them. "Mommy would hold her by the feet and hit her head on the floor."

Social workers find out about Rachel, Joe, and Maureen—all dead.

Carl tells them that Julie was detached and flippant when Rachel died. He says Julie had abused Mary as well. He says, though it isn't immediately clear how he knows, that Julie's former husband, Joe, used to beat her a lot and that Julie had scalded Maureen before she died officially of pneumonia.

The Department of Children and Family Services presses for immediate termination of parental rights, so Nancy and Mary won't ever be returned and so they can be adopted.

Judge Angelo Pistilli of Will County Circuit Court, who now refuses comment on the case, says then: not so fast. He expresses his contempt for social workers and what they do. Rather than suggesting possible criminal charges, he suggests that they all try to work toward getting the family back together.

Julie and Carl begin shopping for a psychiatrist who will tell Pistilli they are normal and that they should have their children back.

It takes a long time to find one. Psychologists and psychiatrists in Oak Park, Joliet, Northbrook, and the Maine Township Mental Health Clinic agree that Julie and Carl don't want help, they just want their kids back so their friends and neighbors think they're nice people.

One psychiatrist recommended by their own attorney says Julie is an obsessive-compulsive person and that "without psychiatric supervision, rearing of children will be most stressful to her and cause her to overreact in the physical punishment of children."

They find another psychiatrist, in Oak Park, who is optimistic about rehabilitation and starts regular family visits. Judge Pistilli, too, is optimistic. Social workers are not.

Meanwhile, Julie and Carl move to Niles and have another child, Sarah. Social workers cannot have the baby taken away. All that has happened previously cannot be brought up in court. All they can do is wait for Sarah to be brought to an emergency room.

She is, at three months, with multiple bone fractures. Sarah is immediately placed with a north suburban foster family, which later adopts her.

A new judge, not Pistilli, hears the case in Will County and parental rights are immediately terminated. Nancy and Mary have now both been adopted.

No charges were ever filed in connection with the apparent murder of three babies and the severe beating of the three others, all of whom were hospitalized.

When Sarah was adopted, Julie—who has never acknowledged that she is a child abuser—called before the proceeding to say she would contest it.

That was the last social workers heard from her. Before hanging up, she told one of them that her dog had just had some cute little puppies but that for some reason they were dying, one by one.

THE INSANE ONES

The young men rose late and drifted into Jersey City's Hamilton Park, where they sat on park benches and, seeing no future, talked of the past. They seemed old. Late in the afternoon a few roused themselves for a basketball game, one in which most of them tried to score on the impossibly long shot.

Across the street in the St. Michael's rectory, Antonio seemed not too keen on the idea of washing dishes, a job opportunity that Sister Antonelle Chunka was telling him about. She left him to think about it for a minute, threw open a window, and yelled, "Jose!" at one of the basketball players. "Be here at seven o'clock."

The burly youth, wearing a yellow satin jacket with "Zodiacs" emblazoned in purple across the back, sheepishly replied, "Yes, sister."

Sister Antonelle is five feet four inches of unflagging faith and determination—some around here call it naivete—who left the sanctuary of administrative positions with the Roman Catholic Church last summer to work among the street gangs of Jersey City.

The city is attracting new business to its abandoned buildings and vacant lots, as well as middle-class professional people to its large inventory of brownstones and three-story brick flats. Still, there are neighborhoods where one youth will shoot or stab another for the shoes on his feet. She walks among them unafraid, wearing a maroon "St. Anthony's Varsity Champ" jacket over her habit.

Something is happening to Richie Perez, leader of The Insane Ones, that he and the members of his gang do not fully understand. He talks freely of having engaged in a series of burglaries at local shops and of standing trial this year for the murder of another youth after a dance in the St. Michael's gymnasium last summer. He was found not guilty.

"Some of my boys think I'm going soft," he said. "Here I am hanging around with a nun."

Sister Antonelle had welcomed the eighteen-year-old gang leader this evening to one of her regular night meetings at the church rectory after relieving him at the door of a butcher knife carried beneath his sweatshirt. The shirt was adorned with drawings of skulls, roses, snakes, and the name of his gang. He is at a loss to explain just why he is drawn to these meetings, as are other members of gangs and clubs. But they come.

"Things would be different around here," he said, "if there was some hope of jobs or something. But it ain't like that for us." At the meetings, Sister Antonelle talks to them about personally intervening to stop gang fights and about setting up a "peace council" to negotiate their differences. And she talks of their futures: getting jobs, becoming involved with neighborhood projects, and helping the younger kids. They all seemed to agree that they did not want the young children in the neighborhood to end up as they had.

For some reason, they come to the meetings and for some reason they respond. Gang violence in the neighborhood is being reduced by degrees, according to residents and gang members, and some of the gang members are, at the nun's suggestion, setting up recreation and cleanup programs in the park—the park where the youth was killed last summer.

Sister Antonelle believes that they attend her meetings because they have problems and no one else is listening. Sometimes they show up bleeding, yes, or hungry or in need of a suit of clothes for a job interview. One of the young men is living at the rectory now.

On her walk through the neighborhood this day, three young men sitting in the park perked up when she told them about a program that would pay $100 a week while they trained for jobs ranging from computer programming to dealing cards in a casino. She talked to others about a course that would prepare them for the Graduate Equivalency Diploma examination. The dozens of youths she talked with, ranging in age from fourteen to twenty-one, were all high school dropouts.

She grasped their hands softly as she talked with them. They did not try to pull away. They did not talk tough street language to her and seemed for the moment completely incapable of the illegal acts attributed to them. But there are the police records.

When they talked of getting the runaround at various social service agencies, the nun softly replied: "Come and see us. We can help you." As she walked away, one of them, named Gregg, replied, "I sure hope so, sister. This just ain't no good."

She stopped young men here and there, telling those who might qualify about openings for counselors to younger offenders in a probation program that she is establishing with the cooperation of a judge. She circled "help wanted" advertisements in a local newspaper and handed it to one of the youths and said that she would be asking him how his interviews went.

Next she happened upon the aftermath of an incident in which the police had arrested three young men in an abandoned building for trespassing and had charged one, thirteen years old, with possession of marijuana and cocaine. The nun told the youths gathered on the corner "playground"—a small lot of buckled asphalt, broken bottles, burned mattresses, and swing sets without swings —to come to one of her meetings. Henry, a short, baby-faced fifteen-year-old, said he had dropped out of school. Would the older boys advise him to go back to school? she asked. "Yeah," said Max, seventeen, but Henry smiled a smile that seemed to say he never would. An eight-year-old boy carrying a book entitled *Growing Up Healthy* looked up at him.

"Jose," said a priest in the neighborhood, speaking to Sister Antonelle about one of the boys just arrested, "was doing extremely well at school, but he got no support from his mother or his friends or anyone else."

"There's a bunch of kids on this corner," she said, "that we must reach before it's too late." The priest said, "That will be soon."

Angel Hernandez, leader of The Zodiacs, arrived for the seven-o'clock meeting, embracing Sister Antonelle and greeting her with "Heyyy, sis." He said he was working with Sister Antonelle "because it is to the point where you or your sister couldn't walk down the street without being attacked.

"I talked The Insane Ones out of a fight," he said, "and came in and told the sister, 'There's been a miracle.' "

Jose had arrived and was listening to rock music through earphones and perusing some of Sister Antonelle's books, such as *The Pope Speaks* and *Casebook in Psychopathology,* when he spotted a youth named Vince walking in. "You got him, sister? You are good!"

She talked to the group about their personal goals and what their next steps might be toward achieving them. They discussed the start of the recreation and cleanup programs in the park. Some rehearsed with Sister Antonelle what they would say at job interviews she had scheduled for them.

The sister asked Angel Hernandez if he could help bring in the group that was involved in the arrests that afternoon. "No, sis, that's a bad group," he said. "They tried to steal my father's hubcaps." The others looked at him in shocked disbelief. Sister Antonelle laughed: "They said we'd never get you here either."

A couple of hours later they went out the front door and vanished. The streets around the small park were quiet. From somewhere on the far side of the park came a whistle, one that was answered with a whistle from someone unseen on the near side. A passerby picked up his pace.

OFFENSIVE FENCES

This is the city Chicago, Illinois. I'm not Sergeant Joe Friday, and I'm not a cop. (Sometimes I think I am, but I'm getting professional help.)

I was working the graveyard shift for the paper in the suburbs when the call came through. Things were getting ugly on a 4A in progress out in Palatine.

The thought goes through your head. Is our whole society sick? What makes these people unduly demarcate their property lines?

You shake off those thoughts that make you turn in your pencil for pipe and slippers at an early age. "Let's go," I say to no one in particular, flicking a Lucky into the gutter and sticking a white "press" card into the band of my brown fedora.

It wasn't pretty out there. Carrol and Yvonne Caynor live at 842 Willow Walk Drive, Palatine, in the ninety-eight-home Willow Walk subdivision across Roselle Road from the posh suburb of Inverness.

The Caynors had put up a four-foot-high white picket fence behind their colonial home.

It's no wonder reporters drink when we see stuff like that every day. I guess I don't have to tell you that there are laws against things like this, a direct violation of Rule 4, Section A, of the Willow Walk subdivision rules.

You've been around the block a couple of times and think you've seen it all. But how do you figure a guy who would do something like this?

We pulled a confession out of the guy in five minutes. "I'm in a job where I'm transferred a lot," Caynor, forty-six, says. "We've moved seven times, and we've always had a fence. We have a dog." He says it almost without emotion.

Pretty flimsy. The Architectural Committee of the Willow Walk Homeowners Association hit him with Property Line Demarcation, unduly demarcating more than 10 percent of his property line. The homeowners association sued him, and Judge Arthur Dunne of Cook

County Circuit Court ruled May 11—in his wisdom—that Caynor must remove the fence. Last week, Caynor appealed Dunne's ruling.

Norbert F. Vandersteen, president of the homeowners association board, has taken a hard line: "These people who don't want the rules are wrong, and there won't be any peace until they back off."

Vandersteen says that if Caynor is allowed to violate the law, others will, too. Caynor might also go on to a life of crime, moving up to trying to grow hedges on the property line, planting a garden larger than the rules allow, having a TV antenna higher than five feet above his roof, or actually trying to hang the laundry out to dry on a clothesline! It turns your stomach.

It has taken someone strong like Vandersteen to see this thing through. The public doesn't understand a crime so devious as property-line demarcation, especially when everyone agrees the fence is attractive, and the neighbors on either side of Caynor aren't complaining. And it doesn't help when property values—the reason for all these restrictions—are going up astronomically. Caynor bought his home three years ago for $76,000, and realty agents now estimate its value at $135,000 or more.

Caynor has learned that crime doesn't pay. He has already been billed $5,405 by his attorneys, and he hasn't received a final statement for the trial he just lost in Circuit Court. His attorneys say it will cost another $5,000 to $10,000 to appeal the case. Caynor says he can't afford all this and that anything like taking a vacation or replacing his six-year-old car is out of the question.

There are other costs. The Caynors have many sympathizers but few, if any, who will associate publicly with them, having actually expressed fear of rocks being thrown through their windows or having their children lose all their friends.

Rather than an all-American white picket fence, you'd think from the reaction they'd put an E-Z-Go station, a chinchilla ranch, or an International House of Prostitutes back there.

Vandersteen says that without Caynor's fence, all of the yards in the development look larger.

But the people, Norbert, look a whole lot smaller—you; the judge who gives this the force of law; and neighbors who gladly send old ski sweaters to Guatemalan earthquake victims but who won't walk across the street to comfort Yvonne Caynor, who sits home alone and cries.

IX

GOVERNMENT
AND
FOREIGN RELATIONS

WHO, EXACTLY, IS NOT RUNNING FOR GOVERNOR?

Last year it was disco roller-skating and riding mechanical bulls; this year it seems to be running for governor of New Jersey.

The Garden State is offering up to $600,000 in public funds to help finance the campaign of anyone who wants to run in the June 2 gubernatorial primary election, and a record number of candidates are taking advantage of the offer.

By the close of business yesterday, twenty-four had filed with the State Election Law Enforcement Commission, and the filing deadline is still more than two weeks away.

The question around the statehouse in Trenton, according to one official, has become: "Who isn't running?"

Paul Kovolisky, manager of the International House of Pancakes in Parsippany, told this reporter last week that he would not run for governor. Also not running, according to an informal sampling, are Chris Jakubowski, a secretary at Bayonne Welding and Boiler Repairing; Frank Dell Aglio, owner of a Sunoco gas station in North Bergen; Laura Rouba, owner-operator of the Curley Cue beauty salon just outside Trenton; and Maria Granado, an employee of the Hoboken Bilingual Keypunch School.

So, it only seems like everybody is running for governor of New Jersey. Thousands, literally, are not.

"I don't think it's apathy," said Michael Murphy, a Newark computer software salesman and noncandidate. "Some of us just have prior commitments."

Ellen Palombi, of Fort Lee, said, "I'm not old enough to run." Adela Weyer, of Weehawken, said she was waiting until she became a citizen. Michael Lamolino, of Fort Lee, said, "I'm too tired to run."

Mrs. Rouba said that although she met a lot of people at her beauty salon in Hamilton Township, "I'd need more name recognition." Jeffrey Kaplowitz, of Jersey City, said, "I will not run, and if elected I will not serve. If I did, I wouldn't be able to complain."

All of those surveyed said they found the enormous field—fourteen Democrats and ten Republicans, and counting—extremely confusing. One man suggested giving New Jersey residents public funds not to run for governor. Another suggested

175

letting the candidates handle the job on a rotating basis, something on the order of "Governor-for-a-Day." Most expressed resentment over the new campaign-financing law, which was intended to prevent special-interest groups from gaining influence through large campaign donations. Under the law, a candidate who raises $50,000 is eligible to receive $2 from the state for every $1 raised privately thereafter. It has since come to be known facetiously in Trenton as the Politicians' Full-Employment Act and will cost the state far more than the original estimate of $4 million.

It is pointed out that $1.5 million in state funds has already been given to nine of the twenty-four candidates who have filed with the election commission, even though only one has officially filed with the secretary of state's office to be placed on the ballot. A candidate may lawfully collect hundreds of thousands of dollars, drop out, and not even appear on the ballot.

"If they want to be big shots, let them use their own money," said Rita Pantoliano, a waitress at Pizzaburg in Palisades Park. Mack Albus, manager of Kimura's Karate School in Hackensack, said, "Some are just running for the prestige. It's a waste of money." The two said that they planned to pursue their interest in pizza and karate, respectively, and would not enter the race.

Several of those interviewed said they particularly resented their tax money going to finance campaigns for the primary election, which one characterized as "just a party squabble to find a candidate."

All of them believed that most of the candidates would not be running if it were not for the campaign-financing law. "An official of my little township is running," said Mrs. Rouba. "He has no chance at all. He's just trying to get his name around."

Several others agreed that many candidates are taking advantage of the new law as a cheap way to build some recognition. Mr. Dell Aglio, however, said that even the public financing could not draw so many candidates and concluded, "It must just be a simple job."

"I'm not running myself," said Don Warner, a Paramus liquor salesman, "but I do know several of the candidates personally." Hearing that, a bystander commented, "In this election, it's hard for someone not to know a candidate personally."

It has reached the point where some politicians not running for governor are finding it necessary to declare their noncandidacies.

Governor Byrne, who cannot seek a third consecutive term, has an "I'm NOT Running for Governor" button. Even Mr. Byrne—who made passage of the campaign-financing law a top priority of his administration—said he was alarmed by the enormous field of candidates, and he has tried unsuccessfully to increase the threshold for public financing from $50,000 to $150,000.

Assemblywoman Barbara W. McConnell, Democrat of Flemington and one of the candidates, said the Legislature had considered the $150,000 threshold but decided on the $50,000 figure so that no citizen would be denied the opportunity to run for governor.

It appears that few will.

☛ THE MOOD OF THE ELECTORATE IN PRECINCT 2B

What is the mood of the electorate on this election eve?

Hundreds of thousands of dollars have been spent by newspapers, television and radio stations, and the candidates to gauge voter sentiment and reveal: the electorate has a "negative association" or is otherwise upset with high taxes and inflation; is still undecided about Percy and Seith; favors Thompson over Bakalis; and so on.

But in an apparent abandonment of journalistic tenets and First Amendment responsibilities, no news organization has taken the pulse of the majority of the public—those who apparently just don't give a damn.

To get the story, your reporter went to the scene of probably the greatest display of voter apathy in election annals: Precinct 2B near north suburban Libertyville.

No one in Precinct 2B voted in the last election, the March 21 primary. No one.

Election judge Marilyn Carsten and two others had their little table set up over in the Oak Grove School gymnasium. They had the binder with the names of registered voters, and they had the rest of the election paraphernalia—the flag, the "Polling Place" sign on the door, and all that. But no one showed.

"You don't expect to get many voters in the primary," Mrs. Carsten says. "We thought we'd get some early or around noon, but that didn't occur. It was kind of quiet."

Election officials describe the turnout as "abysmal" and said they believe that it is probably the first time anywhere that no one has voted in an entire precinct. One election official called it "amazing," even though he is used to seeing things like 150-percent voter turnouts in some Chicago precincts—if the weather is good.

Rudy Stolarek, in precinct 2B, said that he would have gone to the polls in March except he was "monkeying around and forgot."

And what is the mood of the electorate? "Pretty good," Rudy says. "I cut the grass today and I always like to get that done. Then I had some old-fashioned potato soup, one of my favorites. You just put some potatoes in and boil them, then add some Carnation milk and some salt, pepper, garlic . . ."

No, Rudy, I mean politically. There's an election Tuesday. Millions of dollars have been spent on advertisements. Candidates who could lose their power and their livelihoods, and journalists paid to care, are going wild.

"I'm sixty-six," he says, "and have found that no matter who the President, the congressman, or the governor is, we still live pretty much the same. Life goes on." His wife, Marian, isn't registered and says politicians are "all a bunch of crooks."

Kenneth Lewman would have voted in March if he hadn't "goofed up." And what is the mood of the electorate on this election eve?

"Good," he says. "I shot some squirrels and am going to have a big squirrel dinner. I've been coming home, having a couple beers or a Manhattan, and watching television or reading the newspaper. My mood is good."

No. No.

"I'm concerned about inflation and taxes and all the rest, of course," Lewman says, "but in most of these races they might as well be running yellow dogs as far as I'm concerned. Percy hasn't done anything, the guy before him didn't do anything, and the guy after him won't do anything."

He says, "Politics is getting to be a pretty good-sized joke as far as I'm concerned." He and others say they're tired of "fanatics wiretapping and forging signatures on petitions." They say the candidates are like all the other products advertised on TV, promising to make you happy "but not delivering when you buy their bill of goods."

"If it keeps going this way," says Levina Paul, "with all the insincerity, and the big promises they know they can't keep, someday nobody will vote."

NO PETS OR COMMUNISTS ALLOWED ON BEACH

The past week has been an eventful one here at Exit 39N of the Long Island Expressway. The Welcome Deli received its long-awaited beer license; Landing Cleaners swept the local softball playoffs; a wallet found at the 7-Eleven grocery was returned to its owner; and the city council drew the ire of the world's two superpowers, both of which have threatened retaliation—in some nonnuclear way, one hopes.

After voting to repair a garbage truck and to reappoint a nursing home aide, the city council expressed outrage at reports of electronic spying by Russians who occupy a mansion in the community, and voted 6 to 1 to revoke their beach passes. The council renewed the ban, originally voted in May, which also excludes Russians from the city golf course and tennis courts. The council ignored a warning by the U.S. Department of State to stop meddling in foreign affairs.

While John Foster Dulles might have applauded the council's action in the days of the cold war, the State Department has asked the Justice Department to consider taking legal action against Glen Cove, New York, for treaty or civil rights violations. The Soviet Union has mentioned that it could retaliate in kind against our diplomats in suburban Moscow.

The reaction among the city's twenty-seven thousand residents has been mixed, ranging from one man on Glen Street who said that the action was "ludicrous and embarrassing to Glen Cove" to the next man, who compared it with "President Kennedy's courageous stand in the Cuban missile crisis."

Many in the city are bemused. Bill Conologue, a sunbather on Prybil Beach, contended that he was not at the beach relaxing but rather watching for Russian gunboats. At the Glen Cove Yacht Club, Paul Shein looked out upon several dozen small sailboats moored in Hempstead Harbor and pronounced the fleet ready to defend Glen Cove's shores against Soviet naval power "or, perhaps, the Philistines."

On a sign at the Morgan Park beach saying, "No Dogs, Bicycles, Roller Skating, Ball Playing, or Frisbees," someone had penciled in "Russians" and added the statement "Nuke Their Beach Tags."

Three of four boys carrying fishing poles through the park gave
widely varying opinions on the situation, with the fourth—perhaps
coincidentally the one wearing a Sony Walkman—saying he had
never heard of the dispute.

One hard-liner contended that the threats by the Russians to retaliate constituted mere saber-rattling. He added that there were no
beaches in Moscow and that, what's more, Russians did not play
tennis.

Indeed, a spokesman at the U.S. Embassy in Moscow said yesterday, "The Russians have more to lose in this than we do." Glen
Cove seems to be exploiting a recreational-facilities gap. The Glen
Cove estate, used by the Soviet Mission to the United Nations since
1946, is, according to local officials, a forty-nine room mansion on
thirty-seven acres, with tennis courts across the street and the
beach and golf course just down the road. The counterpart for
United States diplomats in suburban Moscow is a five-bedroom
house with a volleyball net stretched between two trees, the embassy spokesman said.

The Russian mansion here, known as Killenworth, sits behind
iron gates and out of view on Dosoris Lane between the YMCA and
the Glengariff nursing home. Local rumors have it that agents of the
Central Intelligence Agency work at the nursing home. The Russian
estate is actually a monument to capitalism, built by Charles Pratt, a
founder of the Standard Oil Company.

The neighborhood was once known as the Gold Coast, populated by wealthy industrialists until the advent of high income taxes
during the New Deal, and there went the neighborhood. J. P.
Morgan lived here, and the Russians sun themselves on a beach still
owned by his family and leased to the city.

"Glen Cove Loves America" stickers adorn car bumpers and
trash cans in what residents describe as a patriotic city. Mayor Alan
M. Parente said that the hundreds of calls and letters coming in
overwhelmingly supported the council's action. "They express
two themes," the mayor said. "They are mad at the State Department for butting in, and they believe the Russians here are a threat
to us.

"The Soviet Union has used brute power in Afghanistan and
Poland," said Mayor Parente. "There has been a feeling of frustra-
tion that the United States has lost power and influence and cannot
help."

When Glen Cove had finished with the Russians last week, a spokesman in the Soviet Mission to the United States said, "It's a pity they've deprived us from using those beaches. But what can be done?" The mayor and council have more in mind than punishing the Russians. They face a $2 million budget deficit and have made it clear that if the federal government will pay the annual $75,000 to $100,000 property-tax bill on the tax-exempt property, perhaps they would have a change of heart.

A production of *Bye Bye Birdie* appeared at the high school auditorium over the weekend, but there were those suggesting that another 1950s production, *The Mouse That Roared*, might have been more appropriate—the latter about a small, financially troubled country declaring war on the United States in order to lose the war and gain enormous sums in postwar reparations.

Many in the city are opposed to the council's action. "I think it's time to back down," said a sunbather at Prybil Beach, Bob, a city worker who declined to give his last name. "These are nice families. The wives and children are the ones we're punishing."

A former city official, who asked not to be identified, said that he was a longtime friend of many people at the Russian estate and that they were still being smuggled onto beaches as guests of local people. He said a number of the Russians had received telephone calls inviting them to play tennis at private clubs since the council's vote.

Others were maintaining a hard line. "You have to draw the line somewhere with the Russians," said an elderly woman at Prybil Beach. "Yes, I am concerned with the spying. I think it's affecting my TV picture."

☛ BUMPER STICKER BRIGADES ROLL

As difficult now as it is to believe, just a few short weeks ago there were those in the international community who were questioning America's willingness and ability to respond effectively to acts of international aggression.

This may have been because a short, primitive people with bad teeth recently defeated the combined armed forces of the United States of America without ever changing out of their pajamas. I don't know.

What fools. Within hours after a bunch of students with abominable deportment seized the U.S. Embassy in Tehran, "Iran Sucks" T-shirts were being convoyed to stores in suburban Chicago and airlifted to shops throughout the fifty states.

"Put A-Hola in the Ayatollah" bumper stickers were deployed here instantaneously, courtesy of Danco Distributors of Hinsdale. Also in the company's arsenal are "Deport Illegal Iranians" and "Bomb Iran" stickers, among others.

More T-shirts were sent into the fray by Creative Screen Design: one with a picture of Uncle Sam saying "A Sleeping Giant Is About to Be Awakened" to the Ayatollah; a second (perhaps designed to confuse the enemy) showing the Shah sitting on a bomb with the inscription "A New Cure for Cancer"; and a third showing the American flag on a pole driven into the Ayatollah's forehead. Al St. John, owner of the T-shirt company, is putting $1 from the sale of each shirt into a Families of the Hostages Fund in a Park Ridge bank. "There must be some way the hostages can use the money," he said, "they have been out of work for eighty days."

A Carol Stream service station operator put up a large sign saying: "We Reserve the Right Not to Serve Iranians." One can only guess the financial sacrifice involved in such a bold move. In any event, he took it right down when told it might violate civil rights laws.

A number of local suburban governments mobilized, issuing saber-rattling resolutions denouncing Iran and putting up flags to show their support. South suburban Dolton lined its streets with 110 flags, about 100 of which have been stolen so far.

Franklin Park lowered its flags to half-staff, and the White House called to thank the mayor. The Franklin Park-Park District, however, believed lowering the flags to half-staff was an act of mourning and decided to fly its flag at full staff, along with the Gadsden Flag—a coiled rattlesnake with a "Don't Tread on Me" motto.

In south suburban Lansing, local officials decided to secure a safe and speedy return of the hostages by blowing the civil defense siren six times each night until their return. One resident complained that blowing the sirens is like "group shock therapy," and she had the gall to suggest that it may not be helping the hostages all that much. She is also upset that the only person who can stop the sirens is the Ayatollah Khomeini: "If I'd wanted a seventy-nine-year-old bearded lunatic with a towel on his head as a village trustee, I'd have voted for him," she concluded.

One west suburban police chief told a reporter privately that he was going to stop any motorist in his town who even looked Iranian. Several suburban police forces are wearing arm bands, some black, some white.

The eleven suburban newspapers of the Addison Leader chain are running their mastheads upside down to protest the Iranian situation and speed the safe release of all hostages.

At least four would-be singers here in the suburbs have recorded patriotic songs denouncing the Ayatollah. Dale Press, of suburban Bedford Park, is turning out effective propaganda posters to whip up fervor of our boys in uniform and the folks back home—in this case, one and the same. A company spokesman says almost five hundred thousand posters of the Ayatollah with a target drawn on his face have been sold.

If foreign aggressors need evidence of the fighting mood of this country, they need look no further than Dale Press. The company, which had never before printed posters, has had to move to larger quarters with the overwhelming success of the Ayatollah posters being used as dart boards and at shooting-range targets across the country. Calls started coming in for other posters, and now the company sells "The Shah," "President Carter," and "Jane Byrne," all with superimposed targets. "It's weird," one spokesman said. "People are frustrated and want to shoot everybody."

Iran and Russia were foolhardy to test the mettle of the United States of America.

The Ayatollah and Leonid Brezhnev couldn't sign up for aerobic dancing at the Franklin Park-Park District now on a bet.

TEED OFF

"I'll tell you what the Japanese are," said a disgruntled member of the Haworth Country Club. "The Japanese are just too . . . too damned successful."

The Japanese have recently settled in great numbers here in northern New Jersey, most of them employed by about seventy Japanese corporations in the immediate area. And the growing Japanese community is presenting something of a problem to the old-timers at this country club.

Members of the club contend that they are not such a prejudiced lot, really, just angry. They say that they would be lashing out at the Little Sisters of the Poor if it were they who bought the country club and raised the fee for playing weekend golf from about $300 this year to between $5,500 and $10,500 next season. But it was three Japanese businessmen who made the purchase.

"There have been a lot of jokes about installing geisha girls in the locker room," said Frank Giordano, a club member who had gone to the home of another member, Fred Cicetti, to discuss the turn of events.

"And about Tora! Tora! Tora! golf carts," said Mr. Cicetti, who has a public relations firm in Leonia. "But the jokes have turned to resentment. A lot of the members are very bitter."

Mr. Cicetti calls the situation "a real switcheroo" on the classic case of suburban country clubs discriminating against minority groups. "It's obvious," he said, "they're trying to boot us out so they can make this an all-Japanese club." Another member, George W. LeBolt, has threatened to file a discrimination suit. "It's to the point," Mr. Giordano, a plumber, said laughingly, "where the other day a guy I was playing with said, 'Look! There's an American!' and started waving."

Paul Sashikata, who became a manager when the club changed hands last January, rejects the charges of discrimination and denies that there is any intent to cultivate an all-Japanese membership. "We are making major improvements in the golf course and the clubhouse," he said, "and upgrading the club from a semiprivate to a private club appealing to a different clientele." He said that anyone who can afford the fee is welcome to join but acknowledged that the club advertises on New York television alongside Japanese-language programming, and he said that he can envision the membership becoming, "say, seventy percent Japanese."

For his part, Mr. Cicetti said, "This is a classic case of how bigotry is created. I've always admired the Japanese people for creating a great society and culture on a small island and everything else. I think they are astute and industrious and always very polite. If three Japanese families moved in on this block no one would mind. But all of a sudden, I find that I don't like them.

"Raising my fees from $275 to $5,000 to drive me out is heavy-handed," he said. "It's rude and impolite and frankly out of character." Mr. Cicetti attributed the situation to what he called a fanaticism for golf among the Japanese, which he said was creating long lines at local golf courses and driving ranges.

Mr. Sashikata will not argue with the notion. He explained that playing golf was extremely expensive and quite difficult in Japan, a densely populated country with few courses. He and the club's golf pro, Toshi Morioka, told of $200,000 initiation fees at some clubs in Japan, of $100 to $200 green fees for one round of golf, of having to schedule tee times weeks in advance, and of driving ranges several stories high that charge $40 an hour and have $2,500 initiation fees. There is a religion in Japan, the Perfect Liberty Kyodan, known to many as the golfing religion, which claims about one million members and has driving ranges atop many of its churches.

"Some wives of Japanese businessmen here," Mr. Morioka said, "go crazy—literally—because their husbands play golf all weekend, every weekend during their two- and three-year assignments in America."

"It's a shame," Mr. Giordano said. "It was a nice club. I'll miss the camaraderie." Mr. Giordano is a member of a club-within-the-country club, informally known as the men's club, which has about two hundred members, holds golf tournaments and social functions, and has been in existence since before the country club opened in 1968. Spokesmen said the men's club would probably be disbanded because new guidelines preclude reserving large blocks of course time for its tournaments.

"It galls you," said Ed Brett, president of the men's club, "that these people can come to this country, take over, and squeeze you out. They bought the club and next thing they'll be buying homes. They seem to be the only people who can afford them now. You don't like to be pushed around. A lot of our members fought in the Pacific in World War II and there's a lot of talk about forgive and forget, but some can't forget."

"It frightens me," Mr. Giordano said, "it really does, that outsiders—Arabs and Japanese—are coming in and buying things up and pricing Americans out of the market, making us second-class citizens." Mr. Cicetti argued that Americans have been doing this around the world for many years: "This is just the Japanese version of the ugly American."

"But it's frustrating," Mr. Giordano said, "There's nothing you can do. You start to get an idea of what the auto workers must feel."

"Except," Mr. Giordano said, "this is just some silly game."

"It's more than that," Mr. Giordano said.

ONE McBOMB TO GO
You start at the top.

Mayor McCheese refuses to comment. Eight hours, twenty-five phone calls, and a trip to corporate headquarters later, you realize nobody wants to say much about bomb threats at large corporations.

A suspicious-looking briefcase sitting unattended is spotted one morning this week in the lobby of corporate headquarters of McDonald's, purveyors of more than 25 billion all-beef, 1.6-ounce, 3.875-inch patties.

The headquarters are in west suburban Oak Brook, a couple of blocks from the polo fields of one of Chicago's most posh suburbs. You might expect the closest thing they've seen out here to foreign terrorists is a Mexican with hedge clippers.

Oak Brook police are notified. And the national security manager and security coordinator for the huge chain are brought in.

Suburban police departments are easily excited. The McDonald's Corporation has something of a reputation for paranoia. Reporters and other guests are received just inside the front door, not allowed to go into corporate offices, where they might glimpse a Top Secret document listing the number of sesame seeds on those buns.

The Du Page County sheriff's office is contacted. It could be international terrorists; the bomb unit is on its way. Members of the unit are thrilled. Like the Rolling Meadows S.W.A.T. team, the Du Page bomb unit doesn't get a lot of work. Sergeant Allan McKechnie, who heads the crack unit, arrives in a specially equipped van at McDonald's Plaza, Twenty-second Street and McDonald's Drive.

It is morning and hundreds of people are already at work in the eight-story office complex. It is determined that no one will be evacuated. Bad press.

The case is X-rayed with mobile equipment and shows wires and canisters inside. Not good. The case is cautiously moved to the van and placed in a protective container. The lid is left open so that if the bomb explodes, the blast will go straight up and hopefully not harm anyone.

The van moves out—cautiously—and travels more than a mile to a remote, open field of weeds at Jorie Boulevard and Kensington Road. Luckily, there are no bumps of any kind in Oak Brook streets.

The squad readies to blast open the case with a piece of equipment called a water cannon. The cannon is used to open cases without totally destroying them, to allow members of the bomb unit to study the contents.

When the bomb is determined to be a safe distance from motorists on Illinois Highway 83 to the west, workers in new office complexes to the north, and anyone who might be in the lavish public park to the south, the case is blown.

The bomb team waits for a moment, approaches the case, and peers inside. They see a broken makeup mirror and wires for the lights around the rim of the mirror. They see jars of makeup.

McDonald's officials make a positive identification.

They have blown up Ronald McDonald's makeup kit.

X

DOMESTIC
RELATIONS

☛ THERMAL NUCLEAR FAMILY WAR

Barbara O'Connor says that she and her husband are "about to strangle each other" in a desperate struggle for control of the thermostat.

Mrs. O'Connor heatedly charged that he prefers to keep their three-bedroom suburban home at a temperature more appropriate to a walk-in meat locker. He implied that if she had her way they could cook a roast in their home simply by setting it out on the coffee table.

"We have to dial down like everybody else," John O'Connor argued, explaining that their monthly fuel oil bills would go up by $200 during January and February. She countered, saying that the nation is caught up in an energy-saving frenzy and that "some people are just carrying it too far."

"There are so many fanatics," she said, expressing dismay over her husband's frigid tendencies, while looking skeptically upon wood stoves that he had brought her to see in the local Sears, Roebuck store. "You go to fanatics' homes and they tell you how great the new stove is and how much money they're saving, and you're sitting there absolutely shivering."

"Today," Jack Beineix, a salesman, interjected philosophically, "each family must decide how much discomfort they can live with."

Another customer, who thinks of herself as part of an energy-saving backlash, said she knew of a well-to-do man in her neighborhood who kept his house at 60 during the day and in the 40s at night: "His wife turns it up to 70 when he's gone and opens the windows to let the heat out before he comes home."

The owner of a stove store in Peekskill said that a few of his customers set their thermostats at 55 and close off all but two or three rooms of their suburban houses to cut fuel bills. An increasingly popular item at area stores is a lock for the home thermostat that keeps whimpering spouses, children, and guests from seizing control.

"You wear a lot of clothes these days when you're invited to someone's home," said Mrs. O'Connor. She and others said most homes in their area are equipped with new energy-saving thermostats set to decrease heat automatically in the evening. They said these automated thermostats have no consideration for human beings and can often turn a dinner party into what they describe as something of a quivering Madame Tussaud's, where guests pray the dessert is flambé. It would not surprise Mrs. O'Connor if white gloves came into vogue for even the most informal affairs.

Woe unto the person who suggests that the heat be turned up, they said, for this would compromise energy-saving goals. They agree that fuel economy has become so fashionable that such a request would be a considerable faux pas. To date, books of etiquette hold no answers. One suburban man suggests that a warm room is fast becoming a status symbol.

Conversation at such suburban social gatherings invariably turns in these energy-conscious times to such things as "flair-stack-pack-vent-dampers" and to kerosene heaters, which the fuel-efficient now carry with them from room to room much as their ancestors did candles.

Roadside kerosene stands are sprouting in some suburban areas like Christmas-tree lots. Heating boutiques with names like The Energy Option Shop have opened in Westchester to vie with the likes of the more traditional Henry's Plumbing and Heating. Chimney sweeps are again a common sight as fireplaces are retrofitted to make them more heat efficient and in constant use.

Some homeowners are said to be purchasing practically anything with an "energy saver" tag on it, and merchants have been quick to pick up on it. Socks are said to be tagged "Energy Saver" at one store here, and one wonders if door stops and paperweights can be far behind.

Sales of comforters and electric blankets—as well as hot-water bottles—continue to climb at stores in the area. Ceiling fans to blow warm air back down and insulated draperies have become popular items. "Insulated window shades" are advertised. Newspaper and broadcast advertising campaigns attempt to persuade homeowners to switch from oil to gas heat, while counterpropaganda tells them they're foolhardy if they do.

For the militant energy saver, rolling metal shutters used by shopkeepers to keep burglars out at night are being offered by merchants to cut fuel bills, and for those who have thrown appearances to the Arctic-like winds, three-sided aluminum and plastic entryways to attach to the house and keep drafts from the door. The last line of defense would seem to be the "Snug Sack," essentially a sleeping bag with armholes. It is nearly sold out at the Sears store here, where a clerk explains how one goes about zipping, snapping, and finally tying oneself into the insulated bag—to wait for spring while watching television, reading books, and praying, all the while, that the telephone doesn't ring.

New rites of fall have taken their place alongside leaf raking in the suburbs: caulking, weatherstripping, and laying yet more strips of prickly pink insulation in the attic. Al Cohen, who is "just browsing, thanks" in the stove department at Sears, is what has come to be known as a fuelish person, saying that he does not take part in these new rites. Rather, he stuffs an occasional sock or dish towel where the chill is seeping in around the windows and lets it go at that.

"The subject bores me," he said of energy conservation. "I let my wife pay the bills and try not to think about it." For people like him, a black cast-iron stove in the living room would only serve as a grim and constant reminder that these are hard times, energy-wise. Mr. Cohen could not think of a thing that he does to save energy other than allowing his cat to sleep on the bed before he retires for the evening.

The O'Connors could not bring themselves to buy a stove. Even Mr. O'Connor feared that it might be more trouble than it was worth. With the price of firewood running as high as $195 a cord in the area, he agrees that foraging for dead trees in the neighborhood has become like a second job for many stove owners.

Mrs. O'Connor simply could not picture a black cast-iron stove sitting next to an Oriental rug, amid the chintz-print chairs and love seat in her living room. She departed with some vague and troubling feeling that she was a Bloomingdale's catalog woman living in a *Whole Earth Catalogue* world.

☞ P LAYING SECOND STRING

Many women in the Monday night class describe themselves as "football widows," women who have lost their husbands to televised football. They come to learn about I-formations, nickel defenses, and hang time, that this might enable them to communicate once more with loved ones lost.

They are enrolled in a new course entitled "What Is Monday

Night Football All About? A Course For Women," taught by Sheila Peck, a psychotherapist who knows how to diagram a down-and-out pattern. She teaches football and counsels the afflicted.

"I hate football," Harriet Shapiro told her understanding classmates. "I'd like to blow up the TV sometimes." It would be quite an explosion; her husband bought a set with a six-foot screen to watch sports.

"First there was Saturday football," said Linda Goodrich, who blames televised football for her divorce, "then there was Sunday football, then all-day Sunday football, then Monday night football, and now there are Thursday night games and new football leagues playing almost all year. It's a very, very serious situation."

"Soon," cried out another in the class, "there will be no family life!"

"Monday night football," Mrs. Peck told them, "is a fact of life that we must learn to deal with. It is an institution."

Indeed. Several bars in the suburban Lynbrook, New York, area pack in the customers for Monday night football on what used to be their slowest night of the week. Municipal officials tell of sharply reduced attendance at Monday night meetings since the inception of Monday night football in 1970. Hundreds of New York metropolitan-area residents are card-carrying members of the California-based Church of Monday Night Football.

Women in the class told of trying to cope with the intruder in their homes that is televised football. Mrs. Shapiro told of her attempts to have Sunday dinners ready at the precise moment of halftime of the second televised game. She grew weary of that and began ordering carry-out Chinese food, but even that was difficult. "You should see the Chinese restaurant at halftime of the second Sunday game," she said.

Another woman told of being driven "half crazy" by the *huuuut-huuuut-huuuut* of the quarterback emanating from the family room during Thanksgiving dinner. Mrs. Goodrich told of one woman she knew who had finally cut the plug off the television.

The class discussed the various theories of why professional football is so popular with men: that it is controlled warfare; that men like violence and aggression; that watching football is one of the last male preserves; that it is an escape from the problems of touch with their boyhoods; that it is a game that allows men to hug and pat each other; that Monday night football extends the week-end.

"To a point," said Mrs. Peck, "this is healthy. But it can become an addiction, a distancing from the family members, an excuse to tell them to be quiet and go away."

"Women may watch TV," said Mrs. Shapiro, "but not with such lust! My husband lies on the bed watching football in *our bedroom* and doesn't even want me in the same room because I might make noise. It's disgusting!"

The husband of one woman taking the course has asked if Mrs. Peck could accompany the two of them to football games to answer his wife's questions so he won't be distracted.

"I don't know," said Mrs. Shapiro, "maybe it's my fault. I feel excluded when my husband and my two sons are watching the games. But I've never asked to be taught."

Mrs. Goodrich said that she understood the feeling of exclusion, explaining that in her previous marriage "it was an all-male club watching the games, with me doing the cooking.

"He was always a fan," she continued, "but we were married in the early 1960s when we did other things and there wasn't so much football. Finally, there wasn't time for anything else."

Mrs. Peck had to admit that her husband was home playing the piano, and Enid Feldman, founder of the Learning Nexus of Valley Stream, New York, which is offering the course, said that her husband was teaching a bread baking course. "That can be a problem, too," she said. "He practices a lot and gets very involved with reading his recipes."

On a blackboard, Mrs. Peck outlined the National Football League by conferences, divisions, and teams. She also diagrammed a "pro-set offense" facing a "three-four" defense, identifying each position. She also used an electric football game to explain formations. The women were perplexed.

Mrs. Peck brought the women up to date on professional football news of the week, including the Jets' announced move to New Jersey, the fracas at Studio 54 involving Jets players, and Bubba Smith's charge that the 1969 Super Bowl game was fixed. One woman said that she would bring these "important issues" up at the dinner table.

Some were taking the course for reasons other than pleasing their husbands. Arline Dreyfus wanted to learn about football to determine a safe position for her teenage son. After three weeks of class, she had determined that position to be "bench."

Lisa Muscarella had said that she was attending the class because she had been a cheerleader in high school and never knew what she was cheering about. Harriet Rand said that her daughter is a football fan and "needs somebody to watch the games with."

Then came the practical exercise, with the class watching the first half of the Jets-Buffalo Bills game, during which Mrs. Peck pointed out the significance of such things as the "man in motion" and "field-goal attempts."

She had said that teaching the women too much could be a problem, because their husbands might feel threatened, but this fear seemed groundless.

"Do you know what a field goal is?" she asked Mrs. Rand. "I know nothing," Mrs. Rand responded, asking Mrs. Peck to point out the quarterback. "Should we be cheering now?" she asked.

When she explained that the defensive team was not allowed to touch the punter, Mrs. Marsh looked at her and asked, "How in the *world* would a person ever know something like that?"

Harriet Schnapp smiled and said, "I just like the part where they say 'Hi, Mom' to the camera. I don't know, I just like that."

Class was dismissed.

LIFE WITH ECO-FATHER

Sol Levine is an ecologist.

His wife and two teenagers are not.

He says, however, that all it takes to live together in harmony are a few compromises.

Like with the television. When Sol became irritated at his kids lying in front of the TV all the time, he built a bicycle generator that they have to pedal to watch it. This saves energy and encourages physical exercise while discouraging TV watching, he explains.

It's this spirit of compromise—the kind that led to the agreement with Hiroshima in 1945—that pervades the Levine household.

Sol and Georgia had been married for many years when he began developing an interest in ecology. Nothing wrong with that, except it was sort of like when Mayor Daley began taking an interest in politics. A few short years later, Sol, forty-three, is president of the North Shore Ecology Center in Highland Park and a changed man.

He recently moved his family into a new, low-energy, solar-heated home in Highland Park. He shows it off proudly. There is a furnace in the house, but he assures me he shopped around for a long, long time to find one that small. There are no pilot lights on the stove, no dishwasher, there are water saving fixtures on all the taps, and his toilet uses little more than half what yours and mine do.

This small, three-bedroom house is a demonstration project for him. He keeps records on use of gas and electricity, because he's trying to prove that this kind of housing is feasible.

He traded in the family car for a little subcompact that other members of the family claim is painfully cramped. He'd like to get rid of the subcompact but is waiting until electric cars are perfected. He has built an electric three-wheel bike that he uses for town travel. He also watches his diet, is leaning toward being a vegetarian, and is trying to avoid junk food.

Trouble is, Sol's demonstration project is his family's home, and Georgia says she really has no interest in ecology.

"I guess I'm a guzzler," she says, speaking of her propensity for common wastefulness. "At first he tried to convince us. Then he saw we would go just so far and he gave up. He decided we were too normal, or 'spoiled,' as he often says.

"I go along pretty much," she says, "but sometimes have to put my foot down, like with the stove and refrigerator."

Sol bragged that his refrigerator used only as much energy as a 100-watt bulb: "We could have had one that used only as much as a seventy-five-watt bulb, but she insisted on a self-defrosting model."

Compromise.

"This house is much smaller than the one we had before," she says, "which is fine for cleaning but not for entertaining. We can't have anyone over." She says she'd like a larger home, a color TV (a major battle Sol won), and another car, because there are three drivers in the family. She won on the electric alarm clock because the windup one wasn't getting the kids out of bed. Neither does the electric, but at least it annoys them while they lie there.

She "source separates," as Sol would say, the garbage, washing bottles and cans and bundling newspapers, all of which go to the local recycling center run by Sol's group.

There have been other compromises. Sol hasn't allowed his son, Bennet, seventeen, to have lizards and other pets, because Sol doesn't think animals should be penned up like that. They do have a dog. Needless to say, Bennet didn't get the car he asked for, but his father has stopped objecting to his playing an electric guitar—Sol thought it should be acoustic, not electric. His using up energy to power his stereo is still a bone of contention.

The hamsters that daughter Lynda, thirteen, purchased were taken back to the store and replaced by Sol with a telescope she can watch bluejays with in the back yard. She has been denied her right as an American teenager to an electric hairdryer.

Does Sol have any secret vices? "My job [advertising]. I make television commercials [for soft drinks, even]. Also, sugar cookies and pound cake, when they're around.

"But vices?" Sol says. "You make me sound like a saint."

No, Sol, you may be an environmental hero someday for trying to save us from ruining our minds, bodies, and planet.

But Georgia; she's the one who woke up one morning with Eco-Man in bed with her and talks about it without a trace of resentment.

She would be the saint.

She has also made a full confession that the minute you leave town she and the kids pop TV dinners in the oven and haul out the Twinkies and Ho Ho's—and bless her heart.

CHARITY BEGINS AT HOME

This is a little story containing several elements central to suburban living: parents, children, shared family experiences, coping with the high cost of living, the station wagon, and the garage sale.

Suburbanites are stealing goods out of Salvation Army and Goodwill drop boxes and selling the goods at their garage sales. They drop their children through small openings (three feet by eight inches on the Salvation Army boxes), have the kids throw the contents out, and load up the station wagon.

A woman from Oak Park called the other day to say she had just seen a sweater at a neighbor's garage sale that she had deposited in a Salvation Army drop box three days before. She was mad. "I give these things for the poor and needy, not so some bitch can make money off them at her garage sale."

The people at the Salvation Army weren't surprised. When they first noticed the phenomenon a few years ago, they were; but now they get several calls a week on the problem. They, like Goodwill, put the vast majority of their boxes in the suburbs to avoid city vandalism and to reap the castoffs of the wealthy and relatively wealthy.

"We've caught two families—fathers and their kids—in the Des Plaines–Park Ridge area in the last six months," says Captain Marcus Stilwell of the Salvation Army. "The fathers drove station wagons and made regular rounds, dropping the kids into the boxes."

Stilwell, who is in charge of about one hundred suburban boxes, says they caught one woman who stole regularly from the boxes for her garage sales and returned the items that didn't sell.

In the affluent north Cook County area, Captain Ron Carlson says he gets two or three calls a week from police or citizens reporting thefts from the boxes. He says he had just signed a complaint in Northfield and had reports of a woman with two kids and a station wagon working the Evanston area.

Brigadier Frank Hovelman, in charge of Salvation Army boxes in the south suburbs, says there's no doubt much of the stuff is being peddled at garage sales as well as secondhand shops. "These people in the suburbs aren't taking it from need, they're just trying to make a buck," he says.

Up in Lake County, the routine has been escalated by a man in a red "Say It With Flowers" truck, who Salvation Army spokesmen say makes the rounds of all their boxes and holds regular rummage sales. "He makes pickups all over—Lake Bluff, Mundelein, Lake Zurich, Waukegan, all over," says Captain Romulo Giudice. "He pops the locks and takes what he wants."

Giudice says he goes through forty locks a month on the twenty boxes in his northern area. He and the others report people cut locks, saw through steel bars, rip off the doors with crowbars, and ram the boxes with cars and trucks to get inside.

"It's incredible what these people do," says Carlson. "They really want the goods."

Giudice, whose territory includes some affluent North Shore

suburbs, says he has "never seen such a nice selection of things" as are on sale at his resale shop. "People cast off things a little easier up here."

Among the castoffs found in the hundreds of Salvation Army and Goodwill drop boxes throughout the suburbs: antiques, fur coats, jewelry, tennis racquets, bowling balls, golf clubs (one set from a fuming golfer returning from a particularly bad day on the links), Bill Blass designer suits, Diane Von Furstenberg dresses, alligator shoes, watches, fine china and glassware, cats, dogs, ferrets, canaries in cages, chickens, bagged grass clippings, fires, sacks of groceries put in by mistake, clothes that were supposed to be left at the cleaners, purses and car keys dropped by accident, and people—a two-hour-old healthy baby in a paper bag in Glendale Heights and a young man in Park Ridge, who didn't stick around to explain why he was sitting in a box clad only in a negligee and a smart fur collar.

MOM VS. THE ASTRO BLASTERS

"There is trouble in Centereach," said Ronnie Lamm somberly—and trouble starts with *T*, and that rhymes with *E*, with *V* and also *G*, and that stands for electronic video games.

"These games are corrupting our youth," Mrs. Lamm said, filling her Mr. Coffee machine and taking a seat at the kitchen dinette. "They are not wholesome.

"They mesmerize our children, they addict them and force them to mindlessly pour one quarter after another into the slots. We see fifteen-year-olds playing these games at ten-thirty on school nights and during school hours. We want them out of our town."

Mrs. Lamm is one of a rapidly growing army that is rising up in communities across the country to beat back the tide of Space Invaders, Asteroids, and Astro Blasters. She sees the onslaught of this technology as a particular problem here in the suburbs, where there are more children—with more money to spend—and where, she believes, there are fewer cultural activities than in the city.

"Suddenly, they are everywhere," Mrs. Lamm said of the video games, "in our mall, the shopping centers, pizza places, movie theaters, little corner delicatessens, and even the laundromat."

She poured a cup of coffee. "We hear unacceptable language

and see antisocial behavior in the arcades," she continued. "Only
the bad kids go into them, and we worry about the young children
not old enough to make value judgments. Those without strong
moral codes can be drawn in. They don't know they are hooked.

"The game rooms teach gambling and breed aggressive behavior," she said. "And so many are operated by scum coming out of
the woodwork, whose only interest is a fast buck. They say that
they do not allow the drinking of alcoholic beverages, but I have
seen bottles in the parking lots."

Mrs. Lamm implied that the video games were driving young
people to crime. "Children snatch purses and gold chains for
money to put in these machines," she said. Others in her crusade to
ban the games from the community have said they believe that the
games inflict emotional, mental, and spiritual damage on young
people and even physical damage to their eyes—not to mention lit-
ter outside the game rooms.

There are those who believe that it is too late for Mrs. Lamm and
her counterparts to stem the tide of this expanding $5 billion indus-
try. They argue that with the games as ubiquitous in some communities like Centereach, Long Island, as slot machines are in Las
Vegas, the battle for the hearts and minds of America's children is
lost. They say that the games are infiltrating our homes—millions
of games on December 25 alone—and that they will soon be offered on cable television.

Mrs. Lamm is unfazed. "We will be victorious," she said, advis-
ing the faint of heart not to underestimate the power of motherhood in this country. She pointed to a number of recent victories
against the likes of Space Panic, Berzerk, and Gorf. When she began
speaking out on this issue, there were seventeen applications to
open video-game parlors on one three-mile strip in her community.
Twelve of those applications have been denied by local officials,
while the other five have been dropped.

She poured another cup of coffee. She persuaded the Town of
Brookhaven, which comprises her community and several others,
to place a six-month moratorium on the issuance of game-room
permits. Her relentless campaign has included circulating petitions,
making speeches before official bodies and community groups,
sending out mass mailings, and talking with state officials about leg-
islation to control the games. Other tactics have included making
calls to the fire department to check for overcrowded conditions at

the more popular amusement centers. Just how far controls can go is expected to be decided in a Texas case now before the U.S. Supreme Court.

Fellow crusaders against the games in other communities call Mrs. Lamm to compare notes, and through parent-teacher-association conventions and other gatherings, a loose-knit army is developing throughout the state and the nation. One member of this network notified her that President Ferdinand E. Marcos of the Philippines had banned video games on November 19 after parents had complained that the games were wreaking "havoc on the morality of the nation's youth."

"We are finding it surprisingly easy, actually," Mrs. Lamm said of the triumphs. "Some of those who want to open these places are the absolute dregs, and they are battling motherhood and apple pie."

Mrs. Lamm spoke of the soul-searching she went through before she decided to speak out on this issue. "Some of the little shopkeepers, the mom-and-pop stores, are having a tough time staying open," she said, "and they can make $500 a month by putting in one of these machines. But our children are more important, and we want the games out.

"There are those who would say that I am a hatchet queen of amusement centers," she said, "but I do not see myself as a hatchet queen of amusement centers. I have even been in these game rooms. I did not play the games, for the same reasons I did not gamble when I was in Puerto Rico.

"Parents are busy these days, and we want them to be vigilant. Like, I am busy, and sometimes I find squishy fruit in the refrigerator and I have to stop and say, 'Whoa!'—my family has not been eating fruit." She said that she sees to it that her children are involved in such activities as gymnastics and religious classes.

At Football World, one of Mrs. Lamm's primary targets, adults, parents with their children, and numerous teenagers pointed out that anything in excess is bad, including milk, and that certainly the silicon chip has an enormous capacity for good and evil.

Speaking for the majority, fourteen-year-old Andrew Bershad looked up from a Pac-Man game and said: "I do my homework. They should give a kid a break."

THE FAMILY DOG IN THE YAP OF LUXURY

Twenty-nine million of the nation's fifty million dogs live in the suburbs. I know. Most of them go to the bathroom in my yard.

Dogs are still very much a part of the suburban dream, and it could be suggested that most owners seem certifiably nuts about them. Pet stores out here sell auto safety belts for dogs, bikinis, wrist (paw) watches, and maternity wear. We have dog psychologists and attorneys who specialize in representing dogs that attack people and violate pooper scooper ordinances. We have Date-A-Dog, a match-making service for dogs. We have a half-dozen large dog cemeteries, one with a chapel where ministers hold funeral services. Last week about one hundred thousand suburbanites attended a pet parade.

Now comes the pet vacation.

"Will Your Best Friend Spend Your Vacation Behind Bars?" asks the headline over the forlorn-looking caged dog in a suburban newspaper advertisement. "Does your best friend worry while you are away? Does he come home with kennel stress? The preferable alternative is a Fido Farms Vacation. Your best friend will be placed in a specially selected, loving rural home where he will receive individual attention and care . . ."

Kennel Stress? Yes, and there's Kennel Cough, too, explains Linda Bush, who heads Fido Farms Vacations.

The pet owner fills out a Pet Information Form listing the dog's likes, dislikes, and details of its homelife. The pet is matched to one of Fido Farms' fifteen to twenty rural families. The pet is picked up at home in a converted thirty-foot motor home with solid oak suites, called a Luxury Land Liner, and driven to the country for a restful respite.

"Owners send along toys and slippers and blankets and run alongside the Luxury Liner waving good-bye," Linda says. "We spoil the dogs and send them home in Fido Farms T-shirts. The only problem we have is convincing some of the dogs to go home."

If a restful respite in the country just isn't your dog's bowl of water, send the dog to the Countryside Animal Spa to be whipped into shape. As spa owner Bernie Brown is wont to say, "Give me your dog for ten days and I'll make a new man out of him." He'll throw that flabby mutt of yours on his patented Dog-A-Sizer, an electric dog walking/jogging machine that runs the little fellas in a circle. He'll toss him in the Jacuzzi. He'll feed him his special custom-mixed high-potency dog food. He'll put him on an herbal diet if he thinks the dog needs it, and give him vitamins.

The specially trained staff at this half-million-dollar fitness palace will massage your dog and give him deep-heat treatments with infrared lamps. They'll get that dry skin and mangy fur back into shape with oil baths.

If your dog doesn't need all this, you can just board him here in a room done by an interior decorator, with a private run, air-conditioning, and FM stereo.

There is also the American Pet Motel, which opened in 1973 as a pioneer in lavish accommodations for pets. With their Imperial package, the dog sleeps on a brass four-poster bed, with a mattress and clean sheets every day. Owners bring favorite toys and specify special diets and treats, according to Robert Leeds, president of the American Pet Motel. "For some we cook bacon and eggs, others, ice cream sodas and sundaes. To one we gave two sticks of Juicy Fruit gum every day. TV dinners are also becoming quite popular."

Leeds says one owner recently gave him a bag with a china plate in it that he said his dog has to eat from. "There was a fork in the bag, too," Leeds says.

Leeds says owners send their pets postcards, "which we guarantee we'll read to the pet." A lot of postcards also come in to the swank Inne Towne Pet Motel, which features limousine service to and from the motel. "We feel kind of silly sometimes," says office manager Joan Kowalczyk, "but we read them. Sometimes owners send taped messages, too.

"The owners call, sometimes daily and sometimes from overseas, to see how their pets are," she says. "We recently had a call from a woman in Colorado who wanted to speak to her German shepherd. We don't have room phones so we brought the dog up and put the receiver to his ear. He wagged his tail and licked the phone."

Pet Vacations is a pet-sitting service. "I find homes to baby-sit pets for people going on vacation," says owner Jeanne Tusler. "I'm very careful with my home studies; I only take about two in ten that want to become part of my network. I'm very careful to match the pet with the right home.

"Sitters cater to all their whims. Shaun, an Irish setter, likes to go to McDonald's twice a week for a cheeseburger, fries, and a chocolate shake. We take him. He brings his own coupons."

☞Turning to News A Little Closer to Home

Today we turn to news a little closer to home.

I am lying there at three-thirty Saturday morning having a nice little dream about being on a scenic trail ride that was just about to reach the Grand Canyon when my wife wakes me up and says she's nine months pregnant!

I look over at her and ask if she could hold it for a few more minutes because I've never seen the Grand Canyon.

"I think I'm going to have the baby," she says softly.

Speaking to her from the nether world, I offer to boil up some newspapers, if that will help.

Then, Consciousness!

I leap out of bed in the darkness and head for the bathroom to get my shaving kit, remembering—as excited as I am—to stub my toe on the bedpost as is my custom. *Aieee!*

I close the door to the bathroom and flip on the light. *Aieee!* I regain partial vision, if not my composure, and begin packing: a tube of Mentholatum Deep Heat Rub to brush my teeth, Milk of Magnesia for shaving, and two 5-Day deodorant pads, torn in half because I only figure to be there a couple of days.

Turning the knob on the bathroom door, a voice inside my head says, "Stupid! Youuu aren't the one staying in the hospital, sheee is." Another example of fuzzy thinking.

Perhaps I've just taken all this Lamaze stuff, where the father gets involved, too seriously. I've enjoyed the classes for the last several weeks, learning the huffing and puffing breathing techniques and talking over coffee during class breaks about water bags and mucous plugs. Delightful. Certainly a lot better, one of the mothers says, than sitting home (with a cold beer) watching Monday night football.

I drop the shaving kit, snap off the bathroom light, and stub—

Aieee—my toe on the bedpost going back. The Lamaze teacher had admitted there would be some discomfort.

Jody, the mother in question and without question (she couldn't fit behind the wheel of the Queen Elizabeth), is packing her suitcase. Just what in the hell was it I was supposed to do? Where are my class notes? I begin tossing things out of drawers. She hands the notes to me. "Thanks," I say. "I'm a little nervous." She says she understands.

My list says I'm in charge of packing:

• A focal point, something for her to concentrate on while she does her breathing, all of which distracts her attention from the labor pains . . . I mean, "contractions." I look around for that photo of Larry Slade, the big nude dancer up at the Sugar Shack.

•Some sour candy or something in case her mouth gets dry from all the panting and blowing. She rejects my offer of Lemon Pledge.

• A washcloth to mop her brow. We have one!

• Knee socks. We have been instructed that the calves chill during childbirth. Good, she got some new argyles for Christmas.

• Phone numbers and dimes. I just throw in the phone book. Good thing we live in a suburb and not Chicago. Less weight to carry. With fewer numbers you don't have to take so many dimes either.

• Counterpressure: something to push on her lower back if that's where the pain—contractions—hits. Two tennis balls, oddly enough, are recommended. I dig through the hall closet and come up with a couple of dirty old gray balls that look to be autographed by Bill Tilden. They don't look like there's much bounce left in them. And this racquet needs restringing; probably no place to drop it off at this hour.

• Lunch for the coach, in case it gets drawn out. That's me. What to have?

I turn to Jody, sitting there with her eyes on the ceiling, doing slow, deliberate breathing during a real grabber of a . . . contraction.

"What do you think I should pack for lunch?" I say.

"I think it's time," she says quietly.

"Probably just a sandwich or something," I continue. "Or maybe I'd have time to hollow a tomato and whip up some crab meat salad."

"I think it's about time to go," she says.

Maybe we can stop for a quick slice of pizza on the way. I grab her suitcase and jerk her down the stairs.

"Willie," I say, addressing our son, who has been awakened by the commotion and is standing by the door, "your mother and myself are going to the hospital. Good-bye."

"He's four," my wife interjects.

I call his grandmother, who arrives forthwith. By this time Jody is huffing and puffing, panting and blowing like something out of a roundhouse. I bring the car around like a drug-crazed Loop parking garage attendant, squealing up to the curb. She gets in, a sure sign of desperation.

We lurch to the hospital. Jody marches past a woman standing at the Registration desk, forms at the ready, and straight into a labor (contraction?) room. Luckily, we're alone when I open the bag and the tennis balls bounce across the floor.

"Still some pretty decent bounce left in them," I say.

"No lunch," she says, smiling. That would be the last smile. After enough puffing to get the City of Miami all the way to where it's going, she announces, "I'm having the baby."

I press the red panic button on the table and people come running. They whisk her out the door and down the hall, tossing me a surgery room outfit, complete with shirt, pants, paper hat, mask, and paper shoe covers. The green shoe covers look like hell with my blue outfit, but I don't say anything.

The doctor suggests, "Perhaps she'd be just as comfortable" on what she was wheeled in on as on the delivery table and—still moving to his left—makes a nice two-handed grab of a stunning eight-pound, eleven-ounce redheaded baby girl. Between the argyle knee socks.

THINGS PARENTS KNOW WITH CHILDREN IN TOW

There are scads of books out on quaint old country inns, but none that I know of describing the basements, attics, and annexes—which is where I always seem to wind up when innkeepers see that I have children in tow.

The attic of the annex of the grand old Chalfonte Hotel in Cape May, New Jersey, had a bare light bulb on the ceiling until a maid came in and snapped some sort of little shade onto it—"so the room won't look so bad," she said. It really didn't matter anyway. It's too hot in the attics of old country inns in the summer to turn on a light. Basements of old country inns are always cooler. Parents know this.

Such things as no air-conditioning and baths down the hall are all part of the quaintness of the currently fashionable inns, but still we were a little disheartened to find that our bath was on a different floor. I suppose that didn't really matter in the long run either, since there was no hot water when we got there. Other curious features of this particular attic accommodation included the lack of a closet, and a door just three feet tall leading to the "veranda," which looked quite a lot like a fire escape to us.

The Chalfonte is a wonderful old postcard of a hotel, known for old-fashioned southern charm, with enough white gingerbread frosting to induce insulin shock. It's just that those with children under five years old have to stay out back in the annex (not pictured in the brochure)—a house that a real estate agent might refer to as "a handyman's special." Although several flights up, the attic was its low point.

When the reservation clerk told us over the phone that the annex was "just as nice as the hotel," it had not occurred to me that she might be talking about some other hotel—probably the one that appeared in a Mel Brooks film with a sign out front reading: "Charming to the Unsophisticated."

"It could be worse," my wife remarked, sitting on a cot provided for the children that was so narrow I thought at first it might be something for the fishing rods. "Did you see *Harvest of Shame?*"

Moments after the staff's party outside our window broke up, we went to breakfast in the restaurant of the hotel, which they advertise as being famous for old-fashioned southern dining. It was old-fashioned all right, harkening back to the times before the Emancipation Proclamation. They wouldn't allow our two-and-a-half-year-old daughter into the dining room, charming though she was with her little barrettes. They made her eat with the other short people in a dim little room behind the kitchen.

New England charm turned out to be better than old-fashioned southern charm. Later in the vacation, at the Dana Place Inn, in Pinkham Notch, New Hampshire (actually, the locals say it's in

Jackson, New Hampshire, but you know how these inn people are about quaintness), they had wallpapered their attic, for which we were grateful, since we were ushered there at the first sight of the kids. It wasn't too bad and fairly quiet, since there weren't any other guests up there. Just the help, and not too many of them, which is probably why it took one hour and thirty minutes before a cracker or roll was placed before us in the dining room that night for dinner. Quaint, but tough on the kids, who were allowed in the dining room. Given the opportunity to come out of the mob rule of "family restaurants," children can develop manners rapidly— particularly when threatened with sharp pieces of silverware.

This inn had something for which it could probably be drummed right out of the American Country Quaintness Association, if there was one: Space Invaders. A clear violation. Does L. L. Bean sell video game gear? Did Thoreau play Ms. Pac-Man? I will say that the infernal device sat unplugged in a corner, but eager children and adults took care of that quickly enough. The adults playing the games said that, after a matter of days or even weeks, they had really had it up to here with mountain trails, trout streams, and town after town of white clapboard houses with dark green shutters.

The video game was the only bow to children we saw in a summer of museumesque country inns, many of which didn't even have a high chair or booster seat around. You could have made do by setting the little tykes on telephone books, except the towns were always so small.

In Landgrove, Vermont, we stayed in the Village Inn, an old country inn that makes much of the fact that it is on a real dirt road. There we were sent to what looked like a special section of the inn for families: two Formica-paneled rooms set apart from the rest of the inn, directly above the Ping-Pong table in the children's game room.

At The Moorings in Southwest Harbor, Maine, a cottage outside the hotel had been suggested by the owner, who took our telephone reservation. She told us there were complimentary breakfasts and baby-sitters. Breakfast turned out to be a box of twelve plain doughnuts for the entire inn, which tended to bring out the basest elements of man.

I digress, but why is it that you never set eyes on a plain doughnut unless it's being given away someplace? Can you imagine wak-

ing up on a Sunday morning to these words: "Honey, wake up. I
went out and picked up some plain doughnuts"?

The doughnuts were plain and the baby-sitters were just plain
not around—lost at sea, perhaps, with the advertised and unavaila-
ble sailing instructor. The owner didn't seem to be around either,
come to think of it.

The attitudes of innkeepers toward families with children
chafe a bit, but then, in a lot of respects, they are right about the
little buggers, aren't they? Parents know this. But what are we to
do? Veterinarians won't keep them while we go on vacation, and
grandparents are always lying on the floor of the living room with
the shades drawn and the lights off.

One can obtain symptomatic relief from the occasional pain of
family vacations by having the children take Dramamine when one
gets sick of them. True, the trip is somewhat less educational for
the kids, passed out there on the backseat, but it sharply reduces
the risk of incidental child abuse.

Stopping for the night isn't always pretty either, trying to get
the children to sleep, with everyone right there in one motel room.
The only way is for all to go to sleep at the same time, say 8 P.M. It's
either that or staying up to read in the bathroom. (I would recommend showering in the morning; otherwise the bathroom is too hu-
mid at night and the pages stick together.)

And, I must admit, the children had little appreciation of the
beauty of the Green Mountains of Vermont, the history of
Portsmouth, New Hampshire, the art galleries of Ogunquit, Maine.
They didn't care a whit for rococo revival and lamb's-tongue facings on the Victorian house tours in Cape May. They wanted to play
Skee Ball and menace everyone on the miniature golf courses. As
for the food, they asked for cheeseburgers when innkeepers
proudly presented their country cuisine. They asked for
cheeseburgers when lobster was cheaper. My seven-year-old son
could write a book: *Cheeseburgers of the Maine Coast.*

I suppose I shall never forget the sensation of hiking to the top
of South Bubble Rock on Mount Desert Island in Maine with a small
group of people. As we stood there in the bright sunshine, breathing cool, fresh morning air, looking down upon the deep green
pine forests and the glistening blue lakes, someone tapped me on
the shoulder and pointed to a man holding up the legs of a two-
year-old, whom he had somehow managed to lug all the way up

there. The man was changing a disposable diaper. Someday this will happen on the surface of the moon.

It can change everything, having kids around. But isn't it bad enough that we have to take children with us on our vacations, without being put up in the attic? Isn't parenthood its own punishment?

CHILD-FREE LIVING

As will happen when a group of old, retired people gets together, conversation at the card tables turned to grandchildren on a recent afternoon.

"They are precious," said a kindly looking grandmother, "as long as they're asleep."

"The noise is the worst part," said another man. "Those new tricycles with the plastic wheels make an awful racket, sometimes at 7 A.M."

"You risk your life on the sidewalks," said another woman, "with all of their bicycles and roller skates."

"That gum children chew," said one man, "smells to high heaven. And they leave it in the damnedest places."

"Don't get me wrong," said Sam Mercurio. "I like kids. I just don't like them around."

Mr. Mercurio and the others live in an apartment complex called The Villas, in Patchogue, Long Island, a childless oasis in suburbia, the nursery of the republic. Outside the gates, they see a world where babies drool and toddlers cry in restaurants, where children trample lawns and flower beds while adolescents squeal tires at midnight and hang out on street corners, up to no good.

In advertisements headlined "We Kid You Not," the complex bills itself as a community of "child-free" living; the word "child" here seems to take on the pejorative connotation of a pollutant or an unwanted additive. It is one of an increasing number of apartment and condominium complexes in the New York metropolitan area that bars children.

The Villas prefers residents over the age of sixty-five and bars any children under eighteen. "We want it quiet here," explained Carole Gagnon, the office manager, who conceded that there might be an infrequent complaint about organ music at 3 A.M. "We won't rent to an eighty-year-old on a motorcycle either," she added. She said more younger people were also applying, eager to keep their distance from children. "This is an alternative lifestyle now," she explained.

Marilyn La Corte, a rental agent, has also noticed an increasing number of applications from younger people, particularly teachers and others who work with children during the day. "They all begin by saying, 'It's not that we don't like children, but . . .' They're very leery of how they put it. A lot of them have had children themselves and have just had it. They want peace and quiet now."

The brochures themselves are something of a mild sedative: The Villas "provides the kind of privacy and tranquility you'll come to cherish," adding, "No neighbors above or below, no children's bicycles, toys, or games . . . none of the hustle and bustle of getting youngsters off to school in the morning or to bed at night."

Indeed, said one of the residents, at night it is so quiet you can hear a tube of Poli-Dent drop.

The brochure goes on to say: "Living at The Villas, you'll enjoy the company of neighbors with interests and attitudes similar to yours."

"We've just had enough," said Ruth Kramer, a resident of the 280-unit complex who seemed to speak for the majority. "Many of us have children and grandchildren and we don't miss all the crying and screaming and running and jumping. I do love children, though."

Children and grandchildren under eighteen may visit. "You certainly know when they're here," Madeline Lapetina said with the flash of a smile. "And the best part, of course," added her card partner, Nancy Clark, "is when they go home."

"Personally, I hate kids," said Joe Pella, causing his poker partners to break into laughter. "We like to sleep in and we so enjoy not having kids outside in the morning to wake us."

However, another elderly man at the table, William Esposito, said he lives across the street, in the La Bonne Vie II apartment complex, which does allow children, because: "Frankly, I don't like old people."

One teenager living in La Bonne Vie II suggested that it was "dangerous" to go across the street into The Villas. "They'll chase you," he said. Fencing has been put up where children tend to venture across into The Villas.

The concept of "child-free" communities reportedly originated in retirement areas of Florida and Arizona and is now spreading throughout the country, despite questions as to its legality. The practice of individual landlords not accepting tenants with children, however, is an old one that is also increasingly prevalent, according to recent studies.

Apartment seekers in Manhattan report they are routinely turned away because they have children. Many museums, movie theaters, and restaurants in the city ban young children and many more give the children and their parents a cool reception. "But there," said one resident of The Villas, "it's young people without children who don't like them."

But if Manhattan sometimes seems to have an antichild bias, children seem to be the raison d'être for the suburbs. "They're everywhere," said one resident of The Villas, speaking of children in the suburbs. Another said that while he "didn't mind" children, he viewed the closing of schools throughout the suburbs, triggered by declining enrollments, as cause for "cautious optimism." One man said he "loves children" but has tired of tripping over roller skates and baby strollers. Another would only say of his desire to live in a "child-free" community, "I have my reasons."

Residents of the complex said they are here for the companionship of others their age, trying to buy a little peace and quiet. They said they came here seeking refuge from sticky little fingers and dirty little hands, from muddy shoes and high-pitched voices that shriek in the afternoon and cry at night. Most of them were grandparents. None offered to show any pictures.

XI

RELIGION
AND IDOLS

☛ SUPER SUNDAY

At 4:21 P.M., Westchester County looked as if it had been hit by a neutron bomb. There were no signs of outdoor life on block after block yesterday afternoon—perhaps the only time of the year when this is so.

This is a country where each is free to observe Super Bowl Sunday in his or her own way. About one hundred million people were expected to watch yesterday's Super Bowl XVI, according to pregame estimates—a lot of them at Walter Peek's house in New Rochelle, New York, it seemed at kickoff time as guests jousted for drinks, dip, and viewing positions.

"It started so simply," said Mr. Peek, a football fan who recalled inviting four couples over to watch Super Bowl I on television. Like the game itself, his annual party seems to have grown more colossal every year. By Super Bowl IV, the party had become so large that viewing it on television was a problem.

Mr. Peek, the fifty-five-year-old owner of a paper company, who was remembered by some at the party this year for inventing a portable backpack Scotch and soda machine in his days at Cornell University, erected bleachers for Super Bowl IV in the then-unfurnished living room of his spacious home. The bleachers collapsed, but even the wounded returned the next year.

Over the years, his daughters and their friends began serving as cheerleaders, dressed in the colors of the two Super Bowl teams. His sons sold hot dogs. Mr. Peek passed out official programs obtained through business contacts. A barbershop quartet began singing at the halftimes, accompanying twirlers of flaming batons.

"My wife is a marvelous woman," Mr. Peek said. Still, when she finally decorated the living room, Mrs. Peek told him to move the bleachers outside, where this year as many as two hundred guests wearing hats and coats watched the game on a giant-screen television under a tent.

For the overflow from the bleachers, there were television sets in nearly every room in the house, including the bathrooms. The house was decorated in pennants, banners, tackling dummies, and other paraphernalia. A Greek statue in the foyer was outfitted in shoulder pads and a football helmet.

"Frankly," said Mrs. Peek, viewing the mayhem, "I cried when I heard the football strike was over."

At the moment of kickoff in suburban Rye, a cheer went up inside the home of Lloyd Dean, where about one hundred people gathered around four television sets to celebrate. More than half the group—some of whom were dressed in football jerseys, helmets, and cheerleader outfits—were unaware that the game had begun. "This is a national holiday," said John Naclerio, dressed in a cheerleader's sweater and skirt. "I don't really care about the game."

Many in Rye were attending traditional Super Bowl parties such as the one in the Dean household, some of which began with brunch at 10 A.M. and took in hours of pregame television programs. Many other fans gathered in boisterous barrooms offering giant-screen televisions and free pizza at halftime, while some others held simple family gatherings. Many zealots chose to watch the game more intently, alone with the phone off the hook, at one with their sets.

Bill Cerasoli, a late-arriving guest at the Deans' party, had watched the game on the way over in his car on a television plugged into the cigarette lighter. He had a packet imprinted "Super Bowl Survival Kit" containing Bloody Mary mix, an ounce of vodka, peanuts, and a kazoo.

"People go crazy during Super Bowl week," said Bill Palmieri, owner of a Westchester TV repair shop. "Their sets break and they come in here like it's life or death. They're panic-stricken." He said many demanded that he rush to their homes in paramedic fashion to fix the sets. "I'm loaning some TVs now," he said Saturday. "I'm a fan. I understand this is an emergency." A few people react in this way when their televisions break down before the Macy's Thanksgiving Day parade or before a popular television series, he said, "but the Super Bowl is important to everybody."

"This is our biggest week of the year," said Giovanni Cozzi, owner of New York Video, which sells and rents video units as large as ten feet in the Westchester area. Most popular is the six-and-a-half-foot screen model that sells quickly during Super Bowl week at $3,300 or rents for Super Bowl Sunday at $425.

"This has always been a big holiday," said Charles Weil, owner of a suburban party goods store, The Party Box, "and it gets bigger every year." He had sold out all four thousand of his Dolphins- and Redskins-imprinted drinking glasses. Also moving well were imprinted napkins and banners, pompons in the colors of the two teams, and centerpieces with miniature football players in the teams' colors. He was stuck with thousands of Dallas Cowboys items he had preordered. "I was so sure," he said.

Food is an important part of watching the game and Mr. Weil sells industrial-sized containers of potato chips and pretzels specially marked "for Super Bowl viewing." Local bakeries were selling Super Bowl cakes. A guest at the Deans' party said she decided not to attend a neighbor's Super Bowl party when she learned that the neighbor was serving "things like popcorn mixed with dried apricots—she saw it on a Super Bowl snacks TV special."

One store in the Rye area was holding a "Super Bowl liquidation sale." Several businesses still open at the kickoff reported that they were largely empty, with clerks listening to the game on radios or huddled around small-screen TVs at checkout counters. A few of the large suburban banquet halls that cater to wedding receptions and bar mitzvahs had booked Super Bowl parties, but most were empty. "Normally we would have six or eight large affairs today," said a spokesman for the Fountainhead in New Rochelle. "But we have none scheduled today. No one in their right mind schedules anything on Super Bowl Sunday."

In some outlying suburban communities, Super Bowl Sunday is described as "the biggest day of the year." In Sayreville, New Jersey, it has long been considered an honor to be among the chosen few to attend the all-male festivities at Swanee's Bar and Grill.

In Manhattan, however, some commemorate in a backhanded fashion the national ritual of watching the game, holding "anti-Super Bowl parties." Said one New Yorker who informed her escort that she had to be home early from a classical music presentation to watch the game: "Manhattan is probably the only place in America where you are embarrassed to tell people you watch the Super Bowl."

At the Deans' party in Rye, one of the guests said that outside one church in the area, the Super Bowl was listed as the topic of today's sermon. After all, the Reverend Dr. Norman Vincent Peale once said, "If Jesus were alive today, he would be at the Super Bowl."

Earlier in the day in New Rochelle, Linda Ann Baker was lugging a case of beer home from the local store for her own Super Bowl party. "It's my favorite holiday," she said, explaining that it was a holiday when the whole family now got together, but one in which she didn't have to worry about buying gifts or sending cards. Things haven't gone that far, not yet.

Mary Murray, a guest at the Peeks' party, suggested after watching televised interviews with even the Super Bowl grounds keepers that the Peeks threw the only party that really befit the Super Bowl: "Large, crazy, and out of control."

After the game began, one guest at that party looked at all the people talking, drinking, and ignoring both the Dolphins and the Redskins on TV. The guest worried that, as with other holiday celebrations, perhaps the whole reason for the holiday that is Super Bowl Sunday had been forgotten.

☛ PRAYER OF THANKSGIVING

We in the suburbs of America are blessed with more of what life today has to offer than any other people on earth, and for this we offer our prayer of Thanksgiving.

Thank you for the world so sweet,
Thank you for the food we eat;
Thank you for the birds that sing,
Thank you, God, for Burger King.

Thank you for Big Macs and Denny's,
Arthur Treacher's, Ho-Jo's, Wendy's;
Rustler, Sizzler, IHOP, Lum's,
Maalox II, Rolaids, and Tums.

Thanks for cans of Spam untold,
For Muzak when we are on hold;
Thanks for Gucci cowboy boots,
And polyester leisure suits.

Thank you for 7-Up in liters,
For Popcorn Pumpers and Weed Eaters;
Thank you for Lite Beer from Miller,
For Open Pit and Weber Grillers.

Thanks for Colortrac and Trinitron,
For regular visits from ChemLawn;
For male dancers in the nude,
Thank you for generic food.

Thanks for aerobics classes at the Y,
For the garage door's electronic eye;
For freedom to pump our own fuel,
And check-cashing privileges at the Jewel.

Thanks for Moose and Elks and Rotary,
For Junior League and K. of C.;
Thank you, Father, for Potscrubber III,
And for RVs with C.B.

Thanks for PTA and granola bars,
For Battles of the Network Stars;
For Tru-Value's sale on driveway toppings,
For Congoleums that need no mopping.

Thank you for garage sale goods,
and station wagons with plastic woods;
For Tuna Helper and Baco-Bits,
Velveeta and No-Pest Strips.

Thank you for right on red,
Thank you, God, for Wonder Bread;
For Barcaloungers and La-Z-Boys,
For Never Paint gutters and Star Wars toys.

Thank you, God, for aluminum siding,
Keep our patio doors sliding;
For S.O.S. in boil-in-bags,
For designer jeans that lift the sags.

We thanketh thee for car pools,
To transport our youth to hockey schools;
For trash bags of polyethylene,
And contented herds of Sizzlean.

Thanks for half-fare coupons, closer shaves,
For Fry Daddys and microwaves;
For Dial-A-Prayer, good for our souls,
Blue water in our toilet bowls.

For Community, Venture, and Kmart,
Thank you, God, for sofa-sized art;
For Bug Zappers crackling in the night,
And to light the darkness, Luvu Lite.

For Polyglycoat and for Zayre,
For friends who sell us Tupperware;
For plastic flamingos that never fade,
Thank you, God, for Ultra-Suede.

We've come a ways since Plymouth Rock,
To Sans-A-Belt and electric woks;
To a feast of turkey loaf that's Stove Top stuffed,
Three hundred fifty years of progress, sure enough.

A CHURCH OF ANOTHER COLOR

On occasion, residents of Litchfield, Connecticut, a little community in the Berkshire foothills, will look up to find tourists standing in their front hallways and living rooms.

They live in a community easily mistaken for a living museum, with its pure white Congregational church overlooking a village green (complete with cannon) and block after block of white clapboard homes with black or dark green shutters. The National Park Service once described it as perhaps the "finest surviving example of a typical late-eighteenth-century New England town."

Now, pigmentation has reared its ugly head in Litchfield, and many residents are strenuously objecting to what they see as this corrosion of colonial charm. The Methodists have painted their white church a color, several colors actually—light gold and dark gold with blue window sash, not to mention the tricolored roof in gold and two shades of brown.

"Horrible," said Gertrude O'Donnell, a lifelong resident, expressing a popular view here. "It's just a lousy shame."

Similarly appalled, Doyle Finan, a member of the Borough Board of Burgesses, has suggested restrictions on coloration in the community and expects a vote next week on restricting the hues of roofing shingles and vinyl and aluminum siding. Arguing that visitors come to Litchfield because of the colonial beauty of the all-white homes, he agreed with those who have speculated that painting the houses and buildings could destroy that charm and stop the tourists from coming.

"I firmly believe the town should be all white," said Mr. Finan, adding that he also feared the painting of the church might "open the floodgates" and inundate the community with all manner of

Valley Forge Greens, Minute Man Blues, Colony Reds, and Spring-field Rifle Grays, available just down the street at Switer's paint and lumber.

The man behind the counter there, Nick Platt, said he did not sell a can of pigmented exterior paint in a month of Sundays. He guessed that most houses in town were an exterior oil-based white, with the shutters a mix of Copper Verde and black, combined to form the darkest of greens.

"I like the look of the church," he admitted. "After all, this is 1982." Then he cogitated, took a puff on his cigar, and added, "But you can't beat white. Face it."

The United Methodist Church suffered extensive damage in a fire a year ago, and the new paint job is part of the reconstruction. After the December 20 blaze, the small congregation did what the Reverend Janna T. Steed described as "some serious soul-searching" on whether the church would or could afford to go on. When the decision was made to rebuild, the vibrant color seemed appropriate. "We wanted to say we're here! We're alive!" she explained.

Mr. Finan's fear of an outbreak of coloration is not without foundation. The Litchfield Historical Society is cited as perhaps the first major offender, having painted two of the town's most histori-cally significant buildings—the Tapping Reeve House and the Law School—"peach" and "gray," respectively, to the utter dismay of many local residents. A fabric store near the church was painted a rusty-red color just last week, to their continuing chagrin. All agree, however, that none of these examples are as egregious as the golden church in the heart of town.

It seems, however, that the so-called traditionalists who favor white may not have history and tradition on their side. A great many of the white, shuttered houses and buildings in Litchfield—and throughout New England—were not white with dark shutters to begin with and became white only through what a local archi-tect, Thomas Babbit, sees as some latter-day crusade of uninformed "Colonialization." The Victorian-style Methodist church was origi-nally dark brown and dark gray.

Mr. Babbit, who has studied local buildings in detail and sug-gested the church's new color, said many of the eighteenth-century buildings and homes were originally not white and did not even have shutters. Shutters, he said, did not come into fashion until somewhere between 1815 and 1830 and were installed not for practical considerations but to soften the lines of the rather stark Greek Revival houses.

Few of the Victorian homes here, which were first built during the mid-nineteenth century, were originally white either, according to Mr. Babbit. Rather, he said, during the last fifty years such things as piazzas, towers, turrets, gables, and porches have been removed from houses in the interest of some notion of colonial homogeneity. "We have lost so many beautiful buildings to an architectural mishmash," he said.

"Historical accuracy," countered Mr. Finan, "can be carried too far."

 **SANTA** Like so many red-suited Israeli commandos, several platoons of Santas descended on the Chicago area this weekend.

Many were airlifted by helicopter to suburban shopping center landing zones, while others arrived in red personnel carriers of various types—fire trucks, "space ships" on wheels, and decorated golf carts.

None parachuted. The Santa-as-paratrooper idea was abandoned several years ago, according to promotion people, when somewhere or other the little chute on one of the elves preceding Santa failed to open, and Santa froze in the doorway, refusing to jump.

Where do these legions of Santas come from? The same place certified public accountants, key punch operators, Israeli commandos, and everyone else in this age of specialization come from: schools.

Santa schools. Western Temporary Services, Inc., the world's largest supplier of Santas, has a University of Santa Claus. You apply, submit a transcript of work experience, and are interviewed.

Though Western recruits for Santas in fire and police stations, colleges, and senior citizens homes (age is not an object), the company is still apparently looking for only a few good men. Company literature claims they accept only one in twenty-three who apply.

Those who make it receive a diploma from the University of Santa Claus only after completing the training and working one season as a Santa, during which time they will be inspected on the job by an instructor.

"We stand behind our Santas," says Pauline Wehr, a USC instructor on the Norridge campus. "They have to be good."

"Our Santas must bring joy and happiness to the retail situation," says Jenny Zink, who is national marketing coordinator for Western's Santa Division and has overall responsibility for the company's more than two thousand Santas in the United States and abroad.

There are three key things they look for in the interviews preceding admission to the USC. Does the applicant like children? Is the applicant jolly? Does the applicant believe in Santa Claus?

Interviewers are told to look for "twinkling, smiling eyes and a fairly full face, and a fairly deep resonant voice." This means trouble for most women who apply. Because of the voice and facial features, most women are washed out here and placed in Western's Mrs. Santa/Santa's Helper training program.

Candidates should "smile frequently . . . be neat and clean in mind and body . . . robust and healthy; it is suggested that eyeglasses, hearing aids, etc., not be worn." They must drive their own cars, have telephones, and not hold other jobs that might conflict.

I audited one of the courses on the Norridge campus last week, just a couple of days before uniformed students took their places in several suburban Marshall Field stores, Goldblatt's in the new Louis Joliet mall, Wieboldt's in Evanston, Sears in Oak Brook, and a variety of other stores, banks, and shopping centers throughout the Chicago area.

School study materials point out: "The Western Santa technique is a proven method . . . it leaves out the margin for error possible in any Santa interview." A "Santa interview" is a child sitting on Santa's lap.

That technique includes promising nothing. One veteran Santa in a Norridge class said he was kicked in the shins three times last year because the Santa the year before had promised toys that didn't come. Jenny Zink says they had one Santa who was bashed in the head with a Tonka truck on this very issue and had to go out and "feed the reindeer"—the excuse Santa uses for all temporary absences—while the doctors stitched up the wound.

One veteran Santa said he was "wet on" twice last year and had to feed the reindeer.

Today's Santa always uses the term "folks" rather than "mother" or "father" due to the high divorce rate. Santa stonewalls it when asked for a baby brother or sister. Western's statistics show 5 percent of all little girls make that request.

Today's Santa does not say, "Ho, Ho, Ho"; Western's research shows it scares the kids.

Western's bonded, fully insured Santas don't get p.o.ed and go home when a teenager pulls off their beard, because Western has legally binding contracts to have a Santa in the store. He feeds the reindeer for a while.

Every night Santa rinses out and drip-dries his white gloves that he is required to wear by state law while handling children.

Santa puts down on his time card only "sitting" time, and never the time to and from his home. Santa will have his time card signed by the store manager or he doesn't get his $3.50 an hour.

Santa does not wear brown wing tips with his outfit: only black shoes, preferably boots.

Santa is not to tell the children that they have to have a $3 photograph taken or they won't get anything for Christmas.

Santa splits fifty-fifty with Western on anything he gets for doing private parties while in his company-supplied Santa suit. This is to protect Santa because his insurance and workman's compensation don't cover him on private parties.

Santa does not smoke or drink alcoholic beverages in uniform.

The people at Western say there are lots of other rules and regulations, too. "We have an image to protect," Zink explains. "Children today become too hardened too quickly. The children in line—those who believe in Santa—are a little younger every year. And Santa is the last vestige of the true, giving spirit of Christmas."

SINATRA

Frank Sinatra is Hoboken's favorite son, and the Spaghetti Frank Sinatra on the menu at Ricco's Ristorante is just the tip of the iceberg.

There is a street named Frank Sinatra, and there are signs on business establishments proclaiming Hoboken, where the idol was born in 1915, his home. Mr. Sinatra's photographs hang, in shrine-like fashion, in restaurants, barbershops, and living rooms. Although he has not been known to make a visit since he hit it big in the 1940s, clerks in the butcher shop speak of "Frankie" as if he might just come in any minute for cold cuts.

Sinatra artifacts are displayed in something of a museum at the library. It is believed that if every local woman who contends she had a date with him is telling the truth, he would have had to pick them up on Saturday nights in a city bus.

"Everybody has a Sinatra story," said a librarian, Doris Corrado. "It's like George Washington slept here." Local folklore has it that Frankie still slips into town without fanfare. It is said by some that he sends checks to Hoboken families in need. It is said by others that this is a lot of nonsense.

So it is that when thirty-seven-year-old Edwin Olivieri discovered he was living in the modest former home of Frank Sinatra, he figured perhaps someone would want to buy it for, say, a million dollars. He paid $19,000. "A lot of crazy things happen in the world these days," explained Mr. Olivieri, who works at the Maxwell House coffee plant here.

This weekend, he held an auction at the four-story, turn-of-the-century, thirteen-by-fifty-foot brownstone at 841 Garden Street, with perhaps as much hoopla and gimmickry as has been seen in Hoboken since P. T. Barnum staged "America's Easternmost Buffalo Hunt" amid the factories and shipyards here more than a century ago.

Barnum could not have done any better with the publicity. Newspaper reporters, television camera crews, and a documentary film group filled the first floor of the house an hour before the auction was to begin, interviewing Mr. and Mrs. Olivieri, their three children, in-laws, neighbors who said that they remembered "Frankie" well, three real estate agents, and, finally, each other.

One neighbor, Eileen Clancy Lorenzo, had been on television so often during the week that she wore extra makeup "to look better on camera than I've been looking" and had taken to saying "cut" when there were lulls in her interviews for television.

As the hour for the auction drew near, wine, cheese, and sausage were placed on the piano, then a birthday cake inscribed "Happy Birthday Frank." It was Frank Sinatra's sixty-sixth birthday, "by coincidence," according to a real estate agent, Don Gordon.

In the kitchen, Giobel Nieves, Mr. Olivieri's brother-in-law from Queens, turned on a "Portrait of Sinatra" cassette tape. The sounds of "Fairy tales can come true, it can happen to you . . ." wafted out into the living room, followed by "Pennies From Heaven." Mr. Nieves said, "Mr. Sinatra could not be here. But his spirit is with us, I believe."

Mr. Gordon, who was to act as auctioneer, was prepared to show to any who had doubts a deed copy showing that Mr. Sinatra's father had purchased the home in 1932. And he had witnesses, the foremost of whom was the fifty-seven-year-old Mrs. Lorenzo.

She was prepared with many anecdotes, including some about Mr. Sinatra's playing in the streets outside—he had lived in the house when he was a teenager—and one about watching Tommy Dorsey and his band debarking from limousines for a real Italian dinner cooked by Mr. Sinatra's mother, Dolly, a ward boss in the community. Mr. Sinatra's father, Martin, was a fireman.

But despite the excitement, not a single person interested in buying the property had come in. When a man carrying neither notebook nor television camera finally arrived at one fifty-eight, two minutes before the auction was to begin Saturday, he might as well have been Mr. Sinatra himself for the attention he received.

Mr. Gordon had talked Mr. Olivieri down from his million-dollar asking price. He began the auction at a minimum of $150,000 and ended it about thirty seconds later, with not one bid. It was announced that the house would go into the Multiple Listing Service, along with the former homes of the less well known.

There had been substantial interest in the house before the auction. Mr. Gordon's daughter, Karen, a real estate agent herself, had shown it to a number of people, one of whom said that she represented a California millionaire who wanted to "relive the life of Frank Sinatra." On her tours, Karen would say, "This is the original foldout ironing board."

"I'm a little disappointed, sure," said Mr. Olivieri. "I hoped for a windfall. It was worth a shot." "I'm happy," said Mrs. Olivieri. "I didn't want to move anyway. This is my home."

Mr. Olivieri yelled for someone to turn off the Sinatra tape, which he said had been his brother-in-law's idea. As a matter of fact, he recalled now, the whole thing had been his brother-in-law's big idea.

XII

RITUALS
AND CUSTOMS

THE HARVEST FEAST RITUAL

The young boy's mother placed one hand behind his head as her other hand guided a heaping forkful of limp, gray eggplant inexorably toward his mouth. The boy closed his eyes, opened his mouth slightly, and gulped down the goo with an awful grimace.

This may well have seemed the longest night in the boy's life, the night of the Vineland Eggplant Dinner, an annual harvest feast ritual that lasts for hours as one eggplant concoction after another is served—nine courses in all, from buffalo soup with eggplant dumplings right through to the eggplant cake. And eggplant wine to wash it down.

Every dish was laced or laden with the fruit of the plant that seems to grow everywhere in this area, the proud producer of nearly half of all eggplants in the United States. "We are here," Mayor Patrick Fiorilli told the audience, "to draw attention to that fact and to pay homage to the eggplant."

Living in Vineland, New Jersey, the young boy at the dinner would learn to take eggplant like a man. In this community it is considered downright unpatriotic not to enjoy eggplant, and residents on the wrong side of the eggplant issue are considered outcasts, according to the mayor.

"We try to win the dissidents over," he said, "by disguising eggplant in various dishes." Those who cannot be won over, he quipped, are not granted full rights of citizenship and often find themselves receiving traffic tickets for the most minor offenses.

"We believe," he explained, "that people can't really drive or do anything else right unless they eat eggplant."

When he was a boy, John Cantoni recalled, he romped in the eggplant fields and played catch with eggplants when he had no baseball. But as wonderful as eggplant is, he said, it becomes a problem for the community at this time of year, when suddenly eggplant is everywhere.

"We have to eat it before it eats us," remarked William Fauretto, an eggplant farmer and operator of one of the farm stands that are almost eggplant to eggplant along the roadways of this southern New Jersey community. Everything grows well here, he said. "They don't call it Vineland for nothing." Eggplant, in particular, seems to like the sandy soil. One of his clerks, Donna

231

Mastalski, added, "The truth is, you couldn't kill an eggplant if you tried."

Some people would like to do just that. Eggplants are so fruitful that no one quite knows what to do with them all.

Mr. Cantoni, who grows eggplant in his garden, consumes what he can—considering there are only three meals a day—and tries to give the rest to friends, neighbors, and members of his extended family.

This is not always possible, he said, a situation that gives rise to the unusual local custom of setting a bushel basket of eggplants on the porch for anyone who will take some.

Local residents don't have to eat half the eggplant in the United States; it just sometimes seems that way. It turns up on their tables baked, stuffed, fried, in soups, salads, cakes, and decorative centerpieces. "You can do a lot of things with eggplant," said Mr. Cantoni, shaking his head. "Maybe too much."

The Vineland Produce Auction, where farmers from miles around bring their produce, is busy selling eggplant and other fruits and vegetables all day every day at this time of year.

At the loading docks, forklifts are constantly filling dozens of eighteen-wheeled refrigerated trucks with tons of eggplant and other fruits and vegetables, bound for points throughout the eastern half of the United States.

Carlis Martin, a worker on the loading dock, suggested that it was all well and good that Vineland grew all of these eggplants. But he wondered why the community had to inflict them on everybody else. "I hate eggplant," said Mr. Martin, implying that many other people around here agreed but were afraid to speak up. "I hate the taste, the consistency, everything about it," he said.

When a forklift driver, William Vaccaro, said the only eggplant dish he could stand to eat was eggplant parmigiana, an eggplant critic pointed out that a tennis shoe can be enjoyed à la parmigiana.

But David and June Seelman drove 275 miles for the fifth annual eggplant dinner, held at the North Italy Hall, because they love eggplant. Mrs. Seelman's brother was visiting from Texas, but they left him to come to the dinner "because you always have your brother, but eggplant is seasonal."

Entertainment was provided by a six-piece musical ensemble, which was distressed by its inability to come up with even one eggplant-related number, and by belly dancers, whose presence seemed to baffle many in the audience. One spectator guessed that perhaps they were "performing some kind of crop-growing ritual."

Mr. Fiorilli explained something of the "fascinating history" of eggplant and told of his dream to someday hold a full-blown eggplant festival, maybe with a parade and people dressed up like eggplants.

The crowd of about two hundred also included some dignitaries. Arthur Brown, the state secretary of agriculture, talked of the fifteen hundred acres of eggplant grown in the area and congratulated Mr. Fiorilli for "his long history of promoting vegetables."

Victoria Schmidt, state director of travel and tourism, received a commemorative eggplant-purple shirt with the menu printed on the back. She made brief remarks but did not address the issue of how eggplants might enhance tourism per se.

Kristin Charlson, Miss Vineland, wore a crown and an aubergine-colored dress that closely matched the color of the eggplant centerpieces. She said that she had always liked eggplant.

"Eggplant was always there," she recalled. "Always."

T HE LEAF PEOPLE

Jane Bishop of West Cornwall, Connecticut, locks up Fred when the leaf people come around. Fred is her cat. The leaf people are the hordes that invade New England every October to relish the resplendent fall foliage. "They'd run him over or steal him if I didn't," Mrs. Bishop explained.

As the tinctured tidal wave of yellowing birches, crimson sugar maples, and bronze hickories sweeps down from the Canadian border, it is met by Gobi-beige Audi 5000s, Surinam-red Volkswagen Rabbits, burnished silver Dodge 400s, and hundreds of thousands of other vehicles from the metropolitan Northeast and beyond.

The leaf people also come by train and plane, on bikes and hikes, on weekend and weeklong fall foliage bus tours, even on fall foliage hot-air balloon expeditions. Residents in this northwest corner of Connecticut, where every photograph taken at this time of year could adorn a calendar, see it as somehow fitting that city folk sit in traffic jams viewing nature. Some local people will tell you there is a degree of madness in the leaves.

"It's unbelievable, terrible," said Jane Bishop's husband,

Philip, who owns Yutzler's Country Store. "They cause traffic jams and throw trash on the streets and park in people's driveways. We have no parking facilities. We don't have sidewalks, so they block the streets. They just take over."

"The leaf gawkers drive so slowly it's irritating," said Deborah Petersen, of the adjacent town of Sharon, adding that she meets leaf people there from as far away as California and Arizona.

Rudolph Eschbach, a farmer living just across the state line in Amenia, New York, said he found the leaf people more amusing than anything else. "They look at my sheep," he said, "and say, 'That's interesting. I didn't know cotton grew on sheep.' "

"It's awful," said Robert Osborn, an artist and resident of Salisbury, "but the terrible truth is: it really is so beautiful, you can understand their coming."

West Cornwall is particularly hard hit by the invasion of the leaf people because it has a covered bridge. "The leaf peepers," as they are known in this community, pour out of buses and cars, cameras clicking. They line up, waiting their turn to pose spouses, friends, and generally uncooperative children between the bridge and the yellow-leafed maple.

One woman living on the river next to the bridge had plastered her property with "No Parking" and "Private Property" signs that went unheeded. Another local resident recalls with a devilish grin a leaf peeper posing by the river and falling in.

Jean Norton of Niantic, Connecticut, was picking up elephantine sycamore leaves near the bridge. She planned to place them under the glass cover on her kitchen table for decoration. "It was my husband's idea to come," said Mrs. Norton, confessing that she would just as soon be back at the motel drinking beer. "It's beautiful, sure, but people make too big a deal out of the foliage."

Michael and Donna Goldman of New York City worried—in what some would say was typical New Yorker fashion—that they might not have seen "the absolute best" foliage.

"Is there a better place?" Mrs. Goldman asked of others at the bridge. "I told her," said Mr. Goldman, "that we should have come last week. Now, I would say, thirty to thirty-five percent of the leaves have dropped off. I told her."

Bert Fitch, an eighty-five-year-old Connecticut Yankee, allowed as how he didn't understand all the fuss over a bunch of dead leaves. Sporting a flannel shirt, suspenders, and a cap, he looked so stereotypical as he raked mounds of sugar maple leaves that one suspected he may have been placed there by the department of tourism.

"To me, the leaves are a problem," said Mr. Fitch, not missing a stroke of raking in a twenty-minute conversation, in which he explained that he makes his own syrup from the tree. "If the city folks like the leaves so much, I wish they'd stop and help. It's bad. You can hardly sit on the porch for the *bzzt-bzzt-bzzt* of the traffic.

"I guess," said Mr. Fitch of the leaf people, "the local businessmen are glad to take their money." Todd Aichele, owner of The Corner restaurant, next to the covered bridge, has mixed feelings about the leaf watchers. "This leaf season has been busier than ever," explained Mr. Aichele. "It causes problems, but it's a very important part of our business."

Local residents sell everything from quilts and apple cider to costly antiques and summer homes to the leaf people. Local children have been known to sell plastic bags of leaves. All manner of weekend festivals—apple, chrysanthemum, clam, jazz, art, craft, antique, heritage, cauliflower, and leaf—are held in various communities that are competing for the leaf people trade. In nearby Amenia, Iris Sincerbox said the local rescue squad takes the opportunity to solicit contributions from leaf watchers at the town's only stoplight.

Leaf watching has become so popular that it now ranks with the summer vacation and winter ski seasons as a draw for visitors in many New England areas. Some states have established toll-free "Leaf Report" hotlines, and the competition for leaf watcher business has erupted into public bickering by officials of various New England states over which has the better leaves.

The Connecticut Commissioner of Economic Development invited leaf people to this state, charging that towns in Vermont and New Hampshire were "somewhat depressed looking"; to which the governor of Vermont said that he supposed the leaves of Connecticut, like its ski slopes, might be all right for beginners.

The leaves are falling now, but that doesn't necessarily mean life here will return to normal. "As bad as people think this is," said Mr. Eschbach, reminded that deer hunting season starts soon, "it is nothing like next month when they all come back with guns."

THURSDAY NIGHT IN ROSLYN

"Sometimes you look out the window at dusk," said a resident of Roslyn, Long Island, "and you don't see any, and you think maybe they won't come, maybe finally they are gone." But as surely as bugs to the porch lights, they do return on summer nights to this small village—at first just a few, then later in swarms, covering sidewalks, driving patrons away from businesses, causing some property damage, and keeping people awake until all hours of the night.

On Thursday nights hundreds of them—teenagers—fill the sidewalks in front of the historic buildings in the quaint shopping district, now retrofitted with fashionable shops. The youths spill out into the street, where the police man barricades to keep the swelling crowd from making Old Northern Boulevard impassable to the bumper-to-bumper cars and occasional motorcycles.

"What's going on here?" asked a middle-aged man, caught unaware in the traffic. To which one of the youths answered, "Good question." Another one explained that the young crowd was simply engaged in the time-honored tradition of hanging out on a summer night.

The police said that in the three or four years of this phenomenon that is Thursday night in Roslyn, there have been surprisingly few problems with drinking or drugs, fighting or rowdiness—even though the crowds have sometimes numbered as many as two thousand. Some parents drop their children off here to hang out.

Asking the teenagers why they are in Roslyn on a Thursday night seems to them to be questioning a law of the universe. "Because this is the time and the place," explained one in the crowd. Residents contend that signs reading "Thursday Night in Roslyn" have been spotted at colleges half a continent away. Disc jockeys dedicate records to those gathered here.

Residents feel as though they have been visited by a plague. The picturesque village has gone from outdated and dilapidated to historic chic in recent years, through the painstaking restoration of dozens of homes and buildings. It is a village—said one resident—of "us old-house nuts," where talk at parties tends to be of rococo revival mantels and lamb's-tongue window facings. The regular

Thursday night infestation of teenagers is as unwelcome as a horde of door-to-door aluminum-siding salesmen.

"Things are fragile here," said Millard Prisant, who lives in an 1845 Greek Revival home that he and his wife, Carol, have restored. "The whole village is an antique." Mr. Prisant told of waking on a Friday morning to find an eight-foot section of his half-solid, half-swag picket fence, which he and his son had built from scratch, lying in the street. He regularly finds pickets broken off the fence, he said, and once a beer bottle was tossed through his window.

Police say serious incidents are rare, however. Of the teenagers who gather here, many of them are young women ranging in age from about fourteen to about twenty-one, who are dressed "in the very latest Bloomingdale's has to offer," in the words of Larry Krause, twenty-one, of Manhasset. The young men, who on the average are perhaps a year or so older, are dressed more casually, but rarely in anything that would embarrass parents at a country club.

"It's the biggest fashion show in the world," explained Michael Posillico, twenty, of Old Westbury. "The girls come here to show off. The boys come here to look and maybe get a phone number. It's like a shopping center for girls."

Said Jackie Steele, nineteen, of Woodmere, "You come here to get dressed up and show off your tan." A young woman with her questioned if this was so different from why adults go places.

"It's a meat market," said Danielle Sedlak of Plainview, who said she had picked up two telephone numbers and a date for Friday night. "No," said Mr. Krause, echoing the view of many others, "it's just a place to see everybody." He was renewing an acquaintance with Neil Feirick of Jericho, whom he had not seen for ten years, since they went to camp together.

"This is not real," said Bruce Introp of Queens, who had driven out to witness a Thursday night in Roslyn. "Everybody is just standing around in fancy clothes and hairstyles and jewelry." Someone standing nearby described the scene as "Woodstock 1982." A local homeowner commented, "They just stand and stare, a whole lost-generation thing."

U.S. Blues, a bar and restaurant with live music and a dance floor, is a focal point. Many in the community would like to see the establishment closed. They believe that the crowds might go away, even though there are several other bars here on what one sweatshirt advertises as "The Hottest Strip on Long Island."

Ironically, the crowds are bad for business at U.S. Blues. "People see the crowds, the barricades, and all the parking places taken," said the night manager, Ron Joy, "and they keep going." Most of those in the crowd, he said, just stand out on the sidewalk all night, some of them because they are under eighteen and too young to get in. "I pray for rain so they'll come in," he said.

But, said Diane Texin, twenty-one, of Bellerose, Queens, "I've driven by on rainy Thursdays and seen hundreds of them out here with umbrellas." "There's very little to do in the suburbs when you're sixteen," said Mr. Joy. "You can't drive, go to a bar, or even to an R-rated movie."

On a recent Thursday night, the crowds did not begin breaking up until about 1 A.M. and many were still around at two. When they were asked what time they had to be home, a typical answer was, "Whenever."

"I suppose it's not so different from our cruising the drive-ins in the 1950s," said Mrs. Prisant, standing at her fence, watching the traffic whiz by. What the Prisants and seemingly everybody else in this sleepy little village would like to know is: Why do kids hang out? Why, Lord, in Roslyn? And why Thursday night? Science holds no answers.

☞THAT TUPPER FEELING

"Tupperware is beautiful,
  Tupperware for me,
  Tupperware is beautiful, so beautiful, to me."

The Tupperware ladies are singing early on a Monday morning.

"I've got that Tupper feeling
  up in my head,
  up in my head . . ."

The Tupperware National Anthem fills the meeting room at Prime Time Party Sales in west suburban Berkeley. Tupperware, the plastic food container par excellence, has become a symbol of middle-class family life—and something of a symbol of the suburbs.

As have Tupperware parties (you can't buy Tupperware in a store), where you play games, meet your neighbors, and buy translucent polyethylene boxes and bowls with the patented Tupper seal. Man may not live in a vacuum, but his kumquats can.

A Tupperware party begins every ten seconds somewhere in the world. Tupperware is sold throughout the United States and thirty foreign countries. There are Tupperware fiestas and Tupperware sukiyaki keepers. Ayatollahs may come and go, but Tupperware parties continue unabated today and every day in Iran.

The sun never sets on Tupperdom, where $500 million a year changes hands in living rooms.

So, it's really more of an international anthem these fifty women are singing this day in a Berkeley industrial park. On the walls are the felt banners of the sales teams in the Prime Time distributorship: Leading Ladies, Go-Getters, and eight others. Attached are green and blue ribbons recognizing sales achievements.

The Troubadours sit in row three, their presence announced to all by chair-back coverings of brightly colored felt, with "Troubadours" emblazoned across the backs.

One here today doesn't sit in a yellow plastic chair. Sue Long, supersaleswoman, sits in an orange director's chair with her name on the back, in row one on the aisle.

The chair recognizes sales achievement. Tilling the fertile suburban area, she sells tons—tons—of Tupperware every year. She is one of the top Tupperware saleswomen in the Midwest and manages a unit that some weeks is the best of the more than six hundred in the Midwest.

Sue receives an award at this weekly Assembly for tops in sales, having sold $1,110.30 of Tupperware last week. This is almost twice what the second-place award winner has sold. If she goes over the $1,100 mark once more, she gets to keep the director's chair. She has been with Tupperware almost four years and has a basement full of director's chairs.

Sue, twenty-six and perky, stands to receive her award—one of three she'll get this day—revealing a two-foot-long strip of cloth hanging from her waist filled with medals and ribbons the likes of which General Omar Bradley has never seen. These are awards won so far in 1979; Lamplighter Pin for bringing in recruits, Vanguard Crest Pin for sales, and the Diamond Crown (the highest sales achievement).

The Tupperware sales force of fifty thousand dealers and managers is motivated—highly motivated—by incentives and recognition. "A lot of our salespeople have been housewives all their lives," explains an official at company headquarters in Orlando, Florida. "No one ever tells them what a nice job they're doing washing the floor. They absolutely thrive on the recognition and genuine appreciation we have for what they're doing."

Bill and Paula Antonini own the distributorship and run the weekly Assembly. (Distributorships are given exclusively to married couples.) The recognition is applied with a trowel. Sales awards, recruiting awards, individual and unit awards, drawing after drawing for prizes, ribbons, medals, you name it.

Paula tells the women that this begins a period of "friending," when they go door to door seeking women to hold parties. Booking parties is known in Tupperdom as "dating" parties. "Wear a beautiful smile," Paula says, "and you will date. You will date parties and have your datebook filled with parties.

After Assembly, Paula talks about parties and dating and the social overtones. "A lot of dealers are tied down in the home," she says, "unable to make friends since they left school. Tupperware lets them get out, go to parties, and make friends."

There is no doubt that the thousands and thousands of Tupperware parties being held in Chicago's suburbs every year are filling a larger social need. In highly transient, impersonal suburban neighborhoods, people will come to a Tupperware party when invited because it is an opportunity to meet their neighbors and make some friends. And buy a little Tupperware.

Sue Long's Glen Ellyn townhouse is a monument to Tupperware's incentives and recognition. It's packed with prizes, from the color TV, black-and-white TV, dinette set, and bedroom suite, down to sheets and bathmats. She has shelves jammed with trophies, the most recent being gold medals for high sales in Tupperware's World Olympics, where the United States was pitted against the team of Europe-Middle East-Africa.

She puts on her full-length leather coat, a prize, slips behind the wheel of her station wagon, provided free by the company, and is off to a party in West Chicago. She'll hold five parties this week and already has laryngitis from talking too much last week.

At the party, Sue has us play some games to get loosened up—
the kind where four giggling people end up sitting on one person's
lap. Then she demonstrates a few of Tupperware's 140 products.
The company line is that products are sold at parties rather than
stores so the seal can be demonstrated. But Sue's sales pitch is as
much to line up more parties as to sell products. It's called
"chaining" parties.

She lets this group know—in a casual way—that hostess Mari-
anne gets her hostess gift (a small vacuum cleaner and the like) only
if they buy $135 worth of Tupperware and if two of them agree to
hold future parties.

The $135 figure is considered an average party. Not for Sue,
though, who regularly sells more than $1,000 a week at four or five
parties. Last year she had a $2,300 week. Saleswomen clear about
25 percent for themselves.

"It's so neat," Sue says on the drive home. "Where else can
you go except Tupperware and play the same games as six-year-
olds? We laugh together and become friends. It's a real party.

"I started at Tupperware because I was home going crazy with
thirteen-month-old twin boys.

"You gain so much confidence at Tupperware. You saw all the
women at Assembly this morning. They are happy within themselves. They can stand up in front of a group now with confidence.
They are made to be proud."

Tupperware has taken Sue Long from disgruntled housewife
four years ago to supersaleswoman. She was divorced along the
way.

"I believe a woman has the right to be the kind of person she
wants to be. Tupperware gave me that chance.

"Tupperware is like a family. There is so much love in Tupperware. It's a career with me now."

"I've got that Tupper feeling
up in my head,
up in my head, to stay."

GRAND BEGINNINGS: RITES OF SPRING

It was a typical spring day here.

Rain. Thirty-eight degrees. Drivers turning on their brights at noon; flocks of northbound geese making U-turns in the sky.

A day seemingly like all days here in the Chicago area; a good day to stay inside. Maybe sharpen the scissors.

The annual rites of spring in Chicago's suburbs tend less to young men chasing young women, most of whom are influenza victims with runny noses, and more to things like going to spring grand openings of new banks, condominiums, and dry cleaning establishments.

I like grand openings, with their spotlights and pennants and balloons and a chance to meet a Bull, a Bear, a Cub, or a Sock.

The papers were full of announcements of grand openings in the suburbs last weekend, as usual, but one in particular caught my eye. Besides, a friend had received an invitation and had offered to take my wife and me along as guests.

I accepted enthusiastically but somehow wound up there in Downers Grove alone.

"I don't know," my wife said, "I think I'll just stay home and . . . sharpen the scissors." The phone rang. "I can't go," said my friend who had received the invitation. "I'm sick. You go. Have fun."

So there I was at the grand opening of Hallowell and James's new funeral parlor on Seventy-fifth Street in Downers Grove. The gloomy drive out was perfect for the occasion.

More than three hundred people showed up for the open house, confirming my suspicion that suburbanites will go virtually anywhere on a Sunday afternoon, as long as they can drive.

A good time was had by all. I was greeted at the front door by none other than Harry James, undertaker and chairman of the board of Hallowell and James. Harry, a La Grange Park resident, opened his first funeral home in La Grange fifty-six years ago, when he graduated from high school. He has since opened another home in Countryside.

He has laid to rest thousands of suburbanites, from bankers to a biker who was buried in his motorcycle jacket after a service with electric guitars. He is proud of this new facility that can accommodate two funerals or four wakes simultaneously.

It is the ultimate in modern funeral homes, though Harry says he won't offer any of the new gimmicks I asked him about. A Canadian mortician has come out with a $6 coffin, which the family can place inside a rented deluxe model, thereby saving hundreds of dollars. Harry also decided against drive-through services being offered by a Louisiana funeral home. There, motorists can view the body and sign a guest book without leaving their cars. Very suburban.

There are free bottles of hand lotion at Harry's open house, plus Hallowell and James Funeral Home stickers to place right on your phone, in case you have the infirm over a lot.

Guests at the open house munch pastries and finger sandwiches (don't get excited, they got them from the caterer) as they stroll through the showroom looking at the latest vaults, like the Triune SST, and feeling the comfort of the caskets with Simmons ("Beautyrest") mattresses and springs.

They sip mixed drinks and red punch (from the caterer) while examining the modern embalming room. "Fortunately," Harry says, offering me another Scotch and water, "there were no customers in here today. We had three this week before we officially opened."

That was good. The funeral home business, like most these days, is fiercely competitive, particularly with the death rate dropping.

Keeping in mind his fine reputation of fifty-six years of service to the western suburbs, I questioned the mortician as to whether there would be as much business in a mobile suburban area like this, that most who live here wouldn't really call home. And why had he located in an area of homes and condos catering to younger families with kids still home?

"People today want convenience," he says. "They won't return to their hometowns or old neighborhoods even to be buried.

"We find a lot of elderly parents live out here with the younger families, helping them pay for these expensive homes.

"Moreover, it isn't just the old who are dying anymore. With all the pressure and stress today, many more younger suburban men are dying than did ten or twenty years ago."

As for the death rate declining, Harry noted that an industry trade magazine called *The American Funeral Director* reports that there is an apparent bottoming out of this decline and that there is reason for "cautious optimism."

☛ GARAGE SALE JUNKIE

Willard Smith claims he'd never touched the stuff when he moved here ten years ago from a life of clean air and clean living in Colorado.

He says they didn't even have it out there and that he didn't know what it was, much less that it was addictive and could ruin your life.

It's probably too late for Willard now. He's a junkie. Buys junk. At garage sales.

Garage sales, as any teenager with parents in this day and age knows, are mind altering, highly addictive, and dangerous, creating euphoria in some and lethargic indifference in others.

It was once thought that only black jazz musicians attended garage sales, but garage sale abuse is now most serious among suburbanites.

The garage sale has posed such a threat to suburban residents that it is now a controlled substance. Several suburbs require a $2 permit just to "hold" a garage sale. These controls regulate the size and number of signs and the hours, and prohibit the use of loudspeakers and the sale of new merchandise. In one suburb a guy was holding a perpetual garage sale and importing new junk through his brother-in-law in a foreign country. Some suburbs have talked about the possibility of banning garage sales altogether.

Even with these controls, officials report an epidemic of garage sales this summer, as suburbanites attempt to scrounge up extra money during the recession for hamburger, gasoline, and shoes.

You could argue that Willard was asking for it. The guy is a professor at the College of Du Page and you'd think he'd know better than to move to a potential trouble spot like suburban Naperville, Illinois. I mean, all those garages. He moved there with his wife, Joan. They bought a house at 117 Thrush and had a baby. Hard to keep your nose clean with that kind of life-style.

He didn't for long. Willard told me the grim tale of how he became hooked on garage sales, and about his life these last seven years as a garage sale addict, last Saturday as we strolled down the street where I live, where everyone on the block was participating in a gigantic garage sale.

He came dressed like a garage sale addict who'd lost all respect for himself. Actually, he hadn't. Others may have lost respect for him, but he was proud of his outfit, every stitch purchased at a garage sale; the $1 white loafers; gray pants from a $2 Hart, Schaffner & Marks suit; ill-fitting 50-cent dress shirt; 25-cent sterling cuff links; and 25-cent Oleg Cassini tie—in a chicken Tetrazzini pattern.

He said that seven years ago he was just an occasional user but soon found himself attending ten garage sales a week. "I was eventually going to garage sales on Saturdays and Sundays, then Fridays, and on my way to work."

He estimates he's gone to between five hundred and one thousand garage sales. Did he ever go to one where he didn't buy anything? "Not that I can remember," he says. "I had to start having my own garage sales to get rid of the stuff."

There have been no reported deaths from an overdose of garage sales, but Willard almost became the first. His wife said she would kill him if he didn't stop going to them. He was spending all their money on garage sales—though to his credit he never knocked over a 7-Eleven to support his habit.

"I became one of the people who show up at suburban garage sales an hour or more early and I knock on the door to see if I can get first shot at the goods. Some of the real garage sale pros go a day before and say they read the ad wrong.

"Somewhere in there I realized I wasn't spending any time with my family, that these things I was buying meant more to me than people.

"I started going to church and became a born-again Christian."

He still goes to garage sales, but says he is nicer to other buyers and sellers now. And he is trying to beat the habit. Someone at work convinced him to go on the payroll savings plan so he wouldn't have so much cash in hand to blow at garage sales. And when he came to my blockwide garage sale he brought only $6.

Walking along my block, he says, "This is hard for me," referring to the fact that he sees lots of things he wants to buy but doesn't have enough money with him to buy them.

He spots an old camera, identical to one he has at home, and says he just has to have it. Why? "I don't know," he says. "I don't know. I don't know."

He races back to his car and pulls some money from a secret hiding place. "Twelve dollars and sixty cents," he says. "I was supposed to put it in the bank."

But he's too late. The camera has been sold. So, he buys 125 back issues of *Antique Trader* magazine, an angel food cake cutter (he didn't know what it was), a Mother Goose book, something I didn't see for 16 cents (marked 25 cents, he was pleased he got them to bring the price down), a watch case (marked $5, for $1), a silver jewelry pin for $1, a mother-of-pearl collar stay and cuff links ("Now I'm into my gas money," he says, continuing to buy), a little trophy that says "World's Greatest Driver," and more.

I realize as I'm helping him load it into his car that my neighbors owe me a debt of gratitude for inviting him to our block sale. He doesn't buy a thing from my pile of junk. But it's been a good day: lots of fun cleaning out the basement and the garage and playing shopkeeper and just sitting and talking to neighbors and others all day. And I made $60.78 while I was at it, tax free.

I could, of course, have made a lot more. But I won't deal junk to addicts and schoolchildren just so I can trade in my broken-down Volkswagen for a pink Cadillac convertible with wide whitewalls. Not after I've seen what it can do to the lives of people like Willard Smith.

THE LAST CLASS REUNION

A din fills the banquet room of the Riverside Golf Club.

The first reunion ever of the Class of 1928 of J. Sterling Morton High School, Cicero, Illinois, is being held, and the eighty-nine returning class members are making up for lost time.

The layers of conversation and laughter are occasionally pierced by shrieks from people spotting old friends they haven't seen for fifty years.

"I hope the name tags are big . . . I know you! . . . Remember me?. . . You haven't changed a bit . . . Wait a minute, I thought you were dead . . . I'm falling apart . . . Remember the time? . . . What part of Florida? . . . No, he died . . . What have you been up to since graduation? . . . I used to have a real thing for you . . . Sure, I saw her not too long ago; about 1965, I think."

The place was all smiles, with everyone talking a mile a minute and kissing and backslapping and you-old-son-of-a-gun shoulder-punching. And a fair amount of hugging, including a man and a woman who appeared stunned when they first saw each other, then rushed into each other's arms.

The clusters of people were a bit larger around people like Ted Kobza and Karl Long. Ted, a famed athlete who threw a mean fastball for Morton, was said to be an "idol" to both male and female class members. Ted has gained 150 pounds since those days, and one woman goes so far as to tell him she's disappointed.

Karl Long, eighty-four, drove up from Florida for the occasion and will drive back in the morning. He is the immensely popular former basketball coach who guided the 1927 Morton basketball team to a national championship in a tournament held at the University of Chicago with championship teams from forty states.

George Fencl was a starter on that team. He is one of the consensus Big Men on Campus in attendance tonight. There are several others. Joe Ondrus, a class member and now superintendent of the high school district, tells a story about Fencl that is a little risqué for the group: "George stood up at a pep assembly and asked for a big hand for the cheerleaders 'who have been putting out all year.' "

Was Superintendent Ondrus a good student? I ask faculty adviser Hans Andersen, eighty-five. "Hell, no, but he's a good superintendent."

There are also those cruising around to see how the years have treated Eleanor Hall, Jean Perrin, Ann Kveton, and other class beauties. Vlasta Atkins, who wins the award for coming the farthest for the reunion (Monterey Park, California), reminisces about a fellow not in attendance tonight who took her to a dance: "He had the highest IQ in the class."

Cicero is a largely Bohemian town, and Frank Stanley goes to each table during dinner to say hello and to explain fully why it was that he had changed his name from Stachnik. Alice Crosby, it is recalled, was Alice Necrosby. Laddie Lastovicka, Jarmila Jandasek, Blanche Kofist, and all the others in attendance don't seem to really care one way or another.

Tony Kvanic gets an award for most children (six), and someone reminds the group, loudly, that Kvanic was one of the school's top wrestlers. Unsolicited wisecracks fly from the crowd all evening, and you sense they're from the same guys who used to get thrown out of class for it.

The mushroom soup is served. Louis Keller hugs an old grammar school buddy, Joe Ziskal. They talk about getting out of high school and going to work for Western Electric and International Harvester, respectively (two huge local plants where a lot of the class members went to work out of high school), and of fighting to keep their jobs through the Depression.

With all of them standing around in little clusters talking excitedly about sports, romance, boys, girls, and teachers, you half expect the bell to ring and the whole group to troop off to geography class.

They stand as a class, together again after fifty years, and solemnly say the Pledge of Allegiance. The group of kindly, aged faces listens again to the commencement address that they heard fifty years ago: "Four years. They were a day, for in the swift, free race of youth, a passing year's just one full hurried hour. All that's left are memories—of friendship, time-reft; of youthful fun; of heartaches, smiles, brief tears—all milestones on our way . . . eternity has claimed them for her own."

It's almost midnight, and the band is wrapping it up. The couple that hugged and kissed when they first saw each other is leaving the room.

At the front door, they squeeze each other's hands tightly and say how wonderful it's been seeing each other after all this time.

"Take good care of yourself," he says. "See you," she says, turning and walking out the front door, where her husband sits in the car, warming it up.

There's a slight chill in the air, and dry leaves are blowing around in the driveway. The fiftieth class reunion—the last class reunion—is over.

XIII

HOLIDAYS

☛ M EGAWATT MIRACLES OF THE YULETIDE

White Plains Post Road in Scarsdale is aglow this holiday season with the festive brake lights of motorists happening upon the megawatt wonder that is the Prisco family's outdoor Christmas display.

"Santa won't have any trouble finding this house," Denise Dombrowsky, a passerby drawn out of her car by the sight, said to her five-year-old son, Alex. Not to mention intelligence satellites and nonstop flights from London to Chicago.

This is a time in the suburbs for hauling out the ladder and wrapping the bushes in lights—which seem rarely to work from one year to the next—or perhaps stringing them along the gutters. It is also a time for evening family outings to view the outdoor decorations that others have erected. As in all things, some residents carry the decorating tradition a little farther than others, to the great joy of many, the bemusement of others, and the absolute mortification of a few neighbors.

Anthony and Teresa Prisco have draped the bushes at the front of their yard with one thousand pulsating lights. Behind the bushes stands an eleven-piece polypropylene nativity scene, each translucent figure glowing with light bulbs within—all but the two baby lambs, which presumably will glow when they reach maturity.

Across the driveway, which is lined with three-foot-high candy canes, are three incandescent carolers and a wooden soldier. On the porch, which is decorated in garlands strung with lights, stand glowing plastic snowmen, three-foot-high candles, "Noel" lampposts, several Santas, and a drummer boy. Shrubs around the porch are decorated with blinking colored lights, and there is an enormous wreath strung with lights on the front of the house. On the roof is Santa Claus in a sleigh pulled by three reindeer.

While young Alex Dombrowsky found the Priscos' decorations "pretty," a neighbor suggested that they were "a little much," and another neighbor thought the place looked "like Las Vegas." Scarsdale is an affluent suburb where most people put up no outdoor Christmas decorations at all, and most who do keep their enthusiasm for the season firmly in check, displaying tasteful door wreaths of natural materials. The entire subject of outdoor Christmas decorations in such suburbs of studied reserve seems fraught with social peril.

251

It is difficult, perhaps impossible, to find a place in Scarsdale that sells plastic figures, one local resident suggesting that it might be illegal to sell such items over the counter in this village. In a visit over the line to the Flower Time shop in White Plains, Wayne Pritzker was considering the purchase of a four-foot plastic snowman and suggested that "Christmas is for the kids," that people who worry about the tastefulness of decorations "should lighten up a little."

Teresa Prisco loves her displays and said she did not particularly care if her decorations were causing a stir. She would prefer, however, that the other children stop teasing hers and "telling them that their mother is crazy."

Mrs. Prisco has been putting out her Christmas displays for twenty years, adding a few things each year. "Jesus, Mary, and Joseph are originals and do require maintenance," she explained.

"My husband thinks I'm crazy, too," she said. "Every year he says, 'I thought we were going to cut down this year.' " Mrs. Prisco hides the December electric bill from Mr. Prisco.

"I think it's nice," Mr. Prisco observed. "The only problem is she goes a little too far." Many of the passing cars on this busy thoroughfare slow, some stop, and a few come right up the driveway. Some people get out of their cars at this roadside attraction to take photographs or to knock on the door and discuss the lavish display with the Priscos. Some mistake the Prisco home for some kind of store. They knock on the door and ask Mrs. Prisco, "Are you open?"

For all of this, most residents of this community can tell you that the Priscos' decorations are dim compared with those that Dr. John Salimbene used to put up at his house just down White Plains Post Road. One of the doctor's Wise Men moved his arm, by way of a barbecue grill motor, pointing to the star on the rooftop. Some people didn't even notice the moving arm, for all of the wooden elves sawing and hammering in the front yard, Santa and his sleigh on the lawn, the huge "Noel" sign, thousands of lights, the snowmen, the loudspeakers blaring carols, and at times Dr. Salimbene's nephews dressed as Mr. and Mrs. Claus.

"They had to put a policeman on the corner, for all the traffic," the physician said. "We had buses of people coming here."

He said that occasionally someone would make a derogatory comment and that he stopped erecting the bulk of his display about four years ago when a neighbor suggested Dr. Salimbene was less than patriotic—possibly an Arab sympathizer—for using all that electric power on a Christmas display.

Mrs. Prisco said that if Dr. Salimbene is not going to use them anymore, she is interested in buying his animated characters and "getting them out there."

☞THE BEST CHRISTMAS

The mayor of Bridgeport called it "a miracle." Santa Claus himself proclaimed it "the best Christmas ever." Grown men cried.

Just five days after an arsonist destroyed Christmas Village—a chalet-style building in Beardsley Park, where children have come for twenty-six years to see animated Christmas scenes, receive a toy from Santa Claus, and ask of him their fondest desires—Mr. Claus regained his throne.

It was accomplished through the efforts of hundreds of volunteers working around the clock in this Connecticut city for several days, often in subfreezing temperatures, and through donations of toys, money, materials, as well as food for the workers.

An early morning fire last Tuesday, which the fire department said was arson, leveled more than half the 140-foot-long building, with extensive smoke and water damage in what remained. It destroyed several of the exhibits, the costumes for Santa and his helpers, and about $14,000 in toys that were to be given away by the Police Athletic League, which operates Christmas Village. The building's contents were not insured.

At dawn Tuesday, Frank Parlatore, a sixty-five-year-old retired factory worker who has been Santa Claus at Christmas Village for twenty-five years, sat near the smoking ruins, crying.

Karen Bergquist said her seven-year-old daughter, Jennifer, was among many children who believed that Santa had died in the fire. "Everyone was devastated," said Mayor Leonard Paoletta, who called a meeting Wednesday with representatives of local construction companies and building trades unions to see if there was any way the building could be reopened before Christmas.

"Many of them thought I was crazy, and some said so," recalled the mayor, who conceded that he had almost no knowledge of the construction field when he challenged them to rebuild

Christmas Village by this weekend for the children. "If I had any idea what I was asking," he said, watching volunteers working feverishly hours before the reopening, "I never would have gotten the words out."

At the reopening ceremony, some workers cited "Christmas spirit," and others cited "temporary insanity," but for whatever reasons, they had accepted the challenge. The site was cleared of debris, and by 1 P.M. Wednesday the first nail was driven.

The mayor put some city workers on the job. The first volunteers were police officers and firefighters, then came electricians, carpenters, plumbers, roofers, painters, decorators, carpet layers, unemployed people, retired people, Boy Scouts, children after school, and people who took time off from their jobs for a few days.

"They started coming over the hill like a banzai attack," said Nick Zerella, one of the construction supervisors on loan from a local company, "and had to be mobilized."

A contractor in Croton, New York, some sixty-five miles to the east, shut down a job and brought his crew to Bridgeport to work on the project. A carpenter from Monroe, about ten miles to the north, rode his bicycle over.

Jeremy Horner, seven, who lives nearby, was toting some impossibly large boards with his father this weekend. Jeremy said that he had volunteered, with the hope that Santa would take note of his efforts.

Michael Robertson, nineteen, a carpenter, was one of several unemployed building trades workers who volunteered. They so impressed one construction official with their skills and dedication that he said he would try to find them jobs. "This is the greatest," said Mr. Robertson. "You could not get people to work like this for pay. It's quality work. There's so much pride in it."

By Saturday, less than twenty-four hours before the scheduled reopening at 1 P.M. Sunday, work had reached a furious pace. The site was a muddy mess of extension cords and lumber, teeming with nearly one hundred workers who filled the Christmas Village section of the city park with echoes of hammering and sawing, punctuated by the warning beeps of heavy machinery backing up.

The building and grounds changed appearance dramatically from hour to hour. An electrician wired a room with the insulation man hot on his heels, the sheetrock man right behind him, the carpenters and painters closing in fast.

It was a scene that caused onlookers, one after another, to shake their heads in disbelief. The work force was fueled standing up, at a table of sawhorses and sheets of plywood laden with hamburgers, chicken, Italian sausage, pizza, and other fare donated by local restaurants and residents. One restaurant owner, Thomas Caco, set up grills and cooked meals at the site. Women continually appeared from between the dozens of trucks and cars with baked goods. One of the workers, Peter Freer, spoke of a "phoenix rising from ashes" and worried about his weight.

Children showed up with coffee cans full of money collected in their neighborhoods. When a worker was taken to the hospital for a few stitches after a minor accident, the emergency room staff sent him back with $63 in donations. A fireman dropped off a $5 bill given him by someone. A bank gave $2,000.

Several department stores each gave as much as $1,000 worth of toys, and some toy companies from as far away as Long Island and New Jersey sent truckloads of them, as did a Christmas Village in Torrington. One department store had Mr. Parlatore, Santa Claus, spend most of Saturday roaming its aisles with shopping carts.

Sandy Mirsky had taken charge of procurement, telephoning for donations of materials, as the workers told her what they needed. Lifting her foot so the floor could be laid, she explained that her technique was to call local merchants, order what she needed, and then break it to them that she had no way to pay. "Tricky," she said between calls for locks, carpeting, and red flocked wallpaper, "but it has usually worked."

Dolly Goldstone, who is playing Mrs. Santa Claus this year, watched as the work progressed and said it reminded her of the spirit she saw in England during the bombing in World War II.

Ten minutes before reopening, the tree was trimmed and a vacuum cleaner brought in. "Stop vacuuming!" yelled Marilyn Goldstone. "Camp David is calling."

President Reagan called to congratulate the workers, describing what happened in Beardsley Park as "one of the most inspiring Christmas stories I have heard in years and years and years."

Michael Marella, president of the Police Athletic League, said the President's call was "wonderful, but the real thanks is in the faces of the children," hundreds of whom came to see the papier-maché elves hammer and saw once again and Santa arrive in a white, donated limousine.

Snowflakes, large and beautiful, began falling lightly on the chalet and the surrounding pines.

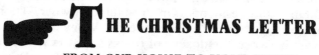

THE CHRISTMAS LETTER

FROM OUR HOUSE TO YOUR HOUSE
ACROSS THE MILES

Hi, Hi!!!

I was saying to Ralph the other day, "Why, Ralph, it just can't be that another year has gone by since I wrote my last family Christmas letter!" And he just looked at me and said, "Why, Mitzi, it has so." That Ralph.

Well, 1979 was another barnburner here in our little corner of God's Country: 191151 Access Road, Interstate Acres, Foulbrook.

The Big Event (And How!!!—900 Bucks!!!) was the society wedding of the year. Our little Bev married Specialist Fourth Class Ralphie R. (middle name: Ralph) Parker from Fort Dix. He is from a nice, well-to-do eastern (Detroit) family that arrived first class on Continental Trailways.

The wedding was situated in the backyard, which our Ralph had freshly mowed—so freshly that many of the guests had to wait in the carport for him to finish. Everyone said the yard looked pretty good (not much you can do about the septic tank). It was an evening wedding that got started a little late, and Ralph had to turn on the brights in the Volare station wagon. It had a military flair, what with the groom in his Army fatigues and the semis on the interstate saluting with their air horns.

The reception was next door in "Flapjacks," the private room at the International House of Pancakes. Then we all came back to our rec room. I argued with Ralph about charging three bucks a head to get in since we did have the cash bar, but it was well worth it. We had shots of bourbon and wedding cake and watched *The Misadventures of Sheriff Lobo,* which Bev will not miss! When it was over, Ralphie R. and Bev hit the road in a shower of Minute Rice and some White Castle hamburgers Ralph picked up from the buffet table. The clerk at the Budget Motel could not imagine how she got the mustard and ketchup and fried onions on her wedding dress.

It was moving for us. Bev had given up a promising career with the McDonald's Corporation. She was a Fries Captain, and also she was taking adult education courses in the Nail Wrapping Curriculum at Foulbrook Community College.

Little Buzz, sixteen, continues to impress, having fully recovered after a tragic accident at the Velvamatic Car Wash. He had been out with his friends (not drinking! not Buzz!) and pulled into the car wash in his convertible at 3 A.M. He suffered hot Carnauba wax burns over 60 percent of his body and was buffed almost beyond recognition.

Look out, Betty Crocker!!! Ruthie, twelve, entered the Girl Scouts cooking contest and took fourth place in Twelve-Year-Old Stuffed Baked Potato!!!

Ralph, Jr., five, has been promoted to Kadet Korporal at military boarding school, which he has attended since running his pet hamsters through the Seal-A-Meal. We love him and see him on major holidays.

Big Ralph had a big job change, moving from Assistant Thinner at Earl Scheib to the door-to-door sales division of Lava Lite. The old Scheib crew threw a big party for him at Pizza Hut. They had two additional ingredients on the pizzas, which I thought was unnecessary since Ralph was paying for it. Also this year, Ralph bought his dream: a new La-Z-Boy recliner chair, which he claims is the greatest thing since remote control TV and Double Entree TV Dinners.

Ralph's father, Ralph, is still living with us in the attic. Sometimes I think he will be with us forever—the good Lord willing, of course. He dropped out of A.A. last week in a policy dispute, and we almost lost him when I buried him with the Toro snow blower. Ralph said I should have noticed him lying there.

Me? You know me, always the activist, always on the go. This year I spearheaded a drive at Woman's Club to introduce a fourth bean—a bean that I thought necessary—into the traditional three-bean salad at the dinner dance. As Ralph predicted, things really "hit the fan" at the club.

I lost that one but took over chairwomanship of the International Committee. I have some of the girls making fudge for the hostages in Iran, and others needlepointing "Ramrod it Khomeini" throw pillows.

Why don't we get together more often?!?!?!?!?!

HAVE A VERY, VERY, MERRY, MERRY,

Ralph, Mitzi, Ralph, Buzz, Ruthie, Ralph—Bev, and Ralphie Ralph

🖛 ADS AND DADS

Some consumer agency or other ought to swoop in and close down Father's Day.

If you think those used shower thongs and other things suburban merchants sell at "Summer Sidewalk Daze" are strange, look at the stuff being hawked for Father's Day.

"Remember Dad," the newspaper ads read, with a $3.19 polyester clip-on necktie of colors not found in nature. Or a gargantuan "home drill press" for dads who apparently like to make things like earth-moving equipment on weekends in their basements. "Dad Is Sure to Be Delighted," the ads conclude.

Can they *say* that? The oft-used "Surprise Dad!" is accurate, but what dad is sure to be delighted with a three-for-$5 mesh top? Show me that dad and I'll show you a man who probably shouldn't have reproduced in the first place.

Where do they get these dads in the ads anyway? These guys who stand there smiling about having their "cool mesh nylon slipons" and their poplin jump suits. What dads are these, standing suspiciously close together in the inserts to the Sunday paper?

The ads are not only saying "Dad Is Sure to Be Delighted" with these Ban-Rol pants and disco hair-styling sets—they are saying it to impressionable children. They are advertising boxes of rumsoaked cigars and sparkly knobs that make it easier to turn the car steering wheel to children who are unwise in the ways of grinningdog merchants.

The kids are then turned loose with $5, $10, $20, and even charge cards to actually *buy* this stuff—big jugs of Hai Karate aftershave, lilac-colored Qiana shirts with a single button at the navel, and something called "precision drill guides."

Bad as it is, the millions of dollars wasted in unwanted gifts is only half of this American tragedy. Take it from me. I am a Veteran of Father's Day. The other half is that fathers have to live with these errant purchases long after Father's Day has faded into an occasional nightmare.

Take for example my 100-percent polyester lavender and silver tie. Won't you? It was a gift from my five-year-old boy on Father's Day last year. His mother helped him pick it out after I gave her a steam iron for Valentine's Day and jumper cables for Mother's Day.

You may know the tie. You see a lot of them in cafeterias after church. The lavender and silver stripes are equally attractive with both brown tweeds and blue pinstripes. Ray Charles wears the tie sometimes on TV talk shows when his valet is mad at him.

If this tie was shrapnel in my leg I could go to a VA hospital and have something done about it. But you just have to live with a Father's Day tie. There are no programs.

You can't get rid of it. Your kids will ask you where it is. And when you plan to wear it next. I find myself slipping it on for special occasions, such as playing Chutes and Ladders with my son in his room with the door closed.

I have been perusing the newspaper ads and believe me, a cheap tie isn't the only thing that can befall the father. White belt and shoe sets are being featured for Father's Day. Lava Lites. Avocado La-Z-Boys. Tie clasps with joggers or fish on them. Frying pans that plug into your car's cigarette lighter. "Handsome" $4 dress shirts. Car air filters. Smoke detectors. T-shirts that say "I'm With Stupid." Three-dollar oscillating sprinklers with minds of their own. Drugstore cologne for $1.97 that shouts "Hey, Sailor." Little $3.99 hibachi grills just right for cooking one cocktail wiener at a time.

If you have young children, you may be lucky enough to receive none of these store-bought items but rather something from school—perhaps a small piece of a tree spray-painted red with glitter on it. This is the best you can do.

The worst is to have older children who know where your charge cards are kept. Then, nothing is too good for Dad, certainly not the "Father's Day Special" $200 coin and metal detectors being advertised, the $380 home air compressor, or even the $1,100 lawn tractor on sale for Father's Day.

If you don't receive a gift, you may spend half the day in line someplace getting brunched. Breakfast in bed also is something dads have to guard against. It is customarily served at 6:30 A.M. on a shaky, overcrowded tray. For thousands of men, Father's Day will get off to a quick start with a cold glass of orange juice down the front of their pajama bottoms.

And for a moment they might pause to reflect on the fact that Father's Day isn't suffered in strata of the animal kingdom where fathers eat their young.

☞ THE FOURTH OF JULY: A SUBURBAN SALUTE

They are: The Lake Bluff Lawn Mower Precision Drill Team, a band of about one dozen white-collar suburban dads, who show themselves for what they really are every Fourth of July. Although little known in the Chicago area because Lake Bluff is such a small town, theirs is probably the finest entry in any Fourth of July parade anywhere.

With deadpan expressions they push their sputtering lawn mowers, stopping at their leader's whistle, to go through their paces—figure eights, intricate weaving patterns, and a number of routines you've seen done by drill teams, drum and bugle corps, and Shriners' minicars.

The crowd goes wild over them. I never miss it.

The team has had a different theme or motif each of their five years: old undershirts, hard hats, and cigars the first year; then top hats and tails; then in drag to commemorate the feminist movement; historical hand mowers in honor of the bicentennial; and last year, bridal gowns to salute a film being shot in that suburb, *A Wedding*.

I called the leader of the group, Kendall Hayes, to see if I could get a scoop on this year's theme.

"I had a knee operation that precludes marching," Hayes said, "and we're not going to be in it this year."

Not in it? I was stunned and managed only a feeble appeal, saying that people would certainly be disappointed. "Yes," he said, "but we did it for five years, and it must cease to be funny after a while."

I called parade coordinator Ralph Kieffer, who confirmed it. "The deadline is past for all entries," he said, adding that he'd contacted the mowers to ask them to be in the parade but that they'd said "no." Other members of the group contacted also said they'd decided to sit it out this year.

Well, they just can't say, "Sorry, not this year." This thing is bigger than they realize, bigger than their whims, something that transcends knee operations (besides, there are ride mowers).

This is a tradition. They can no more just say they aren't marching than Marshall Field's can decide not to have a Santa Claus.

No. I call Kieffer back and ask him if he'll let them in past the deadline if they can be swayed. "Let them in? They're the main attraction. I'll go out there personally and make room."

I call Grace Mary Stern, Lake County clerk, who is to be in the parade, and ask her to issue a statement. She does: "Americanism will suffer . . . Perhaps an overwhelming expression of public sentiment would cause them to reconsider." Dawn Marie Mardoian, Lake County Circuit Court clerk, who is also to be in the parade, issues a similar plea.

U.S. Representative Robert McClory (R-13th, Lake Bluff), grand marshall of the parade, is next on my list. He rushes from his judiciary committee hearing on foreign surveillance, with a short stop to vote on the House floor, to "express deep concern, consternation, and disbelief." He tells a story about the former grand marshall, who became quite controversial by riding a horse at the front of the parade. "I will tell you that you don't ride a horse at the front of the parade," he says, "and I will join you in asking the mowers to reconsider."

Encouraged, I call the White House. The President, I am told by someone in "Media Liaison," is unaware of the situation in Lake Bluff and cannot comment on it. But eventually, a "White House spokesman" issues this statement: "We here in Washington know how disappointing it would be if we didn't have the traditional fireworks display. So we can imagine how disappointed people out there will be if the power mower team fails to make its traditional appearance. We have to hope they're bluffing."

A clincher is needed. A true patriot. No one knows where Kate Smith is, exactly, although this seems inconceivable, given . . .

I catch up yesterday with Bob Hope in a motel room in Sacramento, California, where he is about to address a joint session of the California State Legislature. I explain to his agent about the precision drill maneuvers with the lawn mowers and everything. He wants to know all about the parade, how it goes down Scranton

Avenue and up East Sheridan Place, and all that. "I'm sure Bob will want to comment."

An hour later, Bob Hope issues this statement: "I'm shocked to hear that the Lake Bluff Lawn Mower Precision Team Drill will not be in the Fourth of July parade. Scranton Avenue cannot possibly go another year without being mowed. Please ask them to reconsider."

I do.

They're cracking.

☞ NATIONAL PET MEMORIAL DAY

Yesterday was National Pet Memorial Day, a big day here in the suburbs, home of the dead pet.

Hundreds of humans attended a celebration at Paw Print Gardens Pet Cemetery to sip lemonade, munch on cookies, and hear a talk by a representative of a Georgia pet memorial manufacturer.

Saturday, a gala soiree was held at Arrowood Pet Cemetery and Crematorium, featuring Toby's Angels, a cat and dog act; dedication of a statue of Saint Francis of Assisi, patron saint of animals; cider and doughnuts.

In addition to Paw Print Gardens and Arrowood, there are also nearby: Hinsdale Animal Cemetery, where more than eight thousand pets are buried; Illinois Pet Cemetery, with more than nine thousand animals; Pet Law, part of Elm Law Cemetery; and two new ones said to be opening. They have gone over remarkably well. There are new pet cemeteries all the time in the suburbs, and there will be three hundred to four hundred burials this year at the Hinsdale Cemetery alone.

The sign in front of Paw Print Gardens says it's "A Dog Gone Good Place to Go." At the front of the four-acre lot is Pat Blosser's home. Pat, forty-seven, is the owner of the cemetery and founder of the International Association of Pet Cemeteries, an organization with 218 of the country's estimated 475 pet cemeteries as members, plus several overseas.

In the side yard of her home is Cremation Gardens, a small area of multihued gravels and cement dog statues painted white, surrounded by a short white plastic picket fence. Ashes of pets are scattered here.

Behind Cremation Gardens is the new Shrine of Memories, a

twelve-foot-square structure of cement blocks with a green corrugated plastic roof and adorned with a couple of hanging plants and a statue of Christ. The ashes, or "cremains," of pets will be placed in small square holes in the cement blocks and sealed with engraved bronze plaques.

Next to the Shrine of Memories is a $2,500 replica of "Skipper"—a little mixed breed standing on eleven hundred pounds of granite, and donated by the dog's owner. Skipper is "playing now where angels sing," according to a bronzed plaque attached to the granite.

Then we come to the intimate Paw Print Gardens Chapel. At the entrance, another bronzed plaque reads: "If Christ Would Have Had a Little Dog, It Would Have Followed Him to The Cross."

Inside the chapel is the casket showroom, where prices start at $39 for a styrofoam number suitable for man's best friend—particularly suitable if you consider man's best friend to be a six-pack of Old Style. Prices go to $249 for larger, satin-lined caskets with lace-fringed pillows and mattresses. And even beyond that if you want imported mahogany. Also on sale are such things as artificial-flower bouquets, urns for the ashes in case you want them to go, and of course headstones of granite, bronze, and marble from $79 up.

Say, for example, you want to bury a medium-sized poodle: lots are $55, the inexpensive casket is $49, plus a $20 charge for opening and closing the grave. Total cost, $124, about the same as the other pet cemeteries. That's without a grave marker. Pickup service and embalming are offered at extra charge.

The only actual funeral home for pets in the country recently went out of business, but the Paw Print Gardens Chapel comes about as close as you can get. None of the others in the area has a chapel. This one has a Slumber Room, where customers can view the remains before burial. It has tall, ornate floor lamps on either side of the casket bearer, purchased from an old funeral parlor. There is a kneeling bench and brass candle holders. Baptist, Presbyterian, Lutheran, and Catholic clergymen have performed funeral services here.

There are loudspeakers attached to the back of the chapel to play chimes and organ music during graveside services and on weekends when crowds of people visit their loved ones. Some come out by train and taxi every weekend. Some bring fresh flowers, every weekend.

The cemetery has gravel walkways lined with short, trim hedges. There are white, life-sized statues of dogs on pedestals throughout and a number of "Reminiscing Benches." We walk through the as yet unoccupied Garden of Companionship and Garden of Serenity quadrants to the center of Paw Print Gardens. There Kay Kay Blosser and GiGi Blosser, Pat's own dogs, are buried beneath a statue of Saint Francis.

Most of the pets are buried in the Garden of Love—Oddo, Poopka, Mook, and the others—beneath plaques and $49.95 Memorial Lights, which hold candles that burn for 150 hours. Monuments are restricted to the Estate Sections in the Garden of Love and the Garden of Tranquility.

Not all buried here are dogs and cats. "Buttercup Marovich, 1971-1974," for example, is a duck. A dead duck and one that was actually housebroken. "Tweedle-Dum and Tweedle-Dee" are lovebirds. Buried here and in other suburban pet cemeteries are horses, chinchillas, snakes, pigeons, and even white mice ("The mouse, we only charged him $10").

Some of the plaques and monuments in Paw Print Gardens have photographs of the pets imbedded in them. The epitaphs, currently out of style on human monuments but on all pet ones, are wails of unbridled grief, excruciating pain, incredible loss, and love: "Lamb Chop, Our Beloved Baby"; "So Small, So Sweet, So Soon"; and "Pepe, My Baby, Our Love Will Never Die." (These, in contrast to one I saw on a monument manufacturer's suggested list of epitaphs: "Killed By Hit and Run Driver.")

"Our Pidge, Lillian" is inscribed on one of the larger stones in the cemetery. "That," Pat says, "is our first human."

Lillian Kopp was buried in Paw Print Gardens last year in a family plot alongside Rinty, the family dog. A stone is already up for Cindy, a family dog that's still panting, and is inscribed: "Our Dood Dirl [sic], We Love You Cheech, Take Care of Her Rinty." There are also spaces waiting for Lillian's husband, Henry, and the two children.

There is also a space waiting next to Skipper's grave for his owner. There is a common headstone for the two of them, with only the date of death left to be filled in under the owner's name.

Pat says twelve others have arranged to have their ashes buried with their pets.

Pat Blosser sees nothing at all strange about pet cemeteries. "It just doesn't seem right to us," she said, "to love a living being deeply for fourteen or fifteen years; then when it passes away, throw the body in a garbage can."

☞ TOWARD A SAFE AND SANE HALLOWEEN

Hit him with the spotlight.

All right, kid, freeze!

You have the right to remain silent. I am authorized to give you and your . . . kind . . . oral reprimands, by virtue of the fact you are violating hundreds of Halloween proclamations, resolutions, and guidelines handed down in the past week by suburban, state, and national officials, civic groups, and safety organizations—all prescribing proper Halloween attire and conduct.

You are found to be in violation of the following guidelines drawn up for your own good by these grownups to ensure that you, the child, have good, clean, safe fun.

1. You are found to be wearing a mask in violation of guidelines set forth by the National Safety Council and dozens of suburbs. Halloween masks are not to be worn on Halloween. They impair vision. Instead, parents are to put makeup on you. Furthermore, they are to apply a small amount of the makeup to your arm three days before Halloween to make sure it doesn't irritate your skin.

2. You are out after dark. You are advised to have completed aforementioned trick-or-treating (changed by proclamation in some suburbs to "meet and greeting") and be off the streets in some suburbs by dusk—about 5 P.M.

3. Your outfit is too long and too dark. A proper Halloween uniform is to be light-colored, for visibility, and short, to prevent any possibility of stumbling. It is to be sewn so that last-minute alterations can be made if the weather is cold and clothing must be worn underneath. Billowy sleeves and tattered pantlegs aren't advised, as they can catch on fences and bushes.

4. You have no reflective tape on your costume. You are to wear reflective tape on the front, back, and sides of your costume.

If possible, wear a "retroreflective" costume, approved by safety groups and made entirely of reflective material.

5. You have no flashlight.

6. You are alone.

7. You are eating a candy bar. Even though commercially wrapped, all candy is to be inspected by parents. Unwrapped "noncommercial" and loosely wrapped commercial candy is to be discarded or not accepted by trick-or-treating personnel. Fruit is to be finely chopped before eaten.

8. Your parents are violating a guideline recommending they hold a party for you and your friends so that you won't even go trick-or-treating and the dangers of Halloween can be avoided altogether.

We might go easy on you, if you'll turn in your friends who are violating these other guidelines: Wear "comfortable, well-fitting shoes"; avoid, if possible, whiskers, beards, wigs, and hats, because they might slip and impair vision or become fire hazards; and also avoid boots, high heels, and clown shoes, which might make you fall.

One more thing, kid. Paragraph 19, line 1, of one of the safety group's guidelines reads: "Halloween can be an enjoyable experience."

Smile, kid.

ALL-TRASH DAY

There, shimmering on the shore, in the front yard of a Wilmette lakefront mansion, is a rusty old water heater. Next door, on a lawn that makes Astro-Turf look like natural prairie, is an unsightly pile of broken chairs, stained carpeting, and other debris. A spent, orange and green floral dinette set appoints the parkway at a home adjacent to the Michigan Shores Club.

Appalachian chic? Nope, it is fall, a time for All-Trash Day in the suburbs, when residents can have practically anything hauled away by the village free.

Let others motor through the countryside watching Mother Nature paint the hills with red and yellow hue. In late September I prefer to be near the bobbing sailboats in Wilmette Harbor, in the shadow of the Bahai temple, watching the trash pile up.

All-Trash Day, now in its fifth year in Wilmette, is an event; more of a drive-in debris pageant and rubbish expo than a garbage pickup. When affluent residents of Chicago's North Shore throw stuff away, it attracts more than flies.

"I should sell popcorn," said one resident. "At least fifty cars have stopped here today to examine these broken chairs and old gutters."

The pickers, the rummagers, the scavengers, and garage sale groupies come from all over Chicago and the suburbs to pick up the castoffs. They come in station wagons, cars with U-Haul trailers, and rented trucks, slowly patrolling the streets and almost impassable alleys filled with junk.

"Rubbish expo" information headquarters seems to be the Browning-Ferris disposal company, Deerfield, which brings in huge trucks for the event, capable of handling stoves and water heaters.

"It's wild," said Evie Sullivan, of Browning-Ferris. "A Chicago woman in the flea market business just called to find out our pickup schedule so she'd know where to go today."

She said the scavengers slit open bags filled with grass clippings to see what's inside and that they pick up items in a pile in front of one house, examine them, and discard them in the next. She said one woman called to ask that the truck stop at her house next, because the scavengers kept unrolling her old carpeting in her front yard, and she was embarrassed by the stains on it.

"The scavengers try on clothes in the street and everything," she said. "Last week we received a call from a woman who was laughing that the garbage men got so busy modeling old clothes she'd put out that they forgot to pick up the garbage."

All the scavengers aren't from out of town. Everybody seems to get into the act, though some wait and do their rummaging under the cover of darkness.

"In Winnetka, we call it Exchange Day," said a village spokesman in that suburb, which had its cleanup days program years before Wilmette thought of it. The spokesman lives in Wilmette, however, and admitted to picking up a "good fan" from a trash heap. "But I'm no scavenger," she explained. "I just happened to be driving by. A friend got a great bathroom rug."

"Everybody loves it," said one woman, pitching a broken aquarium on top of an old mattress. She believes that just opening your door and tossing out the trash has therapeutic value for residents of the well-to-do suburb, where "the rest of the time you have to be super neat and tidy."

"The fire department likes fall cleanup, because all that junk in the basement in winter creates a fire hazard," said village official Dave Leach. A village public works employee, John Knapp, said the scavengers seem to like the fall scheduling because the weather is more predictable and they don't like water-soaked furniture.

There is an air of festivity and a few complaints. Knapp said the scavengers once spilled an old can of paint on someone's driveway, and sometimes people object to things being strewn about. Some don't like the concept, because they're too embarrassed to put a stained mattress out for the world to see, Knapp said.

One man who lives in a fashionable neighborhood was having a big party and complained that it wasn't going to be easy to impress his guests with stoves, mattresses, and dinette sets piled up all over the neighborhood.

Police Chief Fred Stoecker said they'd had only one call this year, that call being from a person who was mowing his lawn, momentarily left his mower by the curb, and returned to find the scavengers had made off with it.

Finally, there are reports that people from surrounding suburbs that don't have cleanup days actually bring their old TVs, car seats, and such over to Wilmette and dump it in people's front yards.

Midnight Sunday: a young couple emerges from an alley and looks up and down for signs of life on Isabella Street, the dividing line between Evanston and Wilmette. Seeing none, they fetch some rusty box springs from the alley and cart them across the street.

The woman explained that Evanston said it would pick up the springs but didn't. The city dump has been made into a park. Private refuse companies are too expensive, and so are the dumps where you have to take them. Evanston has no cleanup days program.

"You can get rid of your kids easier than you can your trash," said the woman, a child welfare worker, struggling to hold up her end of the springs.

Those damned things are heavier than they look. Take it from your eyewitness reporter, the guy on the other end of the springs.

HONORING THY NATION'S FATHER

Washington never shopped here. If he had, his memoirs would certainly have mentioned it among his most memorable battles.

At 8:45 A.M. on Washington's Birthday the doors of the Cohoes (New York) Specialty Store opened and Jane Ludik led a thundering herd of several hundred women past cosmetics counters, up the stairs—four at a bound—through the Designer Dress Department, and hit an Aigner leather handbag like a hawk hitting a field mouse. She scooped up another and another and another from a long table until her arms were full, whereupon she retreated to a corner to select the ones she wanted and to give the others to scavengers who had followed her into the corner.

Many of the women had waited all night in subfreezing temperatures outside the store, and they grabbed up five hundred of the leather handbags, marked down to $28 from as much as $115, in about ten minutes. Carol Booth, of Cohoes, sat cowering under some stairs, her nose bloodied, clutching three of the bags, and refusing to trade or sell them.

Bargain hunting has become the traditional way of commemorating the birth date of the Father of Our Country. Newspapers have been filled this week with advertisements of sales on everything from furnace filters and Atari E.T. cartridges to vodka and Bon Jour jeans. In few places, however, does the Washington Day Sales Celebration so nearly resemble a disaster film or the running of the bulls at Pamplona as it does here.

A spokesman for this store, which advertised "designer fashions at the best prices," suggested that the large crowd of sale shoppers, estimated at twenty thousand, many of them coming out from as far away as Buffalo, Rochester, Boston, and Montreal, must have had something to do with "the state of the economy." Other explanations for such behavior ranged from people having "gone overboard on designer stuff" to those in attendance being "nuts."

The shivering Jane Ludik, of Delmar, arrived with two of her friends before midnight in order to be first in line, have first crack at the Aigner handbags, sing camp songs, and play word games for nine hours.

She explained her special technique for carrying twenty handbags at a time while protecting them from "the vultures," who avoid the frenzied crowds at the tables, choosing instead to snatch the handbags from people like herself. One of her companions, Kathy Eck, told of scurrying under racks of clothing at last year's sale to escape the vultures and of eventually lying on top of the handbags to protect them.

"Some people play football," said Miss Ludik. "We come to the Cohoes sale every year." They came in a group of four. One of the other women with them became ill during the night. They would not relinquish their place in line to take her home. A man in line behind them did.

He was Patrick O'Riley, of Melrose, part of a four-member shopping team dressed for cold weather, equipped with a picnic basket, novels, and folding chairs. The team was led by Mr. O'Riley's wife, Laura Morgan, who said she had promised to quit smoking if her husband would join the squad this year as a "runner."

She had come Friday to "case the layout of the store." She had checked off with a yellow felt-tipped pen the sale items listed in a newspaper advertisement, and had then assigned her team members certain purchases, such as Jayna Mode three-piece pants suits, nationally advertised at $580 and selling for $39 today, and $240 Bill Blass down jackets for $19.

Such strategy and tactics were important because there were just thirty jackets and three pants suits. As it turned out, not one of these was in Miss Morgan's size, but correct size and fit did not seem to be a consideration for many of the bargain-crazed.

One of the four, Julie Carrigan, wanted to make clear the point that she was here "strictly as an observer of culture and anthropology," although she did purchase two sweaters, two handbags, three shirts, and a pair of gloves.

Ministering to the thousands who stood in line throughout the day was the Salvation Army's Emergency Disaster Services Mobile Unit, which was parked at the front door of the store, dispensing thousands of cups of coffee as well as tea, chicken broth, hot chocolate, and doughnuts.

"This is not such an unusual assignment," explained Captain Frank Smith, commanding officer of the Salvation Army in Cohoes. "We go to fires and floods, wherever there is discomfort." About seventeen hundred cups of coffee were given out by noon.

While other communities in the area attract crowds of visitors to their pumpkin festivals, apple festivals, leaf festivals, and other celebrations of nature, "this is the big day in Cohoes," in the words of Mayor Ronald Canestrari. The one-day sale doubled the population of 18,400, causing some traffic and parking problems and "some local people to just leave town," the mayor said.

Police Chief Michael Robich held planning sessions before the sale. Some traffic lights were reset, some streets were blocked off, and extra police officers were put on for the day. "The biggest problem for us is ordering off-duty men to conduct crowd control at the store," the chief said. "A lot of the men would rather respond to a fight call at a tavern than go into those shoppers."

Before the store opened, an air of great excitement, accompanied by something of a siege mentality, pervaded the sales force. "Stay off the stairs or be killed," yelled Sanford Zimmerman, store president, referring to the path to the handbags. Terry Waddell, manager of the handbag department, reported that during the initial rush at least one woman had been shoved to the floor and that someone had apparently hired "a big man, at least six feet four inches to grab about twenty handbags." When the screaming and shoving in that department were over, Lillian Lagace of Niskayuna walked away muttering, "I got nothing. These people are nuts."

The main battleground then shifted to down coats and jackets, where the deafening rustle of down-filled nylon sounded like blowing monsoon rains. A woman who had taken off her own coat to try one on turned back to find another woman modeling her coat in a mirror.

Bedlam broke out in the women's shoe department. A bin of Bert Pulitzer shirts selling for $2 might as well have been filled with gold coins.

"I love it, I love it!" said Florence McCullough, an eighty-six-year-old saleswoman with forty-seven years at the store.

"We have to get out of here," Anne Seidler of Montreal shouted to a companion. "I wear a size four and I'm trying on eights. You go crazy."

They did manage to finally get out, through the front doors where a store employee, Beth Bouleris, was allowing ten people in for every thirty that departed, in the hope of toning down the madness. She let eleven in on one occasion, explaining, "You can't break up families."

Outside, it suddenly occurred to Don Barcliff of Rochester that there were four people riding in his car and that there was nowhere to put all of the merchandise.

"She spent a hundred dollars an hour and was in there all day," he said of his wife, Norma, who shot back, "The more you spend the more you save."

This seemed a truth well understood by these shoppers doing battle on the birth date of the commander in chief of our Continental Army: sometimes it is necessary to destroy a budget to save it.

E PILOGUE: TIME TO BE GOING

It's time.

Time to be going now.

Like salmon schooling in the cool waters of springtime for the swim upstream, like birds flocking in the gathering dusk of autumn to fly south, reporters know when it's time to go.

We read stories like the one in the Sunday paper by a Washington, D.C., correspondent informing us that the U.S. Department of Agriculture believes now is a good time to fertilize our asparagus and rhubarb. Or a story Tuesday out of the nation's capital on a moth collection that will be touring the country this month.

We read these and we know. It's time. Time to be going on vacation.

If this is the kind of material our capital correspondents have to work with, think of those of us left behind in the backwaters of journalism.

August is a time of year in the suburbs when competition at the local garden center among Burpees Big Boys, Harris Supersonics, and beefsteak tomatoes qualifies as excitement.

Those who are not on vacation amuse themselves by going to "Sidewalk Daze" sales, where local merchants drag largely unmarketable items, such as dusty old thongs, out on the sidewalk. Many people hole up in air-conditioned family rooms, watching reruns of TV sitcoms or what amounts to reruns of TV sitcoms: the Cubs and the White Sox. Others sit outdoors, watching their lawns turn brown and listening to the sounds of bugs being electrocuted—*zzzzzzt!*—by their new patio bug electrocuters. They can hear their insensitive neighbors frolicking in their swimming pools on the other side of the shrubs, and it is at times like these that the deprived wish they had not made disparaging remarks about the pool-owner's beanie-weenie casserole at the block party.

These are the dog days of newspapering, with Congress, the state legislature, mayors, judges, school boards, village boards, and others taking some time off. Reporters here snap at each other over the Weber grill theft story or the arrests for lawn sprinkling violations.

We begin to feel an ominous boredom in the air. The level of interest in the organism drops. My lethargy starts acting up.

Instinctively, the newspaper shrinks to about half its normal

273

number of pages. There is a milling about in the office. It is almost
time now.

Finally, it comes. The stimulus that triggers the innate vaca-
tionistic behavior: The Call. It is part of the natural process; the
calls come to newspapers at this time of year as surely as bands of
rowdy youths return to the forest preserves.

One summer the reporter sitting next to me received this call:

"Hello. I live in Schaumburg. I have a cherry tomato that looks
like a bunny. What should I do?

"It has two ears," the caller continued. "I thought of drawing
a face on it and putting it on my daughter's plate.

"Then I thought the tomato is so weird maybe I should keep it.
I thought maybe I should put it in formaldehyde. Or just put it in
our refrigerator for a long time.

"I thought maybe *Playboy* magazine would be interested in
it."

The caller said they'd finally decided to keep it and "show it."
The caller's husband showed it at work. She showed it to her neighbors. They took several pictures of it.

Another summer a man called the suburban office to say he had
"a squash you could actually sit on." I took the call and actually refrained from telling him to, by all means, do so.

Last year, this was the call that sent me on my way:

"Do you happen to know the world record for the tomato?

"Well," said the caller, "you should send a photographer over
to my house because I'm going to have tomatoes this year the size
of my head."

"Cherry tomatoes?" I asked.

"No, beefsteaks," he said.

I told him I couldn't come over because I had to go on
vacation. He had let me know. It was time.

This year was a little different. A woman walked into the office
with a squash. The receptionist, knowing my interest in these
things, sent her over to my desk. I picked up the phone to tell my
wife to start packing the car.

Then it dawned on me. This couldn't be it. This was the first
week in April. She had the small round squash in an Easter basket
with little green polyethylene grass underneath it.

"See," she said. "It's like a little Easter egg."

I thanked her for bringing it in but admonished her that it isn't wise to meddle with the forces of nature. "Come back in July," I said.

In July I was called by people asking me if I wanted an exclusive interview with a doctor setting up a chain of Hotlines across the country for acne sufferers; if I wanted to write an article about the Texas Burger being added to a suburban restaurant's menu; or if I wanted to write about a Lake Forest socialite being sawed in half by a magician with a power saw for charity.

I checked the air in my tires and dug through the closet for my tennis racquet.

A few days ago, a colleague in the newspaper business who knows how I feel about these things called to say he was putting the finishing touches on a filler item about an important upcoming VFW steak fry when his phone rang.

"It was a guy with a spaghetti squash the size of a small beach ball," he said. "Have a nice vacation."